DEMOCRATIC PROCEDURES AND LIBERAL CONSENSUS

D0209865

Democratic Procedures and
Liberal Consensus

GEORGE KLOSKO

OXFORD
UNIVERSITY PRESS

OXFORD

UNIVERSITY PRESS

Great Clarendon Street, Oxford OX2 6DP

Oxford University Press is a department of the University of Oxford.
It furthers the University's objective of excellence in research, scholarship,
and education by publishing worldwide in

Oxford New York

Athens Auckland Bangkok Bogotá Buenos Aires Calcutta
Cape Town Chennai Dar es Salaam Delhi Florence Hong Kong Istanbul
Karachi Kuala Lumpur Madrid Melbourne Mexico City Mumbai
Nairobi Paris São Paulo Singapore Taipei Tokyo Toronto Warsaw

and associated companies in Berlin Ibadan

Oxford is a registered trade mark of Oxford University Press
in the UK and in certain other countries

Published in the United States
by Oxford University Press Inc., New York

© George Klosko 2000

The moral rights of the author have been asserted

Database right Oxford University Press (maker)

First published 2000

British Library Cataloguing in Publication Data

Data available

Library of Congress Cataloging in Publication Data
Klosko, George.
Democratic procedures and liberal consensus/George Klosko.
Includes bibliographical references and index.
1. Liberalism. 2. Democracy. I. Title.
JC574.K56 1999 321.8—dc21 99–36962

ISBN 0–19–829234–1

1 3 5 7 9 10 8 6 4 2

Typeset by Hope Services (Abingdon) Ltd.
Printed in Great Britain
on acid-free paper by
Biddles Ltd.,
Guildford & King's Lynn

For
Meg, Carrie, Sukey, and Debby

Die Vernunft als die Rose im Kreuze der Gegenwart zu erkennen . . .
(To recognize reason as the rose in the cross of the present . . .)

(G. W. F. Hegel, Philosophy of Right)

PREFACE

In this work I develop principles of 'political liberalism' capable of being justified to and providing a basis for unity among liberal citizens. Readers familiar with recent work in political philosophy will recognize my great debt to the work of John Rawls. In a series of articles beginning in 1980 and culminating in *Political Liberalism*, published in 1993, Rawls raised the basic question of what he termed 'political liberalism': how is just moral and political union possible in pluralistic, contemporary societies? Subsequent work on this and related issues has been carried on in the shadow of Rawls's contributions. But I do not believe Rawls's approach to his own question is the most appropriate.

Since 1987, when Rawls's article 'The Idea of an Overlapping Consensus' appeared, I have felt that major questions of political liberalism have a deeply empirical dimension. To the extent that Rawls recognized this, many of his views about contemporary liberal societies struck me as improbable. Clearer understanding of the facts would have caused him to revise the principles he developed. In subsequent years Rawls apparently recognized the empirical implications of his early forays into political liberalism. For fear of being 'political in the wrong way' (see below, Chapter 7), he largely abandoned the subject's practical and empirical side. But I believe his original question is of great importance, and address it in the following pages. My central claim is that principles of political liberalism must be worked out with close attention to the facts of modern societies, and that these drive resultant principles in a definite direction, as seen below.

My account of the principles of liberal consensus should not be deeply surprising to anyone familiar with research in American public opinion. Political scientists and sociologists generally agree about central views of liberal citizens. The evidence shows that many liberal citizens are markedly intolerant and would not endorse a strong conception of rights. The view I work out is a variant of procedural liberalism. Its primary focus is democratic political institutions, rather than a specific conception of rights or principles of distributive justice—although the evidence shows that Americans generally support a particular distributive principle, but far removed from what Rawls puts forth.

This work has been long in the making and I would like to acknowledge my many debts. Earlier versions of several chapters were presented at the University of Jena in 1996, the University of London in 1998, and the Catholic University in 1998, at meetings of the American Political Science Association in 1993, 1997, and 1998, and to the Virginia Philosophy Department in 1996 and 1998. I am grateful for comments and criticisms at all these sessions. Earlier versions of several chapters have appeared in print: 'Rawls's "Political" Philosophy and American Democracy', *American Political Science Review*, 87 (1993), 348–59; 'Rawls's Argument from Political Stability', *Columbia Law Review*, 94 (1994), 1882–97; and 'Political Constructivism in Rawls's *Political Liberalism*', *American Political Science Review*, 91 (1997), 635–46. I acknowledge my gratitude to the publishers for allowing me to use this material here.

Financial assistance was provided by University of Virginia Summer Grants in 1994 and 1995 and a University of Virginia Sesquicentennial Grant in 1994. I benefited from the research assistance of Gregg Stelmach, Maureen Morrison, Ann Witkowski, and Eric Sands. I am also grateful to James Hunter, of the Sociology Department and the Post-Modernity Project at Virginia, for organizing a highly stimulating conference on American democracy in the fall of 1996, which I attended and which did much to shape my thinking.

My greatest debts are to friends and colleagues with whom I have discussed my ideas over the course of several years. Virtually every claim in this work has been debated with Ernie Alleva, from whose vigorous and penetrating criticisms I have benefited enormously. My colleague Steve Finkel was a patient guide through the public opinion literature during the early stages of this project and also read and commented upon drafts of several chapters. He also allowed me to sit in on two graduate courses in quantitative research methods. Other colleagues and friends from whose insights and criticisms I have profited include Colin Bird, Talbot Brewer, Richard Dagger, Daniel Devereux, Joshua Dienstag, Paul Freedman, Jerry Gaus, Dante Germino, Mark Hall, David Klein, John Leech, Debra Morris, Jonathan Riley, John Simmons, Mark Warren, and Jonathan Wolff. I am also grateful to anonymous reviewers of the articles listed above, several anonymous reviewers from Oxford University Press, and Dominic Byatt, of Oxford University Press, who has been a model editor at all stages of this project, and Amanda Watkins has expertly guided it through production. Discussions with all these people have helped me improve my manuscript considerably, although I have frequently not followed their advice and am of course responsible for the problems that remain.

As ever, I am deeply grateful to my wife, Meg, and daughters, Caroline, Susanna, and Deborah, for moral support.

CONTENTS

1

Liberal Commitments

THIS work addresses the problem of identifying political principles that can be generally accepted in diverse contemporary societies. I will attempt to outline a foundation for agreement among people with widely different moral, religious, and overall philosophical views. In a basic sense, seeking agreement of this kind requires detailed knowledge of modern citizens and their beliefs. But the resulting principles must be acceptable on moral grounds as well. Details of appropriate moral constraints will be discussed in this chapter, while a central theme of this work is tension between the kind of principles many people—including, presumably, many readers of this book—might wish to see and those liberal citizens would be likely to accept.

Before proceeding, I should make clear that I do not claim that the questions addressed in this work exhaust the concerns of political philosophy. Principles of justice, rights, political obligation, and other important issues can of course be defended on grounds other than that liberal citizens would accept them. But, on the whole, attempting to establish principles that are 'metaphysical' rather than 'political'—to paraphrase Rawls (1985)—is not my purpose. Nor will I explore more than a fraction of the interesting questions that could be raised in regard to the relationship between the approach I pursue and other normative concerns. I believe that identifying the principles of liberal consensus is an important undertaking and concentrate on that.

This study's most distinctive feature is heavy reliance on findings of recent social science, especially survey research on the beliefs and attitudes of liberal citizens. Because principles of political philosophy address the circumstances of actual polities, they have an unavoidable empirical dimension. But although social science is of great relevance to political philosophy, it has been largely ignored by political philosophers. I attempt to remedy this situation by examining important social science research and tracing out its implications. As we will see, arguing from the best available empirical evidence pushes normative theory in a particular direction. Although I do not claim that empirical data themselves are able to establish normative principles, they have definite tendencies, and so prod normative principles as well.

The starting-point of this study is the view that people should be governed on the basis of principles they are able to understand and accept. I believe that political arrangements are necessary, that people could not lead acceptable lives without them. The features of such arrangements, however, are not ineluctably given, but must be able to be explained and *justified* to modern citizens. A set of basic requirements can be identified as central to the liberal tradition and subscribed to by most citizens, although there is considerable variation in how people interpret them. Accordingly, I begin with a brief look at central elements of the liberal tradition and liberal political theory.

1. 'POLITICAL' LIBERALISM

The principles discussed throughout this study fall within the liberal tradition. The empirical studies on which I focus concern people's attitudes, which are shaped by, and are generally supportive of, existing institutions and practices. Since ours is a liberal society, both institutions and practices are primarily liberal. The liberal tradition is broad and diverse, and exactly where boundary lines should be drawn is a question I will not discuss.[1] But important themes of the tradition should be noted here.

Since its origins in the seventeenth century liberal political theory has been concerned with defending the individual and his rights. There is great variance within the tradition concerning claims about the precise natures of both individuals and rights. At different points our discussion will touch on these issues. But beginning with the need to resist arbitrary and unjust political authority, as classically espoused by Locke, liberal theorists have concentrated on defining and justifying a protected sphere within which the individual can pursue his (later, his or her) own aims, free from outside interference—especially coercive interference by other people.[2] A notable early statement of liberal commitments is Locke's *Letter on Toleration*, which centres on the individual's right to practise his own religion, to paraphrase J. S. Mill, to pursue his own religious good in his own way.[3] This emphasis is apparent in classic works of liberal theory,

---

[1] See Ruggiero (1959), Hobhouse (1994); on the American liberal tradition, Hartz (1955), Young (1996).

[2] For earlier roots of the liberal tradition, see Tierney (1955, 1982); Franklin (1969), Klosko (1993*a*, 1995).

[3] Mill (1978: 12); for Locke's view of rights, see Simmons (1992).

through Locke, to Mill's *On Liberty* and Robert Nozick's *Anarchy, State, and Utopia*.

Since its emergence from the tangled medieval world liberalism's defence of political rights has had a strong intellectual component. Rejecting prior, religiously based grounds of political authority—e.g. the divine right of kings—early liberal theorists presented the demand that political authority be justified: it must be shown to benefit society and/or the individual on the basis of reasoned arguments. This requirement is bound up with the familiar idea that individuals have the right to consent to political authority, advanced, again, most notably by Locke: 'Men being . . . by Nature, all free, equal and independent, no one can be put out of this Estate, and subjected to the Political Power of another, without his own *Consent*' (Locke 1988, Second Treatise, sect. 95). Similarly, the authors of the Declaration of Independence declare that governments 'receive their just powers from the consent of the governed'. In recent years, consent theories of political obligation have fallen out of favour. According to consent theory, governments cannot justifiably command the obedience of their subjects unless the latter consent to governmental authority. The problem, of course, is that few liberal citizens can be shown to have consented expressly. In his classic formulation of the doctrine Locke addressed this difficulty, arguing that, even if most citizens had not expressly consented to their governments, they had done so tacitly (Locke 1988, sects. 119–22). But careful examination of this claim shows that it cannot be sustained.[4] However, in spite of its problems in grounding political obligations, consent theory expresses a permanent theme in the liberal tradition, the idea that people *should* be able to consent to their political arrangements. So understood, the requirement of actual consent can be construed as one of 'hypothetical consent', that citizens *would* consent to their government if given the opportunity.[5] The implications here are epistemological as well as moral. Political arrangements should be able to be understood by each member of society as a necessary condition for granting his consent.

The central role a particular view of justification plays in liberal theory is eloquently expressed by Jeremy Waldron (1987). Waldron describes the characteristic liberal attitude as 'impatience with tradition, mystery, awe and superstition as the basis of order, and . . . determination to make authority answer at the tribunal of reason and convince us that it is entitled to respect' (p. 134). Waldron connects this particular attitude with the

---

[4] See Simmons (1979, ch. 4); the most important defence of a consent theory of political obligation is Beran (1987); criticized in Klosko (1991).

[5] Pitkin (1965); see also Kant, 'On the Common Saying: "This may be True in Theory, but it does not Apply in Practice" ', in Kant (1970), esp. pp. 79–80.

rise of the Enlightenment in general, and its conviction that human reason could make sense of the world, by explaining it fundamental principles and regularities (p. 134). According to this point of view, society too could be understood. As Waldron says, society should be *transparent*. Its fundamental principles should be capable of being understood by everybody, and accepted by everybody (p. 146).

Important theorists besides Waldron recognize liberal theory's commitment that principles be understood and accepted. In the first formulation of his version of social contract theory, 'Justice as Fairness', John Rawls roots his conception of fairness in the possibility of discovering moral principles that everyone could accept. He describes this as 'the possibility of mutual acknowledgment of principles by free persons who have no authority over one another' (Rawls 1958: 179). When this condition is satisfied, people should be able to 'face one another openly and support their respective positions, should they appear questionable, by reference to principles which it is reasonable to expect each to accept' (p. 178). The need for principles that can be generally acknowledged has been a consistent theme in Rawls's work for almost forty years. In his recent work *Political Liberalism* Rawls appeals to the 'liberal principle of legitimacy': 'our exercise of political power is proper and hence justifiable only when it is exercised in accordance with a constitution the essentials of which all citizens may reasonably be expected to endorse in the light of principles and ideas acceptable to them as reasonable and rational. This is the liberal principle of legitimacy' (Rawls 1993: 217).[6]

Within liberal political theory, then (or at least, a strong current of it), individuals should be able to assess and accept the principles according to which they are governed. Principles should be *generally* acceptable, thus reflecting a consensus of citizens' beliefs. Our question, then, is how consensus can be obtained in contemporary liberal societies. I will concentrate on the United States, though with frequent references to other liberal societies. But as soon as we turn to contemporary liberal societies, a problem arises. Given the diversity of moral and religious views these societies contain, it is difficult to imagine how all citizens could agree on a single set of political principles. The differences in people's views on numerous moral, religious, and philosophical issues make agreement on political issues an unlikely prospect.

Statement of this problem shows its dependence on two factual assumptions, with which we will be concerned. These can be put forth as assertions here; evidence supporting them is presented throughout this study. First is the fact of pluralism. We can assume that liberal societies contain

---

[6] See also Nagel (1987, 1991); but see Nagel (1991: 163 n. 49).

broad ranges of inhabitants with different moral, religious, and philosophical views. For ease of reference, I will refer to different views of what is important in life, or what people should care about or how they should live, as conceptions of the good life, or conceptions of the good, whether these are rooted in beliefs we would describe as moral, religious, or philosophical. The second assumption is that pluralism is ineradicable. Rawls describes what he calls the 'burdens of judgment' as a series of factors that make it unlikely—highly unlikely—that people with different moral or religious views could ever be brought to fundamental agreement through the force of reasoned argument alone (1993: 54–8). For instance, evidence bearing on moral claims is complex and hard to assess. Even where people can agree about the kinds of evidence relevant to their disagreements, they are likely to disagree about the weight different items should receive. Moral concepts are vague and subject to indeterminacy. As other scholars note, they are 'essentially contested' (Gallie 1955–6; Connolly 1983, ch. 1) The concept of justice, for instance, is internally complex. If people emphasize different aspects of justice, they can easily mean quite different things, with, again, no ready reconciliation in sight. It is likely that the way people view such complex moral concepts and assess particular situations is affected by their overall philosophies of life and experiences. People's thought on moral matters are parts of overall world-views; as long as they subscribe to different world-views, they are unlikely to agree about moral questions.[7] Perhaps the clearest examples of gaps between different citizens' world-views are those between deeply religious and non-religious members of society. These 'cognitive divides' are explored at length in Chapter 4. In view of the material reviewed there, it is far-fetched even to imagine that all liberal citizens could readily be brought to agree on central moral issues.

The conditions indicated by pluralism and the lack of ready agreement confront liberal theory with a formidable challenge. Although general agreement is required, it is difficult to attain in modern societies. There is need for principles that can be generally accepted in spite of widespread and severe disagreements. In recent years this challenge has been taken up by proponents of what has come to be called 'political' liberalism. The idea of political liberalism is indelibly associated with the work of Rawls, especially his book of the same name, while similar concerns are addressed by a range of additional scholars.[8] In spite of possible differences between

---

[7] The unlikelihood of agreement among adherents of different world-views is assumed here. Evidence presented in later chapters will support.

[8] Other recent theories of political liberalism are advanced by Moon (1993), Larmore (1987, 1996), and Gaus (1996).

their precise interests and approaches, proponents of political liberalism generally agree on central concerns, especially problems posed by contemporary pluralism.

As Rawls argues, because of the impediments to consensus in pluralist societies, political liberals should pursue a strategy of attempting to set aside areas of disagreement, where this is possible. According to Rawls, rather than addressing all questions that might concern citizens, political liberalism should be confined to society's 'basic structure', its main political, social, and economic institutions, and how these fit together into a unified system (Rawls 1993: 11). In contrast to a 'political' view that deals with basic structures, a moral view can be described as 'general' if it addresses a wide range of subjects.

Rawls describes a moral view as 'comprehensive' if it contains answers to a full range of difficult and controversial questions, for example, what is of value in human life, ideals of personal character, and other subjects. A view is 'fully comprehensive' if is encompasses 'all recognized values and virtues within one rather precisely articulated system' (Rawls 1993: 13). In contrast to comprehensive views, a political conception is articulated without reference to wider philosophical background. In order to be compatible with the range of comprehensive views found in contemporary liberal societies, a political conception should be as far as possible independent of the opposing and conflicting philosophical and religious doctrines that citizens affirm (pp. 10–11).

Rawls believes that the move to political liberalism can be described as an extension of the growth of toleration that was central to the development of liberal societies. At one time it was widely thought that agreement on religious precepts was necessary for a functioning society. But with the rise of the Reformation and ruinous conflict between adherents of contending religions, thinkers began to argue that the requirement of religious uniformity should be set aside for the sake of preserving civil peace. The *politiques* in France, most notably Jean Bodin, upheld the possibility of living together on terms of social co-operation with other people who upheld different views concerning such questions as the nature of papal authority and the doctrine of transubstantiation (see Allen 1928: 370–7). Political liberalism can be viewed as an extension of this idea. As inhabitants of earlier societies argued for the need to separate questions concerning the status of citizenship from religious affiliation, so political liberals attempt to separate it from conceptions of the good and wider disagreements.

If we accept the standpoint of political liberalism, then we must work out principles that liberal citizens can generally accept, in spite of their wider differences. This overall problem can be approached in different ways, and proponents of political liberalism differ in the angles they pursue. Especially importantly, we can distinguish what we can call sociological and normative dimensions of the problem of agreement.

Given the diversity of moral, religious, and political views in modern societies, there is a pressing practical need to discover an acceptable basis for agreement. At least to a certain extent, society requires citizens' willing acceptance of major political, economic, and social arrangements. A range of rules, including rules of justice, must be maintained. Decision procedures must be established and supported, with general agreement on how they are to function and that the norms they embody are acceptable. Theorists disagree about the extent of agreement that is necessary, and how they believe questions such as this should be addressed. But regardless of exactly where they come down on such issues, most believe that some measure of general agreement is necessary. Throughout this study I will use the terms 'stability' and 'political stability' to refer to conditions in a political system that centre on the smooth functioning of decision-making mechanisms and absence of large-scale, extra-legal opposition, which are central to a given system's preservation.[9] Thus one reason we are interested in consensus is that this is a necessary condition for political stability. The factors that make political regimes stable have been widely discussed since the time of Plato and Aristotle. Though we can assume that ideas play some role, it is difficult to say exactly what this is. At different points in this study I will address this question. But regardless of the precise extent to which agreement is required, it is safe to assume that some measure of agreement is necessary—and so the search for agreement is of practical significance.

The search for acceptable principles is also a moral undertaking. According to the liberal tradition, there is a fundamental difference between societies that govern people on the basis of principles they can accept and others, lacking this, that rule by force. The 'consent of the governed' is essential to legitimacy.[10] This is not an isolated requirement, but exists in the context of other moral demands of liberalism. Not just any principles could satisfy requirements of consensus. They must be of a certain kind and accepted in a particular way. Given uncertainty about the weight of such principles' contribution to political stability, these moral requirements could well be more important than the sociological.

Different kinds of agreements on core principles can be envisioned. It is not unlikely that a kind of consensus could be achieved through the active

---

[9] See Lipset (1960: 30); discussed briefly, below, Ch. 7, Sect. 5; on Rawls's meaning of stability, see the same section, below.

[10] On the meaning of legitimacy, with further references, see Klosko (1992: 67–72, 128–9).

use of political power. Through such means as tight control over education, censorship of mass communications and artistic media, and punishment of dissidents, intellectual conformity could be enforced throughout
even a large modern society. There are, however, obvious reasons to
oppose such policies, both in themselves and because of the dire effects of
total state control throughout society. In addition to the oppression
directly associated with censorship are economic and social costs of the
isolation from other societies that intellectual control would require and
the fact that oppressed masses could well resist state policies, thereby contributing to political instability. But again, in addition to these sociological considerations, some measure of agreement is necessary for the moral
acceptability of a regime—without reference to whether this is required for
the regime to endure. On these grounds, enforced inculcation of beliefs is
inherently objectionable. It flatly conflicts with liberal theory's requirement of general, willing acceptance of principles.

For both sociological and moral reasons, then, the development of
agreement in society is a great good. But again, if we accept pluralism as
a permanent feature of liberal societies, we face the challenge of presenting central political principles upon which diverse citizens can agree. In
this work I concentrate on a rather practical side of this subject; my concern is with liberal societies as they presently exist and the principles their
diverse inhabitants could accept. This is not the only form of consensus
one could envision, but I view it as especially pressing, because of its obvious importance and impediments to the realization of other forms of consensus (as seen in the following chapters).[11] To keep my approach distinct
from those of other proponents of political liberalism, I will refer to my
focus as 'liberal consensus'.

My main contention in this work is that careful assessment of empirical
evidence is necessary in order to develop the most defensible account of
the principles of liberal consensus. I began by noting that political philosophers pay little attention to the findings of empirical social science. But
we can see from the above discussion that the main problem of political

---

[11] In *Political Liberalism* Rawls is more interested in what we can call theoretical
aspects of political liberalism than practical, i.e. uncovering bases for agreement in
actual, existing societies. Scholars who emphasize his attention to the practical side get
Rawls 'exactly wrong' (Krasnoff 1998: 291). Krasnoff presents a convincing account
of Rawls's intentions, and also explains well the moral value of consensus—although
he is far from drawing implications I do in the following chapters. Among those
emphasizing the practical side in Rawls are Rorty (1988), Habermas (1995) (with
Rawls's response: Rawls 1995), and my previous articles: Klosko (1993*b*, 1994, 1997).
The evidence indicates that at one time Rawls did clearly view this as part of his project (for evidence, see Klosko (1994). But he has paid less attention to these concerns
in later pieces, e.g. Rawls (1996, introd.).

liberalism as outlined here depends on factual claims concerning pluralism and the burdens of judgement. Thus one must ask immediately why theorists appeal to the facts of liberal societies to pose their questions, but not, it appears, to answer them. I believe that greater attention to the facts pushes solutions to our main problem in a specific direction, towards what is described in Chapter 5 as 'procedural liberalism'. In Chapter 7 I compare this position to the main theoretical alternative, the view of Rawls, which, I argue, presents liberal principles that are indefensibly broad. Greater attention to the facts suggests that this alternative position cannot be sustained.

If the end is to discover principles that people can accept, then a great deal depends on their existing moral and political views, with which liberal principles must fit. Thus we must inquire into what liberal citizens believe. For good or ill, the best evidence available is often survey research, public opinion polls, and the like. Problems with these sources are discussed in the following chapter, while problems with specific research on which we draw are discussed throughout this work, as different studies are employed. But in spite of the difficulties surveys present, in many cases they provide the *best* evidence we have. In spite of problems discovering the views of liberal citizens, the proper development of liberal consensus requires that we try.

2. LIBERAL COMMITMENTS

Although my main task is to identify principles on which diverse liberal citizens can agree, factors other than agreement must be taken into account. Not just any principles agreed upon will be appropriate. Acceptable principles must conform with central moral commitments of the liberal tradition. In important respects, these are entailed by the requirement of justification itself. Justification is not an isolated moral requirement but is bound up with and entailed by central liberal values, which I will explore.

If we were to ask why justification should be accepted, various answers could be given. But these would all likely be bound up with conceptions of the individual as having dignity and autonomy and the need to treat individuals with respect. In a pluralistic society different accounts of these reasons would undoubtedly be given, and I will not attempt to work out the details of particular variants here. But I should note that my procedure is not strongly deductive. I do not begin by positing the commitments of liberal theory in final form and then require that subsequent principles be constructed to fit with them. Rather, the approach here could be described as dialectical. Though in some form constraints must be posited at the outset, their final form cannot be given until we have explored the evidence concerning people's beliefs—though even then it is important *not* to develop the constraints in great detail.

Among the basic commitments of liberal theory are claims that people have rights, including rights to equal treatment and to some measure of respect. In this section I will describe the commitments in outline. In subsequent chapters they will be 'redeemed' by evidence that liberal citizens overwhelmingly support them—though in rough forms, with considerable disagreement over details.

We can begin with the idea that people must be treated with respect. In moral and political philosophy the notion is epitomized in the Kantian injunction always to treat people as ends, never simply as means (Kant 1964: 95–6). According to this view, people are entitled to respect because they are human beings, not because of particular characteristics they possess. If you see someone drowning and have the opportunity to throw him a rope, you have a duty to do so, without reference to his height, weight, or eye colour, or even his moral character, but because he is a person, a fellow member of the moral community. As Gregory Vlastos says: 'I owe assistance to any man in such circumstances, not merely to good men' (Vlastos 1984: 55).

The precise grounds in virtue of which human beings are owed respect is a matter of controversy. In a pluralistic society proponents of different comprehensive views will understand the concept of respect differently and provide different justifications. But although a detailed account would likely run foul of the views of diverse groups, we can assume that in some form this value is generally accepted.

Within liberal theory, the need to justify political principles to people is generally bound up with respect. Because people have their own views of society and how it should be ordered, the use of governmental power should be shown to be in accordance with their own thoughts and beliefs. As Charles Larmore says: 'The *obligation* of equal respect consists in our being obligated to treat another as he is treating us—to use his having a perspective on the world as a reason for discussing the merits of our action rationally with him' (Larmore 1987: 64). To subject people to the coercive power of the state without providing justification is to treat them without respect.

Although the idea of respect contains a relatively non-controversial core, in a pluralist society, there is less agreement on particular aspects and implications. If we wish to say that respect is grounded on autonomy, the latter concept will likewise be subject to controversy. I will accordingly operationalize the concept negatively. I will assume that there are a number of defensible views of respect and that people can be acceptably treated with respect in different ways. However, beyond a certain point, wholesale disregard of people's worth and dignity is obviously unacceptable. Cases in point include discrimination on racial and religious grounds and unjustified, glaring inequalities in how people are treated. Also included in this are circumstances in which political principles cannot be justified to high percentages of the population.

Human rights are closely bound up with requirements to treat people with appropriate respect. The Preamble to the United Nations (UN) Universal Declaration of Human Rights connects up 'the equal and inalienable rights of all members of the human family' with their 'inherent dignity'. The first article of the Declaration begins: 'All human beings are born free and equal in dignity and rights.' Because of all people's inherent dignity, their rights are necessarily equal (see esp. Vlastos 1984: 57–9). The rights in question are expressed in a variety of official documents, e.g. the Bill of Rights to the United States Constitution, the UN Declaration, and the Canadian Charter of Rights and Freedom, and are generally consistent across documents. Rights generally include freedom of conscience and religion, freedom of thought and speech, freedom of the press, of association, of travel, and a range of procedural protections concerning criminal prosecution by the state. A central feature of these rights is significant weight. According to Ronald Dworkin, rights are 'trumps', ordinarily overriding collective goals of the community as a whole (Dworkin 1978, p. xi). The first article of the Canadian Charter states that these rights can be circumscribed, but only by 'such reasonable limits prescribed by law as can be demonstrably justified in a free and democratic society'. Such cases require that a significant burden of justification be met. An individual's rights to free speech, assembly, association, etc. can be overridden only for unusual and pressing reasons. In general, the collection of rights recognized in a contemporary liberal society can be conceived of in territorial terms, an area of protected space around an individual, within which she should be able to pursue her own projects, free from interference by other people. The distinctive liberal conception of freedom, negative freedom, is freedom from coercive interference by other people, especially in regard to areas encompassed by these rights.[12]

As with respect, up to a point, the existence and importance of a range of basic rights is deeply rooted in the cultures of all liberal societies and so not controversial. Evidence for this claim is presented in Chapter 3. But the precise list of these rights is not agreed upon. For instance, Article 24

---

[12] On negative freedom, see Berlin (1969); MacCallum (1967).

of the UN Declaration guarantees 'the right to rest and leisure, including reasonable limitation of working hours and periodic holidays with pay'. It is, however, unlikely that the majority of liberal citizens view this as on a par with rights to free speech and freedom of conscience. As we will see in Chapter 3, the extent and weight of rights to free expression are themselves deeply controversial issues.

Exactly how rights are justified is also subject to controversy. Once again, as with respect, people with different comprehensive views will understand rights differently and will support them on different grounds. Because of such disagreements, I will generally operationalize rights too negatively, focusing on cases in which conduct or policies would flagrantly conflict with any reasonable view.

Within liberal theory basic features of the political system must be in keeping with people's fundamental rights. Throughout this study I assume the need for the state, that people have obligations to obey their governments.[13] Different forms of political decision-making mechanisms can be defended, and there will be disagreement about which is preferred. But in keeping with the practices of all existing liberal societies, I assume that acceptable governments must be democratic. Article 21 of the UN Declaration reads (in part):

Everyone has the right to take part in the government of his country, directly or through freely chosen representatives. . . . The will of the people shall be the basis of the authority of government; this will shall be expressed in periodic and genuine elections which shall be by universal and equal suffrage and shall be held by secret vote or by equivalent free voting procedures.

Because democracy too allows different construals, this too will be operationalized negatively. Governments that cannot be reasonably defended as democratic will be assumed to be unacceptable. Once again, survey evidence provides strong support for democracy—on a general level.

One reason it is important to recognize a core of liberal commitments is that the view I develop is a form of liberal proceduralism, briefly, that liberal principles are those that emerge from fair procedures. But it must be understood that the procedures are constrained by a set of core commitments. When commitments are violated—e.g. when decision procedures produce results at odds with acceptable views of rights or equality—then the results are called into question. As we will see below, decision procedures are necessary because there is no better way to settle controversial moral and political issues. In many cases the background commitments of liberal theory are able to narrow the range of possible options, but not to

---

[13] For one possible argument for political obligations, see Klosko (1992); this is outlined briefly below, in the Appendix to the Conclusion.

identify single outcomes. Although decision procedures can accomplish this, they do not allow unlimited discretion. Details of procedures, as with other aspects of democratic systems, should be decided on democratically, as well as creation of the preconditions for properly functioning democracy (see below, Chapter 5, Section 4).

3. LIBERAL 'NEUTRALITY'

Because of the circumstances in contemporary liberal societies, the need for principles to be justified requires that they be 'neutral', or, as this is generally filled in, neutral between competing conceptions of the good. Since people hold different moral and religious views, principles cannot be widely justified if they rely on controversial conceptions of the good. Thus ideas of neutrality and consensus are closely related. The requirement to treat people equally entails that the state not favour particular individuals. Just as one group of people should not be treated better than others because of their height or hair colour, or the social class into which they are born, so it is central to liberal political theory that they not receive preferential treatment because of their moral views or religion. The implication is that controversial issues should not be decided on the basis of particular individuals' conceptions of the good. The state must attempt to be neutral between conceptions. (See Rawls 1993, lecture 6; 1997.)

Neutrality is closely bound up with the basic commitments of liberal theory discussed in the previous section, and should be viewed as an additional core commitment. Its central role is noted by important theorists. For instance, Dworkin refers to this as the 'constitutive political morality' of liberalism (1985: 191–2). According to Larmore, neutrality is 'the fundamental liberal principle' (1987, p. x); it is 'the primary idea of liberalism' (p. 46).[14] Neutrality has attracted much attention in recent years, both criticism and defence. Because of the close relationship between neutrality and other core commitments, I will discuss it briefly here, although detailed treatment would take us far afield. Discussion of criticisms and how they can be countered can be relegated to the notes (below, note 23). To some extent disagreements about neutrality have resulted from lack of clarity about what exactly it entails and how it can be justified. But, properly formulated, a particular conception of neutrality can withstand major criticisms.

[14] For discussion from different perspectives, see Goodin and Reeve (1989); also Barry (1995*b*); see below, n. 23.

We should be clear immediately that the requirement of neutrality pertains to governments rather than to individual citizens. As far as individuals are concerned, there is little reason why they should not be able to act according to their own conceptions of the good, though their conduct must be in keeping with rules for mutual protection and the smooth functioning of society. Liberal theorists commonly distinguish between private and public spheres of activity. The requirement of neutrality is reserved for the latter, especially for governmental policies.[15]

Public policies can be neutral in different ways. The *consequences* of a specific policy can be neutral. This will be the case if the policy affects people with different conceptions of the good similarly. For instance, a policy that is not neutral in this sense would be a law forbidding stores to be open on Sunday, which would favour people whose religions recognize Sunday as the sabbath. Or if a given religion regards cows as sacred, a law forbidding slaughter of cattle could be viewed as favouring its proponents. The main alternative conception construes neutrality in regard to the *justification* of public policies as opposed to their consequences.[16] On this view, state actions should be justifiable to people with different conceptions of the good, or, more precisely, justification should not rely on a specific conception of the good. For instance, a law requiring that stores be closed on Easter or Yom Kippur on religious grounds would be disqualified on this criterion, as discriminating against people of other religions. But to return to the law against cattle-slaughtering, this could be acceptable if justified on grounds of public health, as in recent scares over 'mad cow' disease, instead of religious views, since public health concerns are presumably shared by all inhabitants of society, regardless of their specific conceptions of the good.[17]

It seems that a defensible conception of neutrality must rest on neutrality of justification, rather than of consequences. On the latter view, for example, public schools would be allowed to teach neither the theory of evolution nor creationism, since both doctrines affect different compre-

---

[15] Complex issues concerning citizens' requirements to be neutral cannot be discussed in detail here. But briefly, when citizens engage in public activities—e.g. advocacy—and attempt to influence public policy, then they are bound by requirements of neutral justification. But though their positions must be defensible on neutral grounds, they can use additional, non-neutral arguments to advance them. In this respect, private citizens are less bound by requirements of neutral public reason than government officials. For discussion, see Rawls (1997: 769, 797); for discussion of 'inclusive' public reason, see Solum (1994).

[16] Rawls includes an additional sense, neutrality of procedure (Rawls 1993: 191–4).

[17] The cattle-slaughtering example is suggested by Locke (1955: 39–40); for discussion, see Waldron (1989).

hensive views differently.[18] Similarly, mandatory vaccination laws would not be allowed, because they promote certain comprehensive views at the expense of Christian Science. Indeed, if this requirement were interpreted strictly, few state actions would be allowed. In a highly pluralistic society almost any public policy will affect some comprehensive views differently from others.

Neutrality of justification is easier to defend. This requirement is linked to the requirement of consensus. If liberal principles must be justified to everyone, clearly they must be neutral in this sense. And so it is not surprising that most prominent writers defend some version of neutrality of justification.[19]

Neutrality of justification allows the state wide latitude. As has been indicated, this view allows a core of relatively uncontroversial values to be promoted. Neutral liberals differ from non-neutral in supporting a *minimal* conception of the good, as opposed to *no* conception.[20] As it seems to me, much of the controversy surrounding neutrality has resulted from insistence that it be taken literally, so proponents of neutrality must be committed to *no* values. But neutrality so construed is absurd. After all, neutrality is not inherently valuable. If asked to justify it, a proponent must appeal to underlying values, which are therefore compatible with a 'neutral' theory. On a view of neutrality grounded in acceptable values, otherwise problematic cases could well be defensible. Teaching evolution in schools could be justified on the grounds that all citizens of a democratic society in a highly technological age should have basic knowledge of science. Similarly, compulsory vaccination could be justified on grounds of public health, not only the health of the child receiving the vaccine, but

[18] For different ways such education issues can be construed, see Macedo (1995), Gutmann (1995), and Galston (1995). In addition, as Waldron notes, an important theoretical difficulty with neutrality of consequences is that, if the state is required not to act in ways that do not advance the prospects of one lifestyle more than others, e.g. a Christian lifestyle over an environmentalist one, this requires postulation of some baseline against which the differential effects of state actions can be assessed (Waldron (1989: 67).

[19] Examples are Rawls (1993), Larmore (1987), Waldron (1989), and Moon (1993).

[20] Sterba (1992). As examples of public safety and public health show, claims of neutrality give way to strongly established, non-controversial claims of the good. Thus arguments in favour of a particular conception of the good, as in Sher's recent book (1997), if successful, will overthrow neutrality. However, I think it is unlikely that Sher's account yields clear delineations of the good in concrete circumstances, which would take precedence over values of neutrality. Wall (1998) convincingly argues that concerns of justice take precedence over claims of neutrality. But I believe the particular value he defends—autonomy—can be accommodated by a carefully formulated version of neutral liberalism. The strong overlap between Wall's 'perfectionist' view and an acceptable 'neutral' view indicates that these terms have become to some degree outmoded.

also the need to protect other children. The general requirements that the state function effectively, that decision procedures work smoothly, and public order be maintained can be justified neutrally, as important for all people, regardless of their conceptions of the good. As is the case with other values discussed throughout this work, the specific forms and levels neutrality should assume must be set by democratic procedures.

In spite of its importance, neutrality of justification has limits. Not *all* conceptions of the good should be regarded equally. Views that are not reasonable can be excluded (as discussed in the following chapter). Along similar lines, the requirement that public policies be justifiable on neutral grounds commits us to some conception of legitimate justification, or of reasonable argumentation. These notions will be pursued in the next chapter. But we should note here that in a pluralistic society justificatory arguments should be limited to canons of reasoning and evidence that are as uncontroversial as possible. Although no conception of reasoning is entirely non-controversial, permissible arguments should be confined to what is least controversial, e.g. common sense, standard rules of logical inference, and findings of empirical science. Although no canons of argument are completely uncontroversial, these are least objectionable.[21] The liberal tradition emerged historically in opposition to indefensible forms of intellectual authority as well as political authority. The standard of neutrality rules out appeals to certain controversial kinds of evidence, e.g. specific interpretations of sacred texts, which are not accessible to all citizens, the findings of pseudo-science such as astrology, or evidence relying on theories of dubious scientific legitimacy, such as 'recovered memories'.

These restrictions are probably the least we can assert and still be able to achieve consensus. In a pluralist society even these strictures could well be resisted, especially by proponents of religiously based world-views, whose moral epistemologies rely on authority (see below, Chapter 4).[22] Obviously, the consequences of adopting a conception of 'reasonable' justification along such lines would be more problematic than the one proposed here. Arguments based on such reasoning could not be accepted by most liberal citizens, while basing policies on them would be more likely to lead to social upheaval. The liberal tradition has always had at its core ideals of open inquiry and debate that are inimical to authoritative epistemologies. Among liberal commitments we can postulate the need to accept minimal standards of reasonable argument, as elucidated here.

---

[21] See Rawls (1993, lecture 6).
[22] For an alternative view, see Bohman (1995).

APPENDED NOTE

The idea of neutrality has been criticized on different grounds, but these can be countered. The claim that neutrality is objectionable because it is rooted in moral scepticism is easily rebutted, as such scepticism should be viewed as one controversial conception of the good among others (cf. Rawls 1993: 62–3). For Barry's more interesting and more defensible claim for a connection between neutrality and scepticism, see Barry (1995*b*, 168–73). Other grounds for neutrality are possible, e.g. the need to treat inhabitants of diverse societies with respect. Sher (1997) is perhaps the most searching criticism of neutrality that has so far appeared. But his main criticism of neutrality based on respect is easily countered; see pp. 81–2. Moreover, his strategy of criticizing possible bases for neutrality *seriatim* is subject to question, as it is likely that the different grounds can work in conjunction with one another, providing a more secure overall basis.

An additional and perhaps more common ground attributed to neutrality by its critics is a strong ideal of personal autonomy; see esp. Sandel (1982, 1996, ch. 1). However, although Sandel's accounts of the role of autonomy in liberal theory and of the liberal self may be true of particular thinkers, they are not necessary features of liberal theory *per se* or of liberal theorists who are committed to neutrality. Sandel moves illicitly from asserting that (a form of) neutrality *can be* grounded on a highly individualist conception of the good life to the claim that it *must* be. Views of the relevant kind have been advanced by particular liberal theorists, notably Kant and J. S. Mill, in spite of other differences between their philosophies. But they are not necessary features of liberal theory *per se*. Sandel's important claims concerning connections between neutrality and an indefensible conception of the self are decisively countered in Kymlicka (1988).

Although Wall's criticisms are telling, they hold only for strong versions of neutrality and can be accommodated by the view advanced here (Wall 1998; see above, n. 20). Neutrality is criticized from an additional direction, as internally inconsistent. According to this view, expounded, for example, by Stephen Macedo (1990) and William Galston (1991), liberal neutrality is not neutral. In Macedo's words: 'Liberal principles and goals shape our lives pervasively, deeply, and relentlessly' (Macedo (1990: 288). Even if these principles do not directly determine our choices, they limit the range from which we can choose, thereby indirectly structuring our lives. To some extent, this line of criticism is valid. As noted above, liberal theories are not entirely neutral; certain values are favoured over others. Obviously, people whose conceptions of the good make it impossible for them to live peaceably with others must be restrained, as must criminals (see below, Ch. 2, Sect. 1). More troubling issues concern restricting voluntarily chosen ways of life that are inconsistent with liberal values, e.g. a Hindu caste system, that accords the well-being of each Brahmin thirty times as much importance as that of an Untouchable (Galston 1991: 182–3). I will avoid discussing such issues here; suggestions as to how liberal consensus would deal with them are found in Ch. 3.

On the whole, criticisms such as those of Macedo and Galston depend on taking liberal theory's profession of 'neutrality' literally. They are able to show that the values underlying so-called neutral justification have further non-neutral implications. But the response is similar. So-called 'neutral' public policies must be grounded on certain values, which are given priority over others. As long as liberal societies are pluralistic, their inhabitants must agree about certain central matters, even if they cannot be brought to agree about everything.

Finally, rejecting neutrality, Galston upholds a version of liberal theory with a more robust conception of the good (Galston (1991). However, enforced agreement on a wider area rather than a narrower will interfere more deeply with people's pursuit of their own chosen values, and therefore requires that a heavy burden of justification be met that the theorist's preferred values or policies are in fact widely accepted, or implied by other beliefs that are widely accepted, in spite of appearances to the contrary. Alternatively, it must be shown that these values or policies should be imposed on people, although they do not accept them. Especially for theorists who doubt the possibility of being able to argue from objective moral first principles, it is difficult to justify imposing principles on people who object to them.

2

Theoretical Foundations

THE distinctive method employed in this study is construction of principles with careful attention to the actual beliefs of liberal citizens. In this chapter I explain reasons for using this procedure instead of others. In addition, in order to ascertain the beliefs of liberal citizens, I will place heavy reliance on survey research, advantages and drawbacks of which should be discussed.

1. 'REASONABLE' JUSTIFICATION

As explained in the previous chapter, a basic commitment of liberal theory is that political principles should be able to be justified to each citizen, at the bar of his or her own reason. There are, however, obvious limitations here. As a practical matter, because of the diversity of liberal societies, it is unlikely that a set of principles could be developed that would be acceptable to all inhabitants. However, it is not necessary that principles be accepted by *all* citizens. Liberal citizens cannot make patently unreasonable demands; they should be willing to co-operate on reasonable terms with others, which implies willingness to accept principles that satisfy reasonable conditions.

Accordingly, in a classic article Thomas Scanlon notes that, in order to be justified, a given principle, P, need not actually be accepted. Rather, the subject in question should not have adequate grounds for rejecting it. Scanlon appeals to 'the desire to be able to justify one's actions to others on grounds that they could not reasonably reject' (Scanlon 1982: 116). Scanlon notes that this standard can be met even if subjects are not interested in meeting it. A given principle should not be prevented from being justified 'even if others in fact refuse to accept it (perhaps because they have no interest in finding principles which we and others could not reasonably reject)' (p. 116). Thus Scanlon claims that we should focus on what subjects should accept, as opposed to what they actually accept. He notes that one rough way of determining whether a particular justification is adequate is to see if one would accept it if in another person's position (p. 117). Though Scanlon's analysis helps to clarify matters, severe problems obviously remain, especially fleshing out the notion of 'reasonable' acceptance and rejection of principles. Repeated invocation of the term 'reasonable' throughout the discussion here indicates the pressing nature of this demand.

Like other normative concepts, 'reasonableness' is subject to controversy. In a pluralistic society people with different moral views will disagree about its meaning; like other moral concepts, 'reasonable' is essentially contested. As with other concepts we employ, the sense of this term should be determined by our aims. Because the purpose of liberal consensus—political liberalism as discussed in this work—is to develop moral principles that can be widely accepted, we should employ a minimal conception, which can avoid controversy as much as possible. For ease of reference, we can refer to the requirement that moral principles be justified as widely as possible as the requirement of 'general justification'. Because of this requirement, considerations that favour crafting moral principles to allow them to be widely accepted extend to 'reasonableness' as well.

A (relatively) non-controversial concept of reasonableness centres more on how people behave than on what they believe. The concept 'reasonableness' has two main dimensions; we speak of 'reasonable' people in cognitive and attitudinal senses. In the former, a reasonable person is one whose beliefs or opinions are adequately grounded. She has good evidence (good reasons) for holding them; her main principles are securely founded, while others, derived from them, follow according to sound rules of inference. In the second sense, reasonable people try to get along with others. They are open-minded and fair, not demanding more than their share (the Greek *pleonexia*, literally 'having more', which is one synonym for injustice). Reasonable people are willing to live with others on fair terms of co-operation.

'Reasonableness' in this second sense admits a range of construals. According to what we can call a strong conception, a person is genuinely open-minded and tolerant. Important among her motivations is a desire to be able to justify her conduct to others and so to live with them on terms that all can accept. Something along these lines is related to the desire noted by Scanlon. But people can be attitudinally reasonable in a weaker sense. As long as they are willing to live and let live and do not attempt to force their beliefs or practices on other members of society, they can be legitimately considered reasonable, even if their primary motives do not include open-mindedness or tolerance. Additional kinds of reasonableness could be located between the stronger and weaker senses, but, for convenience, we can confine discussion to these two, along with the cognitive sense.

This weaker, attitudinal sense of reasonableness differs from the stronger in possibly being less rooted in moral principles of a particular kind. The stronger sense bridges the gap between cognitive and attitudinal senses, as it contains elements of both kinds. But this does not mean that we should exclude people who are 'reasonable' in the weaker sense. Because of the desire of liberal consensus to encompass as many people as possible, we should view as 'reasonable' people who are willing to live co-operatively with others, more or less regardless of their motivation. Such people should be distinguished from the 'unreasonable', who are either unwilling to abide by the moral requirements of social co-operation or demand to impose their beliefs on others. As long as people are willing to refrain from such objectionable behaviour, there seems to be no a priori reason to exclude them from the requirement of justification. It is an empirical question whether people are able to behave appropriately without particular kinds of moral principle. Without strong evidence that this is not possible, we should not exclude any co-operative individuals from the requirement that principles should be justified to them, and so liberal consensus should take into account the moral principles such people hold.

Construing 'reasonableness' in this way has significant implications. Most importantly, it gives large segments of the population veto power over liberal principles and so could well dilute their content. Obviously, by advancing a more restrictive concept of reasonableness, we could narrow the groups with veto power and so develop principles with more substantive moral content. But such a strategy skirts circularity. By carefully crafting our concept of 'reasonableness', we could ensure the adoption of virtually any principles whatsoever. Restrictions on 'reasonableness' require independent justification. Because the goal of liberal consensus is to provide principles that can be widely justified in pluralistic societies, there is a presumption against a concept of 'reasonableness' that will exclude any group.

Thus it appears that Rawls errs in restricting 'reasonable' comprehensive views to ones with what he regards as appropriate cognitive content.[1] Rawls describes reasonable people as possessing three attributes. First, they are willing to propose fair terms of co-operation, and to abide by them, when others are as well. Rawls notes the close relationship between this sense of reasonableness and the position of Scanlon (Rawls 1993: 49 and n. 2). Secondly, reasonable people recognize the burdens of judgement. They understand that, because of the normal workings of human

---

[1] According to Jones (1995: 526–7), Rawls runs together two senses of reasonableness, which correspond to the two senses under discussion.

reason, people will arrive at different conclusions about fundamental moral matters, and so should expect a range of comprehensive views to exist alongside one another. According to Rawls, this realization 'limits the scope of what reasonable persons think can be justified to others' and so leads to a form of toleration (p. 59). Thirdly, reasonable people will not think it legitimate to use political power to suppress alternative comprehensive views and promote their own (p. 60).[2]

As one can see, Rawls combines essentially attitudinal aspects of reasonableness—his first and third senses—with cognitive requirements, his second. Apparently, he believes that acceptance of the burdens of judgement causes one to moderate one's attitude towards one's own comprehensive view and to tolerate others. For the sake of argument, we can grant this contention and so a connection between acceptance of the burdens of judgement and desirable attitudes towards others. What Rawls has not shown, however, is that acceptance of the burdens is required for the proper attitudes. The fact that accepting them promotes tolerance does not imply that not accepting them necessarily makes one impermissibly intolerant. Clearly, people who subscribe to various fanatical doctrines believe in suppressing alternative views. Rawls quotes Bossuet: 'I have the right to persecute you because I am right and you are wrong' (Rawls 1993: 61 n. 16). Perhaps Rawls would also appeal to the Rousseauian suspicion that, in political matters, there is no legitimate disagreement. If a person disagrees with the majority, this must be because he either lacks virtue or has made an error.[3]

But these connections do not always hold. People can be tolerant for reasons other than accepting the burdens of judgement. For example, people can believe that, on doctrinal matters, even if someone is incorrect, it is wrong to penalize him for his beliefs or to force him to alter them. One of the reasons for religious tolerance Locke advances, in his *Letter Concerning Toleration*, is that only sincerely held religious beliefs matter. Thus it is not possible to enforce conformity: 'the care of souls cannot belong to the civil magistrate because his power consists only in outward force; but true and saving religion consists in the inward persuasion of the mind, without which nothing can be acceptable to God' (Locke 1955: 18).

This is only one justification for tolerance. There are doubtless other reasons as well for people who do not accept the burdens of judgement. If we grant this, then people can be reasonable in Rawls's other two senses without accepting the burdens. Again, there is no basis for ruling out this possibility without strong evidence. Rawls notes that we should avoid

---

[2] Other senses of the 'reasonable' employed by Rawls are discussed by Gaus (1996: 131–2).

[3] See *Social Contract*, esp. bk. IV, ch. 2.

'excluding doctrines as unreasonable without strong grounds' (1993: 59). And so we should leave open the possibility of attitudinal reasonableness based on beliefs other than the burdens of judgement, until careful examination of the evidence shows this to be impossible.

As with other concepts we have examined, the attitudinal conception of 'reasonableness' can be operationalized most clearly in regard to what it excludes. People who do not accept, and act according to, minimal moral principles are not reasonable in this sense. This is clearest in regard to people whose beliefs entail harming others. Such people can be considered unreasonable, and so forfeit the right to be governed by principles they can accept.

We can extend this notion. In order to be included in society's consensus, people must be moved to some extent by virtues of tolerance and civility. They must be interested in preserving civil peace and willing to do their part in this. Because public disagreements must be settled by democratic institutions, they must also possess in some degree the important virtue of being willing to accept decisions made by fair procedures.[4] Thus society owes justifiable principles to all individuals who are willing to live under them with some degree of co-operation. People whose principles are not compatible with this degree of civility or which do not accept co-operative association as an important value forfeit their rights to justification. As Larmore says: 'A liberal political system need not feel obliged to reason with fanatics; it must simply take the necessary precautions to guard against them' (Larmore 1987: 60; also 66).

For the so-called fanatic, society's burden of justification is not withdrawn. He too should be governed by principles that can be supported by strong reasons. But in his case, the reasons will not be convincing *to him*. I take it that the need to exclude people who are patently unreasonable in this minimal sense is not controversial. Any defensible theory must proceed similarly. Rather, given the distinctive thrust of the position advanced here, what is more controversial is the fact that the principles developed must be so inclusive. For instance, although different religious views are based on beliefs that are not 'reasonable' according to many construals, the position outlined here implies that political principles and policies should be justifiable to their proponents, if at all possible. Because of significant differences in how devoutly religious and secular people view the world, including widely different conceptions of persuasive arguments, there are obvious problems in presenting canons of argument that will be accepted by both groups. But doing so is necessary for reasons of consensus in both sociological and normative senses. It is not consistent with the

---

[4] Political virtues required by liberalism are discussed by Gutmann and Thompson (1996, chs. 2–4); and Galston (1991, ch. 10).

commitments of liberal theory not to attempt to justify principles to people who are willing to live co-operatively with others, while it could be damaging to social peace and stability not to attempt to do so. Doing so is especially necessary if large percentages of the population subscribe to religious comprehensive views. A concept of 'reasonable' principles that excludes such people at the outset is obviously at odds with the goals of political liberalism.

2. 'EMPIRICAL' JUSTIFICATION

Since the main task of liberal consensus is to discover principles on which diverse liberal citizens can agree, it seems that the most advisable strategy is to begin by examining the beliefs of the range of reasonable citizens— the large majority of the population—and to look for areas of overlap or agreement among adherents of different comprehensive views. We can refer to this as the method of convergence, or convergence, for short. In attempting to justify principles to a group of people, a great deal depends on what they already believe. If some principle, *P*, is to be justified to Smith, it must fit in with her existing beliefs. However, it could be objected that this course could lead to neglect of necessary restrictions and so to unacceptable principles. But the question, of course, is what the necessary restrictions are.

As it seems to me, the restrictions should be filled in in accordance with the discussion in the previous section. Because the purpose of liberal consensus is to develop principles that are justifiable to a wide range of citizens, requirements bearing on general justification should be as few and non-controversial as possible—including criteria of proper justification itself. 'Justification', like other moral notions, will be understood differently by proponents of different comprehensive views, and so should be dealt with along the same lines as other moral concepts. But this does not rule out restrictions altogether. First, principles developed for a liberal society must be consistent with liberal theory's commitments, as discussed in the last chapter. Principles must guarantee appropriate levels of rights, including rights to democratic government, and not support unjustified inequalities, or treating people without due respect. Beliefs inconsistent with—or that imply principles inconsistent with—these requirements can be set aside.

The subject of necessary cognitive restrictions is complex, and cannot be discussed in detail here. But again, given the purposes of liberal consensus, they should be as uncontroversial as possible. Clear minimal criteria of proper justification are that principle P is justified to Smith (a) if she assents to it, or (b) if P follows closely and directly from central principles to which she assents.[5] Questions of logical implication that arise in regard to (b) should be fleshed out in accordance with the canons of argumentation noted in the last chapter (p. 16). Beyond this point, it is difficult to support additional restrictions. If the principles we seek are to be acceptable to widely diverse liberal citizens, there is a presumption against additional restrictions, which could lead to large numbers of people not recognizing or accepting resultant principles.

A different view of liberal justification is presented by Gerald Gaus, in *Justificatory Liberalism* (Gaus 1996). The issues at stake here can be clarified by looking briefly at his account. Gaus begins by noting the importance the need for justification has assumed in recent liberal theory, as discussed by theorists such as Rawls, Larmore, and Waldron. His claim that public justification 'is the core of liberalism' (pp. 3–4) raises the question of exactly what justification entails. To answer this, he turns to recent work in epistemology and cognitive psychology. He defends a form of coherentism: a given belief is justified on the basis of its fit with a subject's other beliefs. The implications are somewhat relativistic, as beliefs that can be justified to one person may not be to another, in accordance with other justified beliefs they hold. Of more immediate concern, Gaus argues against different forms of 'populist' justification, which depend on beliefs people actually hold. He is willing to set these aside because of flaws in people's reasoning: people 'can withhold their assent because of obstinacy, selfishness, laziness, perversity or confusion' (p. 131).

Gaus focuses on inferential norms. Empirical studies have documented widespread errors in the norms people hold. Examples are common errors in probabilistic judgements, the so-called gambler's fallacy, and others (Gaus 1996: 133, 54–9). Accordingly, Gaus argues that what people regard as common sense is oftentimes 'deviant' reasoning (p. 135). Because what are 'commonsense epistemic norms and practices lead to normatively inappropriate results' (p. 134), correct inferential norms can be substituted for ones people actually employ. By extension, people's actual principles can be set aside in favour of principles they would accept if their reasoning abilities were more sophisticated.

Gaus's discussion shows the need for acceptable epistemological constraints on justification. At minimum, people must be able to reason correctly, and their basic principles must be adequately founded.[6] Just as a

[5] For a good recent account of coherence justification, see Gaus (1996, pt. I).

[6] Given the extent to which many people ground their basic moral principles in religious beliefs, the second condition could well be controversial, though I will not discuss it here.

person can be viewed as unreasonable if she is perversely or obstinately unwilling to assent to principles she cannot reasonably reject, so a person who is not able to realize that she is logically committed to a given principle because it is implied by her other beliefs can also be viewed as not reasonable. However, it is not clear that the implications are as far-reaching as Gaus suggests.

As we have seen, Gaus's project is set in motion by the central role of justification in recent liberal theory, as discussed by Rawls, Larmore, and other theorists. However, he does not explore the reasons why these theorists, and others he notes, are concerned with justification, turning instead to accounts of justification in the literature of epistemology and cognitive psychology. But as we saw in the last chapter, the concerns of Rawls, Larmore, *et al.* are not primarily epistemological. For them, justification is necessary in order to show people proper respect, a motivation which should be taken into account in construing 'justification'. In this study, as I have noted, 'justification' should be construed in the context of liberal consensus and its aims, which require that we pay careful attention to people's existing beliefs and wishes.

The force of the requirement to respect Jones's existing beliefs can be illuminated by looking briefly at the logic of consent. Ordinarily, if Jones consents to do X, this will generate a moral requirement to do it. If he promises Smith to give her \$10, this generates a requirement for him to give her the money. However, under certain circumstances, what Jones has consented to can rightfully be set aside. Theorists have identified 'defeating conditions', circumstances which, if present, can negate an act of consent. These include lack of awareness, lack of competence, and coercion.[7] Thus if Jones consents to some state of affairs while not being aware of what he is consenting to, we would ordinarily say that this is not a proper act of consent and so does not create an obligation for him to do what he agreed to. We would say something similar about a case in which Jones consents to X but for some reason is not competent to do so, whether because he is too young or suffers from a mental condition that prevents him from being able to make normatively binding agreements. Once again, in such a case, this should not be regarded as a genuine act of consent, and the same is true of an instance of forced consent. To deal with cases of these sorts, we can say that, although acts of consent are presumptively binding, they do not always bind.[8] There is a strong presumption that an

---

[7] For brief discussion, see Rosett (1988, ch. 1, sect. 5); Beran (1987, ch. 1).

[8] Promises are generally viewed as creating obligations of compliance for people who make them, although these bind only prima facie, rather than without exceptions. For brief discussion of prima-facie obligations, with references, see Klosko (1992: 12–14). In the cases discussed here, we should probably say that the acts of consent do

act of consent generates an obligation of compliance, unless defeating conditions can be shown to be present—which is frequently not easy to demonstrate. Accordingly, if Jones drafts a will, this should be regarded as creating binding moral (and, perhaps, legal) requirements unless one or other defeating conditions can be shown to be present.

Something similar is true of justification. As noted above, a principle, P, can be viewed as justified to Smith if she assents to it or if it is clearly implied by principles she does accept. The cognitive aspects of these cases allow different construals. It would burden our discussion to explore these in detail, so a rough account must suffice. Clearly, P is ordinarily justified to Smith if she accepts it. The nature of moral theory, however, complicates matters in regard to what her existing moral principles imply. As Rawls says, moral theory is 'Socratic' (Rawls 1971: 49). It is unlikely that all Smith's existing beliefs are carefully developed in a consistent theoretical structure. But also justified to Smith are principles that clearly follow from important aspects of her beliefs, though she does not consciously subscribe to them.[9] In such cases, a given principle, Q, should be viewed as justified, whether or not Smith recognizes this. Presumably, if Q were brought to her attention, she would accept it, because of its close fit with other components of her belief system. Because Q is clearly implied by P, she cannot reasonably reject it. However we fill in the details exactly, it is clear that, in certain cases, principles Smith does not accept can be justified to her. However, if we are required to justify moral principles to Smith in order to show her proper respect, then we can move beyond her existing beliefs only when a heavy burden of proof is satisfied. Especially strong evidence must be produced to show that she should accept Q even though she does not subscribe to it and it is not clearly implied by principles she

not give rise to prima-facie obligations, as they are not overridden by other moral considerations. Rather, the presence of defeating conditions prevents them from generating moral requirements at all.

[9] The qualifications 'clear' and 'important' are necessary here, because, if people's overall beliefs systems contain inconsistencies, a wide range of additional beliefs could be implied by particular existing beliefs—some of which could be inconsistent with one another and with other components of her belief system—and might otherwise be said to be justified. In regard to inferential norms according to which Smiths' beliefs can be fleshed out, we should note that, in order to show Smith proper respect, we should assume that her reasoning is correct, unless it can be shown not to be. Even though, as Gaus argues, widely accepted inferential norms have been shown to be incorrect (1996: 130–6), the norms he discusses are generally fairly sophisticated and have not been shown to be involved in people's adherence to the particular moral beliefs and principles that interest us (above, p. 25). In many important moral cases, the inferential norms employed are simple and straightforward and so unlikely to be incorrect. For the most important examples in this study, see the norms discussed below, in Ch. 5. For discussion of points in this note, I am indebted to Gerald Gaus.

does accept. If Q conflicts with others of her principles, the burden becomes still heavier—and more so depending on how strongly she adheres to these other principles. To meet such burdens of proof in specific instances would require detailed examination, on a case-by-case basis.

Evidence required to move beyond people's existing principles would appear to involve defeating conditions similar to those that justify setting aside acts of consent. These include evidence of lack of competence and awareness, the latter manifesting itself in the form of highly inconsistent or mutually contradictory overall beliefs.[10] A significant defeating condition is the presence of morally unacceptable beliefs. As we have noted, for the justification of moral principles, it is not enough that Smith accepts principle P. P must also be acceptable on moral grounds—in the cases that interest us, according to the commitments of liberal theory. As we have seen, because of difficulties in specifying exactly what constitutes acceptable liberal principles and the importance of personal autonomy, which requires that principles be freely accepted, we should present this condition in negative form. A person's principles can be presumed to be acceptable and justified to him (under the assumption that other conditions are met) as long as they cannot be shown to be clearly unacceptable on moral grounds. But if a given principle is clearly inconsistent with basic liberal principles—e.g. a principle advocating racial or religious intolerance—then neither it nor other principles that follow from it should be viewed as acceptable or as justified. This defeating condition, like the others discussed, requires a heavy burden of proof.

Without strong evidence to the contrary, imposing beliefs on people to which they do not subscribe cannot be justified. Considerations of the kind discussed by Gaus are not in themselves sufficient. The fact that an individual, Betty, makes errors in certain kinds of inference does not justify setting aside her existing moral views unless the errors are closely implicated in her holding them, instead of the views one wishes to impose on her. Demonstrating this in regard to large numbers of liberal citizens raises daunting empirical issues. It is not enough to show that Betty makes errors (or, more accurately, is likely to have made errors), in some general way. One has to show that she makes specific errors that disqualify specific principles to which she subscribes from being justified. In cases where Betty's principles rest on flagrant informational and logical errors, setting aside her existing views may be defensible. But it has not been shown that specific, important, and widely held moral and political principles involve

---

[10] Coercion would appear to be relevant as a defeating condition, when beliefs involve clear indoctrination. But we can assume that such cases are not of concern here.

errors of this sort. Once again, detailed study of actual people's beliefs are necessary.

In this study I will attempt to present the political principles that can be most clearly justified to the large majority of liberal citizens, because people either hold them already or they follow from other important principles they accept. Once again, this requires that we employ the method of convergence. We must look closely at the actual views of liberal citizens and try to identify areas of wide overlap between proponents of existing comprehensive views. Because of a lack of overall clarity in people's views—compounded by shortcomings of the available evidence—we will see that people's basic principles can be formulated only imprecisely and allow different construals. Areas of significant convergence admit only similarly rough formulation.[11] While specific beliefs on which significant numbers of people converge are not ideal from any particular point of view, on the whole they are not clearly deficient and so do not fall beyond the point at which we are justified in setting them aside.

3. TYPES OF CONSENSUS

In Chapter 1 I noted that consensus on basic principles of the political and social order is valuable for normative and sociological reasons. It is important to recognize that different sorts of consensus are possible, depending on the specific values one emphasizes, although the values we have discussed lead us to favour a particular construal.

Three main aspects of consensus on which variation is possible are as follows. First is 'popular breadth', the proportion of the population in agreement on some issue or set of issues. This can range, obviously, from a few members of society to a large or overwhelming percentage. Second is what we can call 'extent' of agreement. Reference here is to the proportion of overall belief systems on which members of the consensus agree. Again, one can imagine differences here, ranging from agreement on a few points to complete agreement on overall comprehensive views. Third is 'depth of commitment', by which I mean strength of moral or psychological adherence to shared beliefs. Other factors could be added, concerning, for instance, the nature of the beliefs agreed upon: moral, religious, political, etc. Or perhaps we could examine different ways consensuses are formed, e.g. through socialization, conversion, coercion, etc. But for our

---

[11] These can be worked out differently from different ideological perspectives, and so disagreements between them can be an important aspect of democratic politics.

purposes, the three most important factors are the ones named. By combining different instances of these, one can arrive at quite different forms of consensus.

It seems likely that particular aspects of consensus regularly combine in certain patterns. For instance, in many cases, we can hypothesize that extent of agreement and depth of commitment are closely related. Roughly, in these cases, agreement on larger proportions of belief systems is accompanied by greater commitment to shared views. An example in which this relationship would hold is a religious sect. A sect is described by Ernst Troeltsch as follows:

The sect is a voluntary society, composed of strict and definite Christian believers bound to each other by the fact that all have experienced 'the new birth.' These 'believers': live apart from the world, are limited to small groups, emphasize the law instead of grace, and in varying degrees within their own circle set up the Christian order based on love; all this is done in preparation for and expectation of the coming Kingdom of God. (Troeltsch 1960: ii. 993)

Given the degree of commitment that such a group requires, it is likely that, as Troeltsch notes, membership would be limited to a relatively small percentage of a given population. As a group becomes more cohesive and tight-knit, it would also become more exclusive. Thus we can hypothesize that extent of agreement and depth of commitment are directly related, but inversely related to popular breadth. At the opposite extreme is consensus founded on a relatively narrow range of points. Because of the lower degree of commitment such unity entails, membership of this group could be far higher in terms of popular breadth. An example here is an American political party, e.g. the Democrats. Will Rogers famously quipped that he belonged to no organized political party; he was a Democrat. But, for the sake of illustration, we can assume that Democrats agree on a range of basic points, e.g. commitment to some measure of civil rights.

Again, for the sake of illustration, let us imagine a continuum between tight and loose consensus. For ease of reference, we can refer to the two extremes as 'sect-agreement' and 'issue-agreement' respectively. It is apparent that consensuses of these kinds would be desirable in different sorts of group, constituted for different purposes. Sect-agreement would be desirable in situations in which strong homogeneity was a value, as in certain religious organizations. Groups of this sort also possess an unusually strong form of commitment and so one can predict that they would have more stable membership than other kinds of group. It is important to realize, however, that consensus of this sort is not likely to be practicable for a modern pluralistic society. Given our interest in general justification, our preferred form of consensus is issue-agreement. The need for extensive popular breadth entails that agreement must be relatively narrow in extent, confined to only certain principles. These suppositions are closely related to what Rawls posits in his overlapping consensus, agreement on only certain points, which adherents of different comprehensive views interpret differently and accept from the standpoints of their overall views. An assumption I am making is that a narrow form of consensus can be adequate for both the normative and sociological requirements of liberal consensus. The evidence examined in the following chapters will support this.

A further set of distinctions, bearing on normative requirements of liberal consensus, is relevant to our analysis here. We have repeatedly noted the requirement that people be governed according to principles they accept. What concern me are different senses in which people accept, or can accept, specific principles. The most obvious sense is what we can call 'empirical acceptance'. Jones recognizes the principle in question as one to which he subscribes, as things stand. We can also include principles that directly follow from ones Jones accepts, according to simple rules of inference, as discussed in the last section. But one must ask if liberal consensus is limited to principles that people actually recognize or could be brought to recognize with relatively little effort. One encounters an entire range of questions—moral, psychological, sociological, educational—in regard to principles a particular group of people could be brought to accept. I do not wish to discuss these questions in detail, and, in any event, it would be of little value to do so on an abstract level, as opposed to in regard to particular groups. Nevertheless, it is important to distinguish between principles that people more or less hold, and those they can be brought to hold through intensive education and training. On the one hand, we have what we can call 'empirical' consensus, founded upon principles to which people subscribe and others that follow closely from central aspects of their belief systems and which they could perhaps be brought to recognize relatively easily. At the opposite pole is consensus based on beliefs that people sharply oppose and would require drastic means to realize, akin to those Plato describes in the *Republic*.[12] Obviously, agreements of this kind need not concern us. More problematic—and more realistic—are forms that lie between these poles. An important form is consensus based on principles to which people are committed, though less closely. Perhaps these follow from certain beliefs they would not view as central, or from particular beliefs but conflict with others. Obviously, innumerable possibilities could be envisioned. But we can assume that conflict with certain

---

[12] For discussion, see Klosko (1986).

of a subject's beliefs is accompanied by psychological reluctance to accept principles at the cost of substantial alteration of her overall belief system. In such cases, subjects could well resist the principles in question, barring intensive persuasion, though less extreme that what Plato describes.

Implications of these variants of consensus will be explored throughout this study. Given the values of liberal consensus, I will generally concentrate on beliefs that fall within empirical consensus. But again, it is most profitable to discuss these in the context of actual beliefs of liberal citizens. Before proceeding, we should note that the method employed to derive the content of a given consensus, or potential consensus, will vary with differences in the form of consensus sought. Clearly, the content of an empirical consensus can be discovered empirically. If members of a group, e.g. the Democratic Party, actually agree on a range of principles, this can be documented through empirical study, by inquiring into what different members of the party think. Other forms of consensus will require different methods. As the content postulated becomes increasingly removed from what members presently believe, then a suitable method will become increasingly elaborate, probably increasingly deductive. For instance, assume that researcher Jones posits that members of group X, while not presently agreeing on principles a, b, c, ... , are committed to them by beliefs p, q, r, ... that they currently hold. In a case such as this, Jones must move beyond empirical investigation of what members of X believe. To be sure, he must devote careful attention to what they think, to demonstrate their adherence to p, q, r, ... But he must go beyond this, to show as well that p, q, r, ... entail a, b, c, ... , which then must be shown to be the basis for a possible consensus. As the connections between people's actual beliefs and the putative consensus become increasingly attenuated, the method needed to derive the consensus is likely to become increasingly elaborate. In addition, if there is a gap between people's actual beliefs and a postulated consensus, then the researcher is confronted with questions of bringing people to recognize that they are committed to the principles of the potential consensus. Our view of the kind of consensus desired in liberal societies should be importantly affected by the practicability of these means.

4. SURVEY RESEARCH

As survey research has become an increasingly important tool in the social sciences, its problems and drawbacks have attracted increased attention. Problems can be divided into three main kinds: sampling error, measurement error, and specification error (Brady and Orren 1992). These can be discussed briefly. In a country of 260 million people, only a small percentage of the population can be polled on any question, and so it is necessary to make sure that those polled are representative of the population as a whole. To ensure this, all relevant members of the population should have known chances of being chosen, and the chance of choosing any one member of the population should not be affected by the chance of choosing another (Brady and Orren 1992: 59). An example of a poll that failed to take adequate measures to avoid sampling errors was conducted by the *Literary Digest*, on the 1936 United States presidential election. Though this publication had conducted accurate surveys on previous elections, the 1936 poll, based on names selected from telephone directories and automobile registration lists, was off by 20 per cent. It estimated Roosevelt's vote at 41 per cent, as opposed to the 61 per cent he actually received. The poll had Alf Landon easily defeating Roosevelt, in what turned out to be one of the great landslides in American history—in the opposite direction. Problems with the survey are easily identified. In the United States in 1936 people who owned telephones or automobiles tended to be more affluent than most Americans and disproportionately supported Landon (Abramson 1983: 16–17). However, although researchers must exercise constant care to choose random samples, the pitfalls are relatively easy to avoid. The surveys we will discuss throughout this study generally succeed in avoiding them—although, it should be noted, a large number of studies in psychology of religion and procedural justice rely on college students, frequently from introductory psychology classes, who cannot be presumed to be representative of the population as a whole. Specific results based on studies of college students must be identified as such. This fact is important in interpreting certain results. But even with this proviso, errors of the other two kinds are more important and troubling.

Measurement errors refer to problems in survey instruments. If an opinion poll is intended to capture the public's attitude on some issue, results should not be affected by elements in the design of the survey. An entire range of factors have been studied and shown to have important effects (see Schuman and Presser 1981). For instance, significant problems have been seen to stem from the wording of questions. Oftentimes it has been observed that rephrasing a question will produce significantly different results. A clear example is from a survey conducted in 1941. Support for free speech in the United States was 21 per cent higher when respondents were asked 'Do you think the United States should *forbid* public speeches against democracy?' than when they were asked 'Do you think the United States should *allow* public speeches against democracy?' (Schuman and Presser 1981: 276–7; my emphasis). Similar results were obtained when samples were asked the same questions in 1974 and 1976, while similar differences between questions with 'forbid' and 'allow' were also observed on a range of social issues, including abortion and use of marijuana. As Howard Schuman and Stanley Presser note, Americans are more likely to support not allowing something than forbidding it, although the practical implications of the two actions would appear to be the same (Schuman and Presser 1981: 276). Given the logical equivalence of 'forbidding' X and 'not allowing' it, it is not surprising that differences in responses diminish with increased education, but they do not disappear entirely (Schuman and Presser 1981: 278–9).

Similar effects have been observed in regard to the order in which questions are asked. An interesting example concerned asking respondents whether they would allow communist reporters into the United States and American reporters into the (former) Soviet Union. Respondents were more likely to support allowing the communist into the United States if they were first asked about allowing the American into the Soviet Union. In a survey conducted in 1948, the percentage who would allow the communist into the United States changed from 36.5 per cent to 73.1 per cent with the change in question order. When the questions were replicated in 1980, percentages still differed from 54.7 per cent to 74.6 per cent. As Schuman and Presser note, the order effect here appears to stem from respondents' desire to maintain consistency in their answers. Accordingly, percentages who would allow an American reporter into the Soviet Union declined significantly when respondents were first asked about allowing a communist reporter into the United States. In 1948 the percentages were 89.8 per cent when respondents were first asked about the American, and 65.6 per cent when they were asked about the communist first. In 1980 the difference narrowed somewhat, between 81.9 per cent and 63.7 per cent (Schuman and Presser 1981: 28–9).

Problems of wording and question order do not exhaust measurement difficulties.[13] Similar changes in results have been observed with other alterations in questions, e.g. to allow responses of 'don't know or no opinion', or to provide respondents with intermediate answer options between 'agree' and 'disagree' (Schuman and Presser 1981, chs. 4–6). Along similar lines, respondents have been found to have a general tendency to agree with statements about which they are asked. This propensity is apparent in responses to the following two statements: 'Individuals are more to blame than social conditions for crime and lawlessness in this country' and 'Social conditions are more to blame than individuals for crime and lawlessness in this country'. In repeated administrations of the statements

[13] Other sources of measurement difficulties not discussed here include simple ambiguity in wording and use of emotionally tinged language.

majorities were consistently found to agree with the alternative presented to them (Schuman and Presser 1981: 207–10). Though much remains unclear about exactly what is at work in so-called acquiescence bias, research indicates the importance of varying questions so that both agree and disagree responses are necessary to capture identifiable attitudes on topics under investigation.

An especially interesting and important measurement effect is achieved by altering the wording of questions to include more than one side of an issue. In a series of experiments conducted in 1974 and 1975, Schuman and Presser presented questions of two different forms on public policy issues, with one of each pair containing substantive counter-arguments. For instance, on gun control, respondents were asked either 'Would you favor or oppose a law which would require a person to obtain a police permit before he could buy a gun?' or 'Would you favor a law which would require a person to obtain a police permit before he could buy a gun, or do you think such a law would interfere too much with the rights of citizens to own guns?' While 28.3 per cent of the first question's respondents opposed the law, 32.7 per cent of the second question's opposed it. Schuman and Presser record similar results on nine variants of this procedure, with a median shift of 8 per cent and six of the nine differences statistically significant beyond the 0.02 level (Schuman and Presser 1981: 184–8). Accordingly, once again, experiments of this sort show that results of attitude surveys can be significantly affected by particular features of questions used.

The difficulties that measurement errors highlight are clearly due in large part to the elusiveness of what is sought. As V. O. Key observed, 'To speak with precision of public opinion is a task not unlike coming to grips with the Holy Ghost' (Key 1964: 8). On certain subjects, opinion polls have been found to be extremely accurate. For example, in twenty-five national elections between 1936 and 1988 Gallup polls were off by an average of 2.1 per cent in their estimates of the Democratic vote. In the eighteen elections between 1952 and 1988 the average error was 1.4 per cent. (Erikson *et al.* 1991: 29). Given this degree of accuracy, it seems clear that the surveys employed were consistently able to avoid measurement errors.

We can hypothesize that cases in which errors can be avoided generally possess certain features. The subject-matter is relatively clear-cut, and so questions can be straightforward—e.g. if the election were held today, which candidate would you vote for? We can also hypothesize that, on such subjects, respondents have relatively clear, set attitudes, which allow their responses not to be affected by specific features of questions. In addition, while liberal citizens have frequently been found to possess relatively little knowledge about political figures and issues,[14] in areas in which they have adequate knowledge their responses are likely to resist the kinds of factors we have reviewed. We can hypothesize a rough inverse relationship between subjects' levels of knowledge and their ability not to be influenced by features of survey instruments. Research consistently shows that measurement effects are strongest among poorly educated respondents. As respondents have increased education and information, their responses are more likely to reflect their underlying attitudes and not to vary because of measurement effects.

Henry Brady and Gary Orren note that an implicit assumption of much public opinion research is that people's minds are like filing cabinets: 'they contain clear opinions on many discrete topics and group them into categories like memos tucked away in file folders' (Brady and Orren 1992: 79). On certain subjects, this assumption may be correct; people do have fixed attitudes, which survey questions can tap. However, this is frequently not the case. On many subjects that interest us, respondents know little about the questions at issue and do not have strong or fixed attitudes about them. Thus measurement errors are a constant concern in the studies we will examine.

One additional measurement problem we should note is that, on certain subjects, respondents have been found not to respond truthfully. Especially when topics are controversial and respondents are reluctant to state their true feelings, either because the interviewer might think less of them, or perhaps from shame, respondents have been found to provide answers that are socially approved rather than accurate. Well-known instances concern black candidates for elective office. For example, when Tom Bradley, the black mayor of Los Angeles, ran for governor of California, in 1982, he was defeated, although public opinion polls consistently had him in the lead. Similar discrepancies between pre-election polls and vote tallies were observed when David Dinkins ran for mayor of New York City, in 1989, and Douglas Wilder ran for governor of Virginia, also in 1989 (see Brady and Orren 1992: 82–5). In these cases, we can hypothesize that respondents were reluctant to tell pollsters they intended to vote against the black candidates. As we will see below, in Chapter 4, something similar has been observed in surveys concerning religion and racial prejudice. Although, in answering questions, certain respondents indicated a lack of prejudice, when differences in their behaviour towards blacks and whites were observed under ingeniously contrived experimen-

---

[14] For information on knowledge levels of US citizens in regard to rules of the political game, political figures, substantive policy areas, and other topics, see Delli Carpini and Keeter (1996).

tal conditions, they were found to be prejudiced (see below, pp. 93–4, 97 n. 15).

In spite of all the measurement problems I have noted, in the subjects that interest us, specification errors are probably a greater concern. Specification errors involve problems in determining exactly what attitudes given survey questions measure. When topics of inquiry are complex and elusive, formidable obstacles must be overcome to make sure survey questions are appropriate to address them. In the words of Brady and Orren: 'Specification error, the most fundamental error, occurs when a theory is inappropriate for the opinion that the poll is trying to measure.' '[P]olls that do not measure what they seem to measure or that are used to prove or disprove poorly conceived theories are useless' (1992: 59). Specification problems are encountered repeatedly in the studies discussed in the following chapters. The nature of the difficulties can be indicated briefly.

In many familiar cases, there is a clear fit between responses to questions and subjects of inquiry. Again, if a pollster asks subjects whom they would vote for, we can assume that answers clearly reflect underlying attitudes. Something similar could be true of asking respondents about their favourite baseball teams. The clear, simple nature of the attitudes in question makes them relatively easy to connect with. Things become more complex as opinions become less tangible. For instance, if respondents are asked about their views on some international trade agreement, their responses are less likely closely to mirror underlying attitudes, because of the likelihood that respondents, many of whom are not familiar with the agreements in question, do not have developed attitudes (see Schuman and Presser 1981, ch. 5). In a case of this sort, one will note, the problem is not the complexity of the attitude researchers wish to study; in this instance, opinions on a trade bill could be similar to those on presidential candidates or baseball teams. The problem in such cases is subjects' lack of information.

In the cases that interest us, the subjects about which respondents are asked are for the most part familiar to them and objects of strong feelings. But the subjects are highly complex and abstract, so much so that survey questions inherently have difficulty tapping into them. Sets of questions, or scales, have been developed in order to record attitudes on many of these subjects, but there is vigorous debate about which scales are best for tasks at hand. Given the complexity of many attitudes that interest us, we must pay careful attention to the nature of the questions designed to tap into them. Just as it would be foolish to rely on generalizations from a single poll, it is not advisable to draw weighty conclusions from polls that employ single questions to measure complex attitudes. By using multiple questions that bear on different aspects of specific attitudes and seeing how responses interrelate, certain specification errors can be reduced.

In certain cases, the value of even multiple questions is limited. On many important subjects, researchers disagree about the nature of the underlying attitude. Consider connections between religion and intolerance, discussed in Chapter 4. 'Religion' is a highly complex notion. Researchers do not agree about what it is; in the literature innumerable definitions have been proposed, and are disputed by theorists. To take one example, Daniel Batson and his colleagues have developed the 'quest' scale, in order to assess an open, questioning orientation towards religion, which Batson and his colleagues view as primarily concerned with the way people approach existential questions. But other scholars ask if attitudes of this sort are really central to 'religion' in the proper sense, and so question exactly what sort of phenomenon the quest scale taps. As this example illustrates, researchers cannot design survey instruments that will be able to tap into an underlying attitude, unless there is clear agreement on the nature of the attitude. Disagreement—especially intractable, theoretical disagreement—about the nature of a given attitude will undoubtedly lead to disagreement among researchers whose questions are intended to capture it. To take another example, in Chapter 3 I explore liberal citizens' attitudes towards rights, or their political tolerance. As we will see, tolerance is basically defined as willingness to respect the rights of people with whom one disagrees. Tolerance is an important subject of investigation in recent social science and a major focus of this study. But scholars disagree about exactly what 'tolerance' is, and so how it should be measured. Intolerance—unwillingness to put up with a group to which one is opposed—can be identified relatively easily, if the target of unfavourable sentiments is clearly legitimate, e.g. scientists who discuss evolution. But what if the target group is so objectionable that tolerating it would be inappropriate? Is willingness to interfere with the rights of sex offenders intolerance? What about the rights of adulterers? Such questions are of great theoretical importance, because one group that many liberal citizens have been found to be intolerant of is homosexuals. But if homosexuality is inherently wrong—immoral, unnatural, sinful—then this is not an instance of intolerance (see below, Chapter 4 n. 15). If people who are more religious (according to different measures) are more willing than others to interfere with the rights of homosexuals, does this mean that religion is associated with intolerance? Along similar lines, if Americans are not wiling to grant full rights to homosexuals, does this mean that American society is intolerant—in spite of recorded increases in willingness to grant full rights to racial, religious, and political minorities? Clearly, the question whether an attitude towards a given group is or is not 'intolerance' requires prior determination as to the moral legitimacy of the group. Because of the difficulties in answering such questions, in many cases the 'tolerance' or 'intolerance' of liberal citizens is inherently resistant to survey methods.

Another problem with the notion of intolerance is its extent. Theorists disagree as to whether tolerance is an attitude towards particular unpopular groups, or whether someone who would abridge the rights of his 'least liked' group is intolerant. Disagreement about this issue is central to determining the evolution of democratic attitudes in the United States, especially in regard to whether the American people have become markedly more tolerant since the 1950s.

Specification problems in these questions concern lack of clarity about the nature of underlying attitudes. Problems of a related sort can arise because of lack of clarity in the relationship between questions and the attitudes they are intended to reflect. One of the most studied sets of questions in American public opinion is the 'trust in government' scale developed by the University of Michigan Institute for Social Research and administered repeatedly since 1958 (see below, Chapter 5, Section 1). These questions have recorded a marked decline in the levels of 'trust' among American citizens, especially in the late 1960s and subsequent years. This change and its implications have been much discussed, with some theorists drawing ominous conclusions about the future of American democracy. Yet there is fundamental disagreement about what exactly the scale of questions has been measuring. Is this people's attitudes towards the political system itself, or their attitudes towards people serving in office, i.e. incumbent officials? If the answer is the latter, then the implications are less ominous. In this particular case, as we will see, the disagreement has been more or less resolved. Most researchers believe that the scale taps into attitudes towards incumbents. But once again, the problems identifying the attitudes recorded by these questions illustrate one type of difficulty encountered when survey questions are used in order to explore attitudes on complex, abstract subjects, especially those which people have not thought deeply about.

Additional instances of specification problems could be provided. But this is not necessary here. Clearly, in many areas of life, people's attitudes are not easy to capture through survey research, even if measurement problems such as those discussed above could be avoided. Because of the apparent intractability of many specification problems, one could well be tempted to throw up one's hands and question the validity of survey research as an effective method of inquiry altogether.

The main reason to continue to rely on survey methods in spite of all the difficulties we have seen is that there is no real alternative. Defence of survey research is Churchillian: it is worse than any conceivable method, except for all others that have been tried. If we are not able to question a representative sample of citizens about their attitudes towards some object of inquiry, then, the only alternatives are anecdotal evidence or trying to imagine how most people feel. These 'methods' call to mind a story about a New York movie critic, who in 1972 thought that Richard Nixon was going to lose the election because everyone she knew was voting for George McGovern. Even with all their difficulties, survey methods are preferable to generalizing from random cases. In a society of 260 million people, anecdotal evidence is largely worthless. Like it or not, survey research provides the best evidence we are able to get. In exploring the attitudes of liberal citizens through survey research, we are making use of the best means available to us, although we must continually be on guard for specification and other problems.

To close out discussion here, I should make clear that in the following chapters I do not attempt to read off liberal citizens' attitudes about complex moral and political issues directly from survey research—certainly not from individual surveys. To begin with, in each of the subject areas examined we have numerous polls, which frequently approach subjects from different angles, asking quite different questions. Not only have results been replicated over the course of many years, under different sorts of conditions, but repeated explorations of single subjects work to counter specification problems. Though such problems remain, we are able to draw on large-scale theoretical discussions among researchers about the nature of the objects under investigation and the questions best suited to capture them.

Even when questions posed in a given study closely replicate those of other studies, the former are valuable as providing confirmation of previous results. Polls are also not the only kinds of studies we examine. In Chapters 4 and 8, on psychology of religion and procedural justice, respectively, evidence of small group experiments is an important supplement to survey research. Other evidence is provided by interviews. As we will see in the chapters on tolerance and distributive justice (Chapters 3 and 6, respectively), interviews provide valuable evidence about how different components of subjects' views fit together. This raises a final, important point.

In addition to examining views on individual issues, I am deeply interested in how particular subjects respond to a range of questions and how their replies fit together. In many cases I observe regular patterns of responses that are evidence of different political views or ideologies, and similar patterns on issue after issue will be seen. In the following chapters survey research and other sources of evidence provide windows into people's overall political moral, philosophical, and religious views. It is not surprising that pluralistic American society contains inhabitants with widely different views in all these areas—which can oftentimes be placed at different locales along a liberal–conservative ideological spectrum. For instance, polls tell us far more than that Americans differ widely on issues of civil liberties. Looked at in more detail, responses to numerous surveys indicate that subjects' opinions on these issues are components of widely different overall philosophical orientations, and that respondents' attitudes towards, say, civil liberties can be predicted accurately from other aspects of their belief systems.

In other words, the evidence of public opinion polls is just that: evidence. It must be interpreted along with other available evidence to shed light on how liberal citizens view central issues. Evidence produced by even repeated surveys does not speak for itself. By moving between different sources of evidence I will attempt to probe beneath the surface and reconstruct overall thought patterns of liberal citizens. In many cases, the evidence does not afford definitive accounts of what liberal citizens believe. But once again, in order for the principles we develop to be as accurate as possible, we must do the best we can. The evidence explored below is far from perfect, but we must make use of it in the absence of anything better. Given the limitations of the evidence, we must take care not to make more of specific results than the nature of the processes that gave rise to them allows. Continual assessment of what particular pieces of evidence allows us to conclude and of the strengths and weakness of the research methods underlying them are integral components of using the data they provide.

3

Democratic Values

IT is commonly held by people who think and write about democratic political systems that a consensus on democratic beliefs among a country's citizens is necessary for political stability. As expressed by Alexis de Tocqueville, for example, such a view has been a staple of democratic theory for hundreds of years. Tocqueville writes: 'For society to exist and, even more, for society to prosper, it is essential that all the minds of the citizens should always be rallied and held together by some leading ideas' (1969: 434). A more recent proponent of this view is Roberta Sigel:

Political socialization refers to the learning process by which the political norms and behaviors acceptable to an ongoing political system are transmitted from generation to generation . . . A well-functioning citizen is one who accepts (internalizes) society's political norms. . . . Without a body politic so in harmony with the ongoing political values, a political system would have trouble functioning smoothly. (quoted by Mann 1970: 423)

But, as we will see, views such as these have problems accounting for empirical findings concerning what democratic citizens actually believe. Discovery of the non-democratic beliefs of democratic citizens raises questions not only about how democratic systems remain stable but about how they function.

According to an idealized account, democratic systems place political power in the hands of their citizens, who make important decisions on the basis of deliberations, or at least according to democratic principles. But empirical studies have been damaging to idealized views. Extensive examination of the beliefs of democratic citizens demonstrates widespread lack of support for democratic values. If citizens were actually to put their beliefs into effect, the consequences could be troublesome.

The literature surveyed in this chapter addresses democratic citizens' attitudes towards rights or civil liberties of various minority groups. This body of studies originated more than forty years ago with Samuel Stouffer's *Communism, Conformity, and Civil Liberties* (Stouffer 1955). Though subsequent studies have generally reinforced Stouffer's findings, researchers disagree about important points and what the findings mean. In this chapter I survey the main findings of this body of research and their normative implications.

In addition to particular institutions ensuring electoral accountability, a working democratic system must guarantee its citizens a range of rights, such as those discussed in the first chapter. Because democratic accountability requires open debate and participation in the political system, citizens must be able to express their ideas, including unpopular ones, free from government interference. Rights are of course also of more than instrumental value. Among liberal citizens, freedom of speech, of conscience, of travel and association, are generally viewed as central to meaningful lives and so are inherently valuable. Thus the finding that citizens of democratic states do not support central democratic rights raises problems. If protection of basic rights for all citizens is a central component of the 'democratic creed' (Dahl 1961, ch. 28), a central finding of empirical social science is that large numbers of democratic citizens do not support the democratic creed.

In this chapter I generally focus on the United States, where the most extensive studies have been conducted, though I make occasional references to other countries as well. General consistency of findings across countries is a notable feature of this body of research. The literature I will examine is generally referred to as studies of 'tolerance', or 'political tolerance'. A representative definition of 'tolerance' is given by John Sullivan, James Piereson, and George Marcus: 'Tolerance implies a willingness to "put up with" those things one rejects or opposes. Politically, it implies a willingness to permit the expression of ideas or interests one opposes' (Sullivan *et al.* 1982: 2). In reference to democratic politics, tolerance implies willingness to accord full rights to participate in democratic processes—rights to free speech, assembly, participation—to individuals who espouse ideas or points of view to which one is opposed. In this terminology, then, large numbers of Americans—and citizens of other democratic countries—have been found to be markedly intolerant. For ease of reference, in discussing the literature I will use terms such as 'intolerance' and 'willingness to deny others basic rights' more or less interchangeably, as also 'tolerance' and 'respect for people's rights and liberties'.

Two main topics are discussed in this chapter. First, by way of background, in Sections 1 and 2, I discuss 'two waves' of contributions to the tolerance literature and the widespread intolerance they reveal. These studies uncover an apparently paradoxical relationship between observed intolerance in particular circumstances but strong support for democratic principles, when stated in abstract terms. This paradox and its implications are explored in Sections 3–4. I attempt to flesh out different views of fundamental rights held by liberal citizens and note important qualifications certain views contain. As we will see, an important factor that has been found to contribute to intolerance is religion. In the following chapter I explore this connection in detail, along with the cognitive orientation of various religious groups that contributes to anti-democratic sentiments.

1. TOLERANCE STUDIES

As noted above, the modern study of political tolerance was initiated by Samuel Stouffer. Stouffer examined Americans' attitudes to civil liberties during the McCarthy period. His study drew on two national surveys, comprising 4,993 interviews, conducted in 1954. These were supplemented with additional interviews of 1,500 'selected local community leaders' (Stouffer 1955, ch. 1). Stouffer was interested in examining Americans' responses to 'two dangers': that posed by a perceived communist conspiracy, and that 'from those who in thwarting the conspiracy would sacrifice some of the very liberties which the enemy would destroy' (p. 13). By contrasting the views of ordinary Americans and opinion-leaders, Stouffer drew influential conclusions about the working of liberal democracies.

As the second of Stouffer's dangers suggests, his study turned up disquieting facts. For example, he examined attitudes toward rights to free speech of socialists, communists, and atheists. Survey respondents were asked, 'If a person wanted to make a speech in your community favoring government ownership of all the railroads and big industries, should he be allowed to speak or not?' Of the sample, 31 per cent responded 'no', 11 per cent, no answer, and 58 per cent, 'yes'. Accordingly, 42 per cent of the sample had at least some doubts about socialists' rights to speak (p. 29). In regard to atheism, respondents were asked, 'If a person wanted to make a speech in your community against churches and religion, should he be allowed to speak or not?' Sixty per cent responded 'no', 3 per cent, no opinion, and 37 per cent, 'yes' (p. 33). In regard to communism, the following question was asked: 'Suppose an admitted Communist wants to make a speech in your community. Should he be allowed to speak or not?' To this, 68 per cent responded 'no', 5 per cent, no opinion, and 27 per cent, 'yes' (p. 41). Clearly, Stouffer uncovered widespread willingness to interfere with the rights of various groups of people.

In addition to his disturbing report on levels of tolerance in American culture, Stouffer presented a series of other findings that were to be of great importance. Exploring the social determinants of tolerance, he discovered a strong negative correlation with religion and a strong positive correlation with education. Basically, he viewed intolerance as an intuitive response to perceived danger or threat, which could be counteracted by 'sober second thoughts' induced by education (ch. 4). Aspects of his findings in these regards will be explored below. Stouffer also discovered the influence of other factors. For reasons he was unable to explain, women were found to be less tolerant than men (ch. 6), while people from rural areas and from the South were also especially intolerant. To some extent the influence of the South can be explained by its higher concentration of rural inhabitants and its lower education levels, but something more in Southern culture was at work, 'something that tends to differentiate' Southerners from other regional groups (p. 130).

In spite of the low levels of tolerance he discovered, two of Stouffer's findings could be viewed as providing reasons for optimism. First, there were significant differences between the tolerance levels of élite groups and non-élites. Stouffer's survey included fourteen different kinds of community leaders—e.g. mayors, Republican and Democratic county chairmen, newspaper publishers, and school board presidents. According to a scale he constructed, 19 per cent of his national sample was found to be 'less tolerant', 50 per cent, 'in between', and 31 per cent, 'more tolerant'. The corresponding figures for élites were 5 per cent less tolerant, 29 per cent in between, and 66 per cent more tolerant (p. 51). Stouffer did not explore the full implications of this discovery, which, when confirmed by subsequent researchers, gave rise to 'élite' versions of democratic theory. His main conclusion in regard to the role of relatively tolerant élites in democratic societies is their responsibility to work against intolerance by helping to increase public education (pp. 232–3). In addition, Stouffer was encouraged by tendencies in society that appeared to be working against intolerance: 'Great social, economic, and technological forces are operating slowly and imperceptibly on the side of spreading tolerance' (p. 236). He believed that increased geographical mobility would erode the insularity of the South and rural areas, while increasing education was especially important.

Stouffer's findings were generally supported by a survey of voter attitudes in Tallahassee, Florida, and Ann Arbor, Michigan, conducted by James Prothro and Charles Grigg (Prothro and Grigg 1960). Like Stouffer, Prothro and Grigg found that large percentages of their respondents expressed willingness to violate democratic norms. But they went beyond Stouffer's study in an important respect. Prothro and Grigg were interested in what they took to be the widespread opinion that 'consensus on fundamental political principles is essential to democracy' (1960: 276). In addition to asking about the rights to be accorded to members of various unpopular groups, Prothro and Grigg explored their respondents' attitudes towards 'fundamental principles of democracy', stated in the abstract. Respondents were asked about five basic principles, bearing on democratic government:

> Democracy is the best form of government.
> Public officials should be chosen by majority vote.
> Every citizen should have an equal chance to influence government policy.
> The minority should be free to criticize majority decisions.
> People in the minority should be free to try to win majority support for their opinions. (p. 282)

As Prothro and Grigg expected, there was general agreement on these propositions, ranging between 94.7 and 98 per cent, 'which appears to represent consensus in a truly meaningful sense' (pp. 284–6). However, there was considerably less agreement when respondents were asked about particular applications of the propositions: 'When these broad principles are translated into more specific propositions, consensus breaks down completely' (p. 286). While more than 80 per cent of respondents opposed barring a legally elected black from office, only 21 per cent supported allowing non-taxpayers to vote. Roughly half the sample supported limiting the right to vote to 'well-informed' citizens, barring a communist from elective office, and allowing bloc voting for professional associations, such as the American Medical Association. While 63 per cent would allow an anti-religious speech, and 79.4 per cent, a socialist speech, 44 per cent would allow a communist to speak. Although 75.5 per cent would refuse to bar a black from candidacy for public office, only 41.7 per cent would refuse to bar a communist (p. 285).

Accordingly, Prothro and Grigg found not only consensus on general principles but, like Stouffer, strong support for what they interpreted as non-democratic views. On four of their ten democratic statements a majority of Ann Arbor respondents expressed undemocratic opinions; on six statements respondents in Tallahassee responded similarly (p. 287). Prothro and Grigg attributed differences in their interviewees' responses to differences in educational level. Controlling for other factors, they found consistent correlations between levels of education and tolerance: 'The greatest difference on every statement was between the high-education group and the low-education group, and the high-education group gave the most democratic response to every question' (p. 291). They note, however, that even among the high-education group, consensus on particular statements was not found (p. 292).

Prothro and Grigg located the connection between education and tolerance in increased ability to recognize the logical implications of abstract democratic principles. They believed that 'the logical connection of the specific proposition with the general proposition is virtually self-evident', and can be expressed in syllogistic terms. For example, major premiss: 'every citizen should have an equal chance to influence government'; minor premiss: 'non-taxpayers are citizens'; conclusion: 'non-taxpayers should be allowed to vote on a city referendum deciding on tax-supported undertakings' (p. 292). But as we saw, although the major premiss was overwhelmingly supported, only 21 per cent of respondents endorsed the conclusion. Presumably, with greater education would come increased intellectual sophistication, which would make people more likely to realize the implications of their broad democratic commitments.

Like Stouffer, Prothro and Grigg were interested in the implications of their findings for the functioning of democratic systems. Although theorists have argued that democratic systems require consensus on fundamental values, Prothro and Grigg believed that their survey overturned this notion. They appealed to 'the functional nature of apathy for the democratic system' (p. 293). More important than what people believe is how they behave. Though large numbers of people express non-democratic sentiments, they are generally too apathetic to act on them. Prothro and Grigg cite the view of Roland Pennock that democracy can tolerate little conscious agreement on principles as long as people behave in accordance with democratic norms of compromise and co-operation (Prothro and Grigg 1960: 294). Their study is important, then, not only in questioning the existence of democratic consensus but in addressing the implications of its absence.

A study conducted by Herbert McClosky confirmed Prothro and Grigg's main findings (McClosky 1964). McClosky drew on a two-sample national survey of more than 3,000 political 'actives' or influentials and 1,500 randomly chosen adults, conducted in 1957–8. The 'actives' had attended the 1956 Democratic and Republican conventions. Like Prothro and Grigg, he found general agreement on abstract principles concerning free speech and opinion—though levels were somewhat lower than those reported by Prothro and Grigg—with the influentials responding more tolerantly than the general public on eight out of eight questions (McClosky 1964: 366). Because McClosky set the requirement for consensus on a given principle at 75 per cent agreement (p. 363), he found consensus among the actives on all statements, and among the general populace on seven out of the eight. (The exception: 79.1 per cent of actives, but only 64.6 per cent of the popular sample, agreed with the statement 'I would not trust any person or group to decide what opinions can be freely expressed and what must be silenced') (p. 366). Once again, however, support fell off sharply on specific applications. For instance, in response to the statement 'Freedom does not give anyone the right to teach foreign ideas in our schools', 45.5 per cent of influentials and 56.7 per cent of the general sample expressed agreement. In response to 'A book that contains wrong political views cannot be a good book and does not deserve to be published', 17.9 per cent of actives and 50.3 per cent of the general sample agreed.

Like Prothro and Grigg, McClosky concluded that consensus on democratic values is not necessary for the stability of democratic societies: 'a democratic society can survive despite widespread popular misunderstanding and disagreement about basic democratic and constitutional values' (p. 376). He too appealed to the benefits of apathy, which keeps people not in accord with democratic values from acting on their views (p. 376). Previous theorists had exaggerated the role that 'cognitive elements'— 'ideas, values, rational choice, consensus, etc.'—play in preserving democracy: 'If the viability of a democracy were to depend upon the satisfaction of these intellectual activities, the prognosis would be very grim indeed' (p. 378).

In order to explain the observed stability of democratic societies in spite of citizens' lack of strong democratic values, McClosky appealed to an élite theory of democracy.[1] Because of their greater intellectual sophistication and exposure to democratic processes, political influentials 'serve as the major repositories of the public conscience and as the carriers of the Creed' (p. 374). As Paul Sniderman and his colleagues note, élite theory attempts to preserve belief in democratic consensus by replacing the general population with different élites as bearers of consensus (Sniderman *et al.* 1996: 17).

McClosky's explanation for discrepancies between adherence to general and particular propositions is somewhat different from that of Prothro and Grigg. While they appeal to logical inconsistencies, especially among relatively uneducated respondents, McClosky fastens on the incompleteness of abstract statements of general democratic principles. When applied to complex substantive situations, general norms, such as principles of religious freedom, conflict with other significant values, such as the majority's right to make laws (p. 376). Different democratic values clash in specific circumstances. Because accommodations must be sought, abstract statements of general norms actually contain tacit qualifications. Thus, for McClosky, the application of general norms to specific situations is less straightforwardly syllogistic than Prothro and Grigg believe. I will return to the relationship between abstract statements and their implications below.

[1] Other prominent exponents include Lipset (1960) and Bachrach (1967); for further discussion, see below, p. 53.

2. THE SECOND WAVE OF TOLERANCE STUDIES

The studies we have seen record low levels of tolerance among democratic citizens, in spite of their stronger adherence to abstract principles. In addition, we have seen important social determinants of tolerance, especially education. Effects of education are discussed throughout this chapter. But we should note here an important implication. According to Stouffer, increased education can bring about increased tolerance. This claim is supported by findings of Prothro and Grigg and McClosky concerning higher tolerance levels among élite respondents, who are, among other things, more highly educated than the general population.

Stouffer's findings were re-examined by Clyde Nunn, Harry Crockett, and J. Allen Williams in a survey conducted in 1973 (Nunn *et al.* 1978). More than 3,500 people were interviewed, along with 649 community leaders. As part of their task, Nunn and his colleagues replicated Stouffer's questions. They received strikingly different results. In the nineteen years that had passed, Americans had become markedly more tolerant. The Nunn group notes that this could be in part because of the harsh times during which Stouffer conducted his survey. But the period preceding 1973 was also one of national turmoil, characterized by increased concerns for national security and personal well-being (Nunn *et al.* 1978, ch. 2). Nunn and his colleagues conclude that, in spite of the times, the intolerance recorded by Stouffer had substantially dissipated. For instance, in both 1954 and 1973 respondents were asked: 'If a person wanted to make a speech in your community favoring government ownership of all the railroads and big industries, should he be allowed to speak?' As we saw above, in 1954, 31 per cent of the general respondents gave intolerant responses; in 1973 this had fallen to 21 per cent. In 1954, 14 per cent of community leaders responded intolerantly; in 1973 this had fallen to 8 per cent (p. 38), In regard to the question whether such a person should be allowed to teach in a college or university, in 1954, 54 per cent of the general respondents responded negatively; in 1973 this had fallen to 38 per cent. The intolerant responses of the leaders surveyed fell from 47 per cent to 26 per cent (p. 39; for responses of the different kinds of leader, see p. 40). In 1954, 27 per cent of the general survey would allow an admitted communist to speak, and only 6 per cent to keep his or her job as a college teacher. The responses in 1973 were 53 per cent and 30 per cent respectively (p. 43).

Nunn and his colleagues constructed a general scale to measure willingness to tolerate nonconformists. Briefly, in 1954, 19 per cent of the general sample was 'less tolerant', 50 per cent 'in between', and 31 per cent 'more tolerant'.[2] The corresponding figures nineteen years later were 16 per cent less tolerant, 25 per cent in between, and 55 per cent, a majority of the population, more tolerant. For community leaders, 1954 figures were 5 per cent less tolerant, 29 per cent in between, and 66 per cent more tolerant. Even these relatively good figures were improved upon by 1973: 4 per cent less tolerant, 13 per cent in between, and 83 per cent more tolerant (p. 51). Nunn and his colleagues describe these changes as 'substantial' (p. 51), and a tone of muted optimism pervades their book. They note that 'the majority of rank-and-file Americans scored as more tolerant' (p. 173), and characterize their results as 'encouraging to those who hope for a more civil society' (p. 176).

The Nunn group believed that the main determinant of increased tolerance was increased education (ch. 4). There was a marked increase of education throughout American society during the nineteen intervening years. In both 1954 and 1973 there was a direct relationship between levels of education and levels of tolerance: 'each step up the educational ladder was accompanied by a noticeable gain in the proportion scoring high on the Tolerance Scale' (p. 59). More specifically, they attribute increased tolerance to increases in 'cognitive development and cultural sophistication' brought about by education (p. 63).

Connections the Nunn group traces between tolerance and one other sociocultural factor will be of concern to us, namely religion. The connection between religion and intolerance was first pointed out by Stouffer (1955, 140–54). Nunn and his colleagues confirm Stouffer's conclusions. As increases in education are accompanied by increases in tolerance, the reverse is true of religion. Increased religious orthodoxy is associated with sharp increases in intolerance (Nunn *et al.* 1978, ch. 8). Exactly which aspects of religion correlate with tolerance will be explored in detail in the following chapter. But we should note the Nunn group's view that one way education contributes to greater tolerance is by undermining certain simplistic religious beliefs (pp. 134–5).

Nunn and his colleagues' optimism was tempered by the realization that tolerance was not increasing on all fronts. For instance, in spite of the results we have seen, they note a 'precipitous drop in academic freedom extended to homosexuals' (p. 55). An explanation for this discrepancy, which suggests disquieting conclusions, is offered by Sullivan, Piereson, and Marcus, in their important study (1982). The Sullivan group made a major contribution by arguing for a new way to conceptualize 'tolerance'. In order for citizen *A* to be tolerant of members of some group, *G*, he must be opposed to the *G*-ites but willing to extend them rights in any case. It

---

[2] On construction of the scale, see Nunn *et al.* (1978: 179–85).

follows from this line of argument that *A* would not be *tolerating* communists or members of some comparable group, even if he was willing to extend them liberties, unless he was opposed to them. Sullivan and his colleagues criticized other studies showing increased levels of tolerance, because researchers had not made sure that respondents were actually opposed to the groups in question (Sullivan *et al.* 1982: 48). Although attitudes towards communists (say) had softened over time, this does not imply that there were not *other* groups which respondents would suppress. Sullivan and his colleagues believed that one reason tolerance appeared to be increasing is that general hostility towards communists, socialists, and atheists had fallen in recent decades (pp. 59–60). Along similar lines, they argued that one reason respondents who were politically liberal had been consistently found to be more tolerant than conservatives is that groups about which they were asked were likely to be more hostilely perceived by conservatives than by liberals (p. 178). In order to counteract distorted results of previous studies, Sullivan and his colleagues developed a 'content-controlled' measure of political tolerance.

The key to their alternative measure was having respondents identify their 'least liked' groups. Rather than asking about pre-selected groups that they assumed were targets of hostile feelings, Sullivan and his colleagues employed a two-step process. Respondents first identified groups to which they were strongly opposed and then were asked about extending civil liberties to them. Sullivan and his colleagues found that respondents varied widely in regard to target groups. For instance, and not surprisingly, respondents with liberal views identified right-wing groups, while right-wing respondents did the reverse (p. 181).

The results of the Sullivan group's survey told against rising levels of tolerance. Sullivan and his colleagues employed content-controlled questions in a survey conducted by the National Opinion Research Center in the spring of 1978 (N = 1,509), and compared this with results of standard Stouffer questions from a survey the year before. As one would expect, tolerant responses to the Stouffer questions had risen considerably, although on many questions, less than a majority of respondents still gave tolerant responses. For instance, 65 per cent of respondents supported an atheist's right to speak, and 63 per cent, a communist's; 40 per cent would allow an atheist to teach in the public schools, and 40 per cent would allow a communist. On the content-controlled questions, although 50 per cent believed that members of their least liked group should be allowed to speak, only 19 per cent would allow members to teach in the public schools (Sullivan *et al.* 1982: 67). Similarly, only 16 per cent believed that members of their least liked group should not be banned from being president of the United States. While 59 per cent believed that members of the group should not have their phones tapped by the government, only 29 per cent believed that the group should not be outlawed (p. 67). Accordingly, Sullivan and his colleagues argued: 'though tolerance of communists and atheists has increased over the years, tolerance as a more universal attitude may not have changed much at all' (p. 66).

Like previous researchers, the Sullivan group argues that American society is generally intolerant and that, in spite of this, society is stable and the civil liberties of most individuals protected.[3] Thus they too question the assumption that democratic stability rests on a consensus among the citizenry concerning democratic beliefs. However, their model of political tolerance has been criticized by subsequent researchers. The content-controlled method undoubtedly represents a theoretical advance over asking respondents about pre-selected groups. As we have seen, if the groups in question are associated with one political persuasion, survey results can be biased. But this problem can be avoided by simply asking respondents about tolerating an ideologically balanced range of groups, without employing content-controlled questions. Since 1976 tolerance questions in the General Social Survey, which is administered by the National Opinion Research Center (see below, Chapter 6 n. 18), have presented a range of groups, and results of these studies are generally similar to those employing content-controlled questions (Gibson 1992*a*). Surveys about balanced groups, moreover, indicate that there is general consistency in people's attitudes towards extremist groups on opposite ends of the political spectrum, in spite of their own political ideologies. In a survey of some 1,200 Americans conducted in 1987 James Gibson asked respondents about both right-wing and left-wing groups, about the Ku Klux Klan, Nazis, religious fundamentalists, and conservatives, as well as communists, atheists, feminists, and homosexuals (Gibson 1989*b*). In general, Gibson found, attitudes towards groups on opposite ends of the political spectrum were positively, not negatively, correlated (p. 566). He surmised that intolerance in general is directed at groups that are perceived to fall beyond acceptable limits: 'the structure of group antipathy in the United States is one of moderates opposing both those who are too far to the left and those who are too far to the right' (p. 566). For instance, almost 80 per cent of Americans identify the Ku Klux Klan as one of their four most disliked groups, while large percentages identify Nazis, communists, atheists, and proponents of military government (pp. 564–5).

---

[3] For their innovative view of the factors responsible for this, see Sullivan *et al.* (1982: 261–3); for criticisms, see Gibson (1989*b*, 1992*a*). For the combination of circumstances under which civil liberties appear most likely to be violated, see Gibson (1988, 1989*a*).

The Sullivan group's study was not concerned with criticizing traditional élite theory and so did not have a separate sample of élites. To the extent Sullivan and his colleagues were able to measure the tolerance of political élites, they found them to be 'substantially more tolerant than the rest of the sample' (1982: 197). However, it seems that early versions of élite theory can be faulted for putting forth overly monolithic views of élite attitudes. In spite of their generally higher levels of political tolerance, élites are not uniformly tolerant. Community leaders, political activists, and other people who have been designated as élites differ widely in their demographic characteristics, including those that have been identified as sources of tolerance and intolerance (see Jackman 1972). As we will see below, studies have shown a relationship between political conservatism and intolerance (McClosky and Brill 1983: 422; see below, pp. 75–7 and Chapter 6, Section 2), an association that has been found to carry over into political élites.

On the basis of a large 1987 survey, Paul Sniderman and his associates argue that in the United States Republican and Democratic activists differ markedly in regard to attitudes towards civil liberties. Though, on average, political élites are significantly more tolerant than average citizens, the distribution of élite tolerance is bimodal. In fact, conservative élites are less tolerant than liberal citizens (Sniderman *et al.* 1991: 364). In the United States, of course, electoral competitions are generally between Democrats and Republicans, and so between members of parties that 'markedly and systematically differ in their attitudes towards civil liberties'. Sniderman and his colleagues conclude: 'The politics of civil liberties can accordingly hinge on which group of élites wins the struggle to constitute the government' (1991: 369; 1996, ch. 2).

For this reason, in spite of the continuing stability of liberal societies, the civil liberties of unpopular minority groups are not always secure. Given widespread intolerance in the general population, the rise of intolerant élites can trigger outbreaks of repression. The McCarthy period serves as a case in point for what can happen when such a confluence of intolerance comes about (Gibson 1988).[4]

To close out this review of findings of tolerance studies, we should note that similarly low levels of tolerance have been observed in other liberal

---

[4] According to Gibson's analysis of repression during the Vietnam War era (Gibson 1989*a*), there is little evidence of élites as protectors of civil liberties, though the dynamics at work were more complex than those during the McCarthy period. An additional danger of intolerance worth noting is that it contributes to an overall atmosphere that discourages expression of unorthodox opinions. Even in the absence of overt oppression, possibilities for political dissent can be constrained (see Gibson 1992*b*).

societies. Other countries have not been studied as systematically as the United States, but the results are generally consistent. I will briefly review evidence for levels of tolerance in Great Britain, Canada, and the European Community countries generally.[5] In surveys reported by David Barnum and John Sullivan, conducted in Britain (in 1986) and the United States (in 1978 and 1987), levels of tolerance were found to be similar in the two countries (Barnum and Sullivan 1990: 722). Nationwide samples were asked whether they would allow members of groups they especially disliked to (1) make a public speech, (2) hold a public rally, (3) run for public office, (4) form an organization that is not banned or outlawed, or (5) teach in a public school, and (6) whether the government should be allowed to tap the telephones of group members. Some sample figures for Britain and the two US surveys respectively are, first, that 27 per cent (Britain 1986), 16 per cent (US 1978), and 27 per cent (US 1987) would have allowed members of the least liked group to run for public office; 34 per cent, 34 per cent, and 33 per cent would have permitted members of the least liked group to hold a public rally; 31 per cent, 29 per cent, and 32 per cent opposed banning (outlawing) the least liked group. Slightly better, 51 per cent, 50 per cent, and 50 per cent would permit members of the least liked group to make a public speech. Accordingly, this evidence indicates similar levels in the United States and Britain (see also Barnum and Sullivan 1989).

Something similar is seen in regard to Canada. Sniderman and associates examined attitudes of the general public and élites towards civil liberties in Canada in 1987. Only 32 per cent of their mass sample believed that their most disliked group should be allowed to hold public rallies. This is in comparison to 61 per cent who responded that 'members of extreme political groups' should be allowed to hold public rallies. But only 20 per cent believed that groups like the Nazis and Ku Klux Klan should be allowed to state their views on public television (Sniderman *et al.* 1991: 355). Fifty-nine per cent responded that police should be able to search a young man who was seen near a house where drugs are sold (p. 358). Not surprisingly, Canadian élites were found to be more tolerant.[6] Sixty-five per cent responded that their least liked group should be able to hold public rallies, 87 per cent that members of extreme groups should be allowed to; 38 per cent agreed that groups like the Nazis and Ku Klux Klan should be allowed to appear on public television (p. 355); 57 per cent agreed that it was acceptable to search a young man outside a drug house. All in all,

---

[5] For studies of additional liberal societies, see Sullivan *et al.* (1985).

[6] The significance of this finding should be qualified, however, in view of the bimodality of tolerance levels of Canadian élites.

these results indicate that the intolerance uncovered by Stouffer and subsequent researchers is not specific to the United States.

The final study we will look at examined attitudes towards civil liberties in a number of European countries. Raymond Duch and James Gibson surveyed respondents in twelve European countries about respecting the rights of fascists (Duch and Gibson 1992). They realized possible problems with this approach, but chose to focus on fascists, who are generally viewed as threatening, for the sake of uniformity. Twenty-two per cent of the sample rated fascists as 'extremely threatening,' and 35 per cent as 'threatening' (p. 245). Remarkably small numbers of respondents were willing to extend full civil rights to fascists. These ranged from lows of 10.5 per cent in Ireland and 10.9 per cent in Belgium, to a high of 30.6 per cent in Italy, who would allow them to run for public office. On the question of allowing fascists to hold public demonstrations, Irish respondents were, again, least tolerant, at 14.5 per cent, followed by Portugal at 14.7 per cent, and Greece at 15.3 per cent. Spain was most tolerant; 39.6 per cent responded affirmatively. Aside from Spain, in which 13.7 per cent of respondents would allow fascists to run candidates, hold demonstrations, and exist as a legal group, positive responses on this cumulative question were under 10 per cent in all other countries, 3 per cent or under in West Germany (0.7 per cent), Ireland, Luxembourg, and Belgium (p. 247).

It is open to question whether, in order to possess democratic values, people in countries that have suffered grievously from fascists in the past must be willing to extend them full political rights. However, as Duch and Gibson note, people who are intolerant of right-wing groups are generally found to be intolerant of left-wing groups as well (pp. 247–8). Perception of threat is generally a strong predictor of political intolerance. The fact that fascists are perceived as so threatening may explain the low level of tolerance expressed towards them, but even if we disregard specific figures to some extent, the overall nature of the responses and their consistency from country to country indicates widespread intolerant tendencies. As Duch and Gibson say: 'There is a strong cross-national tendency for those who feel threatened by a political minority to want to repress it through government action' (p. 249).

3. DEMOCRATIC PRINCIPLES

I have surveyed a range of tolerance studies in order to provide an idea of the tenor of debates and central conclusions. Drawing on this body of evidence, we must inquire into the possibility of general agreement on a single set of rights principles. Although scholars are at odds about particular findings, the overall thrust of this body of evidence is far removed from what many political philosophers assume about the beliefs of democratic citizens.

The evidence, however, contains an important ambiguity. In spite of the low levels of tolerance discussed in previous sections, liberal citizens express strong support for democratic principles when stated in the abstract and so could be considered tolerant for that reason. Such a claim has important implications for consensus theory. If the large majority of citizens accept abstract democratic principles, then this leaves open the possibility of general agreement. But it is hard to know how seriously we should take acceptance of general principles if people are willing to cast them aside in particular cases. We must examine the gap between people's acceptance of abstract principles and failure to abide by their implications in particular cases.

Once again, examples of the gap are found in Prothro and Grigg's study. Although respondents demonstrated overwhelming agreement on the principles noted above when they were stated in general form (above, pp. 45–47), consensus evaporated when the principles were applied to specific circumstances. Similar results have been observed in numerous studies. For instance, McClosky and Alida Brill report that 89 per cent of respondents in a 1958 survey claimed that they believed in 'free speech for all no matter what their views might be'. Over 80 per cent supported the statement that 'people who hate our way of life should still have a chance to talk and be heard'. 86 per cent agreed with the contention that 'unless there is freedom for many points of view to be presented, there is little chance that the truth can ever be known'. In a national poll conducted in the 1940s, 97 per cent of respondents responded affirmatively when asked: 'Do you believe in freedom of speech?' (McClosky and Brill 1983: 49; see also pp. 50–1). Similar findings could be multiplied.[7] But, as we have seen, support falls off sharply when the values expressed in the abstract statements are applied to concrete situations. For instance, McClosky and Brill report that only 41 per cent of respondents in national surveys conducted in the late 1970s agreed that 'foreigners who dislike our government and criticize it' should be allowed to visit or study here (p. 52). Only 18 per cent agreed that a community should 'allow the American Nazi Party to use its town hall to hold a public meeting' (p. 53). Twenty-three per cent agreed that, if 'a group asks to use a public building to hold a meeting denouncing the government, their request should be granted' (p. 53). Obviously,

[7] See McClosky and Zaller (1984: 318) for a list of 'clear democratic norms', meaning that they are supported by at least 75% of élite respondents, in their study, and p. 320 for a list of 'clear capitalist norms'.

such responses indicate that people, or at least many people, hold conflicting views.

To make sense of the gap, two questions must be cleared up: the nature of cognitive processes involved in applying abstract principles to specific cases; and the nature of the principles themselves. The evidence does not address these concerns directly, but it allows us to draw inferences. We are interested in the former question mainly for the light it sheds on the latter.

In the literature there are two main explanations for the gap between abstract principles and their applications. Most simply, respondents could be viewed as making simple logical errors. According to this 'error view', respondents subscribe to general principles of freedom of speech, the implications of which they do not realize when they confront members of disliked groups who wish to speak. According to this line of argument, associated most closely with Prothro and Grigg, movement from abstract principles to particular circumstances is, as we saw, syllogistic. An important reason that education increases tolerance is because it fosters 'greater acquaintance with the logical implications of the broad democratic principles' (Prothro and Grigg 1960: 291). As far as democratic theory is concerned, the error view is necessary to preserve the possibility that large majorities of democratic citizens can agree on a single set of principles, e.g. a right to speak freely regardless of content or circumstances, in spite of non-democratic responses to particular questions. Showing that liberal citizens generally subscribe to sweeping principles that they misapply will allow us to locate such principles at the heart of liberal consensus. On the other hand, however, the fact that recent studies undermine a syllogistic account of the movement from general principles to particular circumstance casts doubt upon the claim that sweeping rights principles are generally held.

The second view can be referred to as the 'tacit qualification' view, or the 'qualification' view for short. According to this interpretation, the broad, abstract principles to which people subscribe actually contain numerous tacit qualifications, though people may not be aware of this until they face uncomfortable situations. Jones may profess an unqualified principle that everyone should be free to speak as he pleases, but in actuality, he does not believe this. His response that Nazis or members of the Ku Klux Klan should not be able to address a public meeting is not the result of an error. It does not contradict his general principle but brings to the surface an exception he had assumed all along—though, again, without perhaps being fully aware of it.[8]

---

[8] This interpretation was first suggested to me by McClosky (1964: 376) and McClosky and Brill (1983: 431–4).

In order to clarify the difference between the error and qualification views, we can introduce a rough distinction between different kinds of democratic principle:

Strong rights principle: Rights cannot be traded off for other values, barring pressing circumstances.

Weak rights principle: Although rights are important values, as a matter of course, they must be balanced against a range of other moral values.

Because all reasonable rights principles admit some qualifications, the two kinds are distinguished on the basis of the qualifications they allow. The nature of the differences can be seen by drawing on the analysis of Joel Feinberg, in his four-volume work, *The Moral Limits of the Criminal Law* (Feinberg 1984, 1985, 1986, 1988).

Feinberg's main concern is explicating liberal principles concerning personal liberty. He presents a traditional view of liberalism: 'A liberal, I suppose one could say, is a person who believes in liberty, as a nudist is a person who believes in nudity' (M. Cranston, quoted by Feinberg 1984: 14). But in spite of the great value liberals place on liberty, they recognize the need for a certain range of restrictions—what Feinberg calls 'liberty-limiting principles'. The clearest cases concern actions that threaten to harm other people. The need to limit liberty in such cases is classically argued by Mill in *On Liberty*. The so-called 'harm principle', or, as Feinberg refers to it, 'the harm to others principle', justifies state actions to restrict liberty in order to prevent avoidable and serious harm to other persons. As Feinberg notes, 'no responsible theorist denies the validity' of some version of this principle (1984: 14).

Liberal theorists generally recognize other reasons for limiting liberty as well. Most liberal theorists argue that certain limitations are justified 'to prevent serious offense to persons other than the actor' (Feinberg 1984: 14, 26). For instance, a concession along these lines is made by Mill, who recognizes restrictions that are required by considerations of public decency:

there are many acts which, being directly injurious only to the agents themselves, ought not to be legally interdicted, but which, if done publicly, are a violation of good manners and, coming thus within the category of offences against others, may rightly be prohibited. Of this kind are offences against decency; on which it is unnecessary to dwell . . . (Mill 1978: 97)

Once we move beyond limiting liberty to prevent clear harms to include preventing actions that are merely offensive, we encounter a range of difficult questions. There is room for considerable disagreement as to where precise lines should be drawn and where measures other than strict state prohibitions are justified. For our purposes, it is not necessary to explore these questions here. However we fill these matters out in detail, it is important to recognize that, for a proponent of strong liberal principles, considerations of harm and serious offence more or less exhaust the grounds for legitimate state prohibition. Thus, according to Feinberg, liberalism is 'the view that the harm and offense principles, duly clarified and qualified, between them exhaust the class of morally relevant reasons for criminal prohibitions' (1984: 14–15).[9]

If strong principles can be restricted only to prevent harm and serious offence, weak principles differ in allowing a wider range of limitations. Most important are concerns that Feinberg describes as 'legal moralism': 'it is reasonably necessary to prevent inherently immoral conduct, whether or not such conduct is harmful or offensive to anyone' (1984: 12). Among the kinds of conduct that can fall into this category are 'deviant sexual activities—homosexual or extramarital sexual intercourse and "perversions" especially shocking to the legislators, even when performed in private by consenting adults—adultery, bigamy, prostitution, even when discreetly arranged, and live sex shows or bloody gladiatorial contests presented by voluntary performers before consenting audiences' (Feinberg 1984: 13; see Feinberg 1988).

Perhaps the most plausible basis for restricting liberty along these lines is preservation of community values (see Feinberg 1988: 81–123). These could justify banning some of the activities Feinberg lists, e.g. live sex shows that people must seek out, and so might not be construed as offensive, and are not obviously harmful in other ways. But even if we grant the importance of community standards, it is not clear how much liberty they would justify restricting. It is beyond the scope of this study to argue that the state either should or should not prohibit conduct along the lines of Feinberg's list. Rather, my main interest in legal moralism is its role in distinguishing strong and weak democratic principles. Principles of the former kind are not qualified for moralistic reasons, while the latter admit this possibility.[10] I should, however, note that even strong principles could contain some minimal moralistic qualifications, e.g. for voluntary public gladiatorial competitions. Arguments for not prohibiting such extreme

[9] For exceptions for other reasons, see below, pp. 74–6. For trade-offs on values in regard to offence, see Feinberg (1985, ch. 8).

[10] The possibility should be noted that wider extension of offence principles or extending forms of legal paternalism (see Feinberg (1986) could also move us from strong to weak principles. The examples I discuss will generally be instances of legal moralism, although some could perhaps also be classified as concerned with these other matters. I will avoid difficult questions of classification here.

practices are not clear-cut.[11] The main difference, then, lies in weak principles allowing liberty to be restricted for a wider range of moralistic concerns.

The need to restrict liberty in order to prevent dangers to personal and public safety can be expressed in terms of providing people with the greatest *possible* liberty. The key idea is that certain rights must be restricted in order to create a framework in which the greatest possible enjoyment of rights—or liberty overall—is available for all members of society. This is the sense of Rawls's espousal of the 'priority of liberty', the view that 'liberty can be restricted only for the sake of liberty itself' (1971: 244). Thus I take Rawls to be advancing a strong rights claim. The main circumstances justifying restrictions on rights concern security; without a given restriction, there would be less liberty throughout society. For instance, there is an obvious sense in which not preventing people from driving while intoxicated would lessen the overall liberty to drive (safely) throughout society. Not preventing people from assaulting their neighbours would also lessen the amount of overall liberty in society. Once again, we can extend claims along these lines to allow limitations on liberty to prevent certain offences. Details of the two kinds of principles and how liberal citizens subscribe to them will be filled in as discussion proceeds.

4. PSYCHOLOGICAL PROCESSES

Having distinguished strong and weak rights principles, we can attempt to determine the nature of the principles subscribed to by the large numbers of intolerant citizens. Once again, the error view leaves open the possibility of agreement on strong rights principles throughout society. The gap between support for strong democratic principles in the abstract but less support in particular cases results from people's misapplying the former to the latter. In contrast, on the qualification view, the principles to which intolerant citizens subscribe contain important tacit qualifications. They do not misapply strong principles but correctly apply weak principles, although they may not be fully aware of the tacit qualifications they allow.

[11] Whether bars to such practices, and so a minimal level of restrictions on liberty for moralistic reasons, can be justified on liberal grounds is a question I will not explore here, but I do not believe the possibility is ruled out. Feinberg notes that cases along these lines are especially troublesome (1988: 328); for discussion, see Feinberg (1988: 128–33, 323–4, 328–31).

I believe the evidence supports a qualification view for a large percentage of liberal citizens.[12] I will look at evidence of two main kinds. First, studies of the psychological processes at work as people apply democratic principles to particular cases show that something more complex than mistaken logical inference is involved. The second kind of evidence shows that, in different ways, people's democratic principles are tightly bound up with their overall moral predispositions, or what we can call their world-views. In the following chapters I will explore relationships between democratic values and world-views in regard to religion, political ideology, and principles of distributive justice. This material will further fill out the nature of the democratic principles that different people apply in tolerance judgements.

According to the qualification view, the rights principles that many Americans uphold contain numerous tacit qualifications, to accommodate a range of values beyond preventing harm and serious offence. Thus what appear to be intolerant responses in regard to specific cases oftentimes result from application of qualified principles. The qualified nature of widely held principles is noted by empirical researchers. For instance, in their recent study, notably titled *The Clash of Rights*, Sniderman and his associates write:

a political culture, above all, a democratic political culture, is not all of one piece. It is pluralistic. In addition to liberty there is a host of other values, including respect for authority, the assurance of order in public life, and the importance of community and conformity. And because a society places a high value on order, for example, it does not follow that it places a low value on liberty. Political societies, most especially including democratic ones, attach and ought to attach importance to a mix of values . . . (Sniderman *et al.* 1996: 24).

On both the error and qualification views, the basic process of making a tolerance judgement can be viewed along the following lines. What is involved are faculties of cognition and emotion, which clash in almost

---

[12] Lawrence's study lends some support to the 'error view'. By carefully wording his questions to bring out the relationship between abstract principles and particular applications, Lawrence is able to eliminate a good deal of the gap (Lawrence 1976). To some extent, as he argues, the magnitude of the gap observed by other researchers is due to lack of clarity in question wording, which makes the application of general norms to specific situations less clear than it might otherwise be. However, the 'general norms' Lawrence examines, though strongly supported (p. 92), are less general than those discussed in other studies. In Lawrence's study these concerned rights (*a*) to petition the government, (*b*) to criticize the government, (*c*) to hold a peaceful demonstration to ask the government to act on some issue, and (*d*) to block the entrance to a government building. The last was, as Lawrence expected, not strongly supported; 5.6% of respondents would allow it always, and 16.4% sometimes, as compared to 78.1% who would never allow it (p. 92).

Platonic terms (in *Republic* IV). We can posit that the general principle is held as a rational conviction. Perceptions of threat play an important role in tolerance judgements. Confronted by the stimulus of a group she dislikes, the subject reacts emotionally, either forgetting the implications of her general principle or qualifying it to allow repressive action against the group, depending on which view of the psychological process we accept. Scholars hypothesize that intolerance is a natural response to fear (McClosky and Brill 1983: 13; Gibson 1987: 439), which can be counteracted by education. The subject who has been properly taught the significance of democratic principles is able to suppress her initial intolerant response. This is the 'sober second thought' of which Stouffer speaks (Stouffer 1955: 57). This rough sketch can, however, be filled in. Recent research provides a more nuanced view of the faculties at work. I will examine three studies.

First, in the late 1980s James Kuklinski and his colleagues examined 553 undergraduates at a Midwestern university and 237 Midwestern residents, in order to test the relative influences of cognition and affect on attitudes towards political tolerance (Kuklinski *et al.* 1991). Briefly, the common-sense view, as they report it, is similar to what we have just described. Intolerance is a visceral, emotional response to a group one dislikes, which can be controlled to some extent by moral principles (pp. 1–3). The Kuklinski group's findings are at odds with this view. Their subjects were asked to respond in different ways to standard questions about minority group rights. One group of subjects (the 'affect group') was asked to respond according to its immediate, emotional reactions. A second group (the 'consequence group') was asked to think about the consequences of the relevant principles before responding. Their instruction was as follows: 'in evaluating each of the propositions you will read, think about what consequences it would have if the proposition advocated in the statement were adopted, or if the event described were to occur, and base your judgment on the desirability of these consequences' (p. 7). There was also a control ('no instruction') group that was not directed how to respond.

Large majorities of all three groups supported civil liberties presented in the form of general principles. Interestingly, however, while views of general principles of the affect and no-instructions groups were similar and along the lines of those noted by other researchers, the consequence group's responses were notably less tolerant (pp. 8–13). Something similar was seen in specific applications. Like previous researchers, Kuklinski and his colleagues noted significant slippage when questions involved generally disliked groups, such as according rights to the Ku Klux Klan. Once again, the responses of the no-instructions and affect groups were similar, while the tolerant responses of the consequence group dropped dramatically (pp. 14–17). Strong evidence that the consequence group was actually thinking about consequences as opposed to responding emotionally is that members of the consequence group whose responses were timed took almost three times as long to respond as members of the affect group. The no-instructions group's average response time was much closer to that of the affect group (p. 18).

In order to explain their findings, Kuklinski and his colleagues hypothesize that when people think about the consequences of general principles, their thoughts turn to adverse consequences and they express their fears (pp. 21–7). In other words, consideration of consequences calls attention to other values with which respect for rights can conflict. Kuklinski and his colleagues note that maintenance of democracy requires adherence to a complex set of values, only one of which is respect for other people's rights. An advantage of contemplation is that it causes people to consider a range of democratic values (p. 23). If Prothro and Grigg's error view were correct, one would expect subjects who reflected more to have higher tolerance scores. Accordingly, the Kuklinski group's study tells against such a view, although there is a complicating factor we should note.[13]

The complication is a peculiarity in the instructions given to the 'consequence' group. Because of the wording of their questions, Kuklinski and his colleagues caused their respondents to think about the *consequences* of allowing the American Nazi party to express their views or the Ku Klux Klan to publish offensive material. In these cases, increased reflection appears to have led respondents to imagine a wider range of adverse consequences, and so to become more fearful. However, the Kuklinski group's study does not cast doubt on other ways in which increased reflection can contribute to tolerance. Once again, a common-sense account of a tolerance judgement is that, confronted with a threatening scenario—with the threat amplified by increased attention to consequences—the subject will react intolerantly unless restrained by consideration of a democratic principle. Increased reflection on democratic principles themselves, as opposed to the consequences of applying them, should therefore increase tolerance. However, because of their instructions, Kuklinski and his colleagues directed the consequence group's attention away from reflection *per se* to one particular aspect of reflection that works to heighten fear. In calling increased attention to consequences—presumably adverse ones—this sort of reflection can be said to have promoted the emotional as opposed to the cognitive element in tolerance judgements. In effect, Kuklinski and his

---

[13] It is conceivable that errors of the kind Prothro and Grigg have in mind could be triggered by increased sensation of threat. On this view, the subject's increased awareness of adverse consequences could upset him and so make him more likely to make logical errors. As we will see, further studies tell against such an interpretation.

colleagues uncovered a cognitive aspect of emotional—fear—responses. But their study does not suggest that increased reflection could not call increased attention to democratic norms, which would, presumably, increase tolerance.

Direct support for the qualification view is provided by Dennis Chong's analysis of civil liberties interviews (Chong 1993). Chong examined thirty interviews conducted in 1977, in connection with a national survey.[14] Although his findings are not supported by quantitative data, the interviews allowed open-ended responses, and so afforded him insight into his subjects' thought processes. Briefly, he found that people's responses depended on how they framed the issues under discussion, which was in turn affected by verbal cues in the questions. As a result of probing by the interviewer, subjects qualified their initial answers, with further reflection leading to responses that were frequently inconsistent with what they had said originally (Chong 1993: 868–73). Respondents' initial answers are characterized by Chong variously as 'off the tops of their heads' (p. 871), 'what comes to mind immediately' (p. 873), due to superficial readings of questions and verbal cues, 'the salient cues in the question itself' (p. 875). One reason for high support of abstract democratic principles is the 'honorific status' these values occupy in the minds of most people (p. 880). And so people initially responded positively to questions about them, about, for example, support for freedom of speech or of religion. When further questioning brought out the complexity of issues involving these norms, subjects qualified their initial responses. For instance, a general response supporting an unqualified right to freedom of speech—'the right to say absolutely anything'—was followed by obvious qualifications, e.g. not being allowed to yell fire in a crowded theatre (p. 879). According to Chong, 'These answers are not so much contradictory as incomplete. they would be contradictory only if the first question had stimulated the respondent to make a broad evaluation of the state of individual rights' (p. 877). Because questions under consideration were complex, further reflection caused subjects to realize competing values at stake, and they grappled to reconcile them. Thus according to Chong, such reasoning does not indicate support for unqualified norms—which, according to Prothro and Grigg, people are unable to apply syllogistically—but adherence to norms that allow exceptions, the nature of which respondents do not at first consciously realize.

Chong's study also casts light on how increased education contributes to increased tolerance. We have repeatedly noted that respondents with

[14] The interviews were a pre-test for the national survey used by McClosky and Brill (1983).

high levels of education have been found to be more tolerant. This in part explains why élites have been found to be more tolerant than members of the general public. Chong observed interesting differences in how different sorts of people responded to civil liberties questions. Briefly, he observed 'strong differences by education level in the way considerations are balanced and weighed' (p. 891). People with greater education, who were more familiar with the issues under discussion, qualified and changed their positions less than others. They were more likely to orient their thinking 'in terms of underlying norms and principles' and to be less influenced by their feelings about the group that wished to exercise its rights (p. 889). Having framed issues initially in terms of individual rights, 'they were more likely to deflect contrary arguments that were brought to mind concerning the nature of the groups in the middle of the controversies' (p. 892). While less educated respondents could be observed to be thinking through the complexities of the issues, the more educated had relatively set positions, formulated through exposure to different lines of argument and acceptance of publicly available interpretations (pp. 889–90). Chong notes that when issues were discussed for which no common frame of reference had been established by public debate, college-educated respondents reacted more similarly to non-college-educated (p. 892).

Thus Chong's analysis provides strong support for the qualification view. People with tolerant responses to general questions but intolerant to specific were seen to qualify their general principles in applying them. Respondents who were better educated and more familiar with democratic arguments tended to respond more tolerantly to specific cases. This suggests that they, unlike other subjects, subscribed to strong democratic principles (which they correctly applied).

The findings of the Kuklinski group and Chong are supported by the most sophisticated examination to date of how people make civil liberties judgements, *With Malice toward Some*, by George Marcus, John Sullivan, Elizabeth Theiss-Morse, and Sandra Wood (Marcus *et al.* 1995). This group of scholars performed a series of experiments in order to identify the thought processes involved.

Their main findings, based on the theory of emotionality of Jeffrey Gray, a British neuroscientist, emphasize the role of contemporary stimuli in tolerance judgements. While previous research on tolerance focused mainly on antecedent conditions—e.g. levels of education, religion, political orientation—Marcus and his colleagues explored how people process contemporary information, especially perceptions of threat. Their basic model is similar to, though more sophisticated than, the view outlined above. Intolerance is a response to perception of threat. Marcus and his colleagues observed that respondents were not affected by information about the likelihood of a threatening group actually gaining power. This calls into question whether desire to suppress the group in question is a pragmatic response to an actual danger, or mainly symbolic or expressive in nature, directed towards the group's belligerent behaviour (pp. 79, 104). I will return to the implications of this finding, below.

Marcus and his colleagues found that intolerant responses were counteracted by appeals to reflection. In an experiment resembling that of the Kuklinski study, respondents were divided into groups who read information concerning threatening behaviour and were then asked, in responding, to 'attend to your thoughts' or 'attend to your feelings' (pp. 64–5). Marcus and his colleagues note that, as we have seen, the Kuklinski group instructed their respondents to consider the consequences of different courses of action, which led to greater intolerance. Their own instruction led to greater tolerance (p. 80): 'When asked to attend to their thoughts, [respondents] may focus on the benefits of tolerance, thereby superseding their natural instinct to be intolerant' (p. 82). As noted above, though reflection on consequences may increase perceptions of threat, reflecting on democratic norms can work to counter intolerant responses.

Marcus and his colleagues measured the strength of their respondents' adherence to democratic norms. Not surprisingly, they found that natural impulses towards intolerance were counteracted by increased commitment. Reminding respondents of specific norms relevant to the situations described significantly increased tolerant responses (pp. 125–32). However, respondents already strongly committed to democratic principles were not affected by being reminded of the principles—to which they already adhered (p. 130). On the whole, Marcus and his colleagues found that different kinds of people responded differently. Those higher in political knowledge and in 'need for cognition'—an individual's measured tendency to need and to enjoy thinking (p. 166)—were not only more tolerant, but responded to situations differently from the less knowledgeable. They adhered more strongly to their principles, unmoved by information concerning the threatening behaviour of target groups. Such people 'have the information base necessary to counterargue contemporary information' (pp. 223, 145). The less knowledgeable were more easily swayed by contemporary information and consistently gave less tolerant responses. On the whole, then: 'People are more tolerant the more they know, the more thoughtful and deliberative they are, and the more willing they are to take a sober second thought' (p. 223).

Marcus and his colleagues were interested primarily in psychological processes underlying tolerance judgements and so paid little attention to the logical status of democratic principles. But their studies demonstrate that respondents who are weakly committed to democratic principles set them aside in the face of threats. Marcus and his colleagues do not comment directly on whether the general principles are qualified or misapplied. But the role of perceptions of threat in contributing to departures from general principles indicates factors at work more complex than the failure of syllogistic logic described by Prothro and Grigg. The Marcus group's studies do not rule out the possibility that people misapply strong principles under the stimulus of threat. But other aspects of their findings tell against this interpretation.

The Marcus group provides a complex account of the psychology of threat. As I have noted, one of their striking findings is that tolerance judgements are influenced little if at all by information about the likelihood that threats will materialize (above, pp. 65–6). Marcus and his colleagues write: 'Probability information simply is not very important in people's tolerance decisions, both in this study and in prior survey research' (1995: 79).[15] Marcus and his colleagues distinguished between different factors that influence perceptions of threat and so tolerance judgements. 'Normative' measures of threat include whether the group in question is violent or non-violent, dangerous or safe, untrustworthy or trustworthy, dishonest or honest. 'Strength' measures bear on whether the group constitutes a genuine danger. Factors here include whether the group is strong or weak, important or unimportant, and likely to become popular. The Marcus group's repeated studies showed that the normative measures 'consistently relate to political tolerance judgments' (average correlation: –0.29). Strength measures, on the other hand, were seen 'to have no influence whatsoever on political tolerance judgments' (average correlation: –0.01) (p. 102). Marcus and his colleagues argue that, in perceiving groups as threatening, people are less influenced by assessment of actual dangers to public or personal safety than by perceptions of 'intrusive and disruptive normative violations' (p. 102). A subject's perceptions of normative violations are, in turn, strongly affected by overall moral attitudes, 'a personality-like predisposition or a long-standing belief' (p. 103). In other words, what constitutes a threat can be traced back to a subject's view of the moral order that is threatened, while his view of this is deeply integrated in his overall personality. For many people intolerance judgements are triggered by perceived normative disruptions rather than by

[15] I should note the possibility that the responses under discussion that Marcus and his colleagues received were affected by respondents' scepticism about whether the hypothetical group described in scenarios—the fictional 'White Supremacist Faction' (Marcus *et al.* 1995: 68–74)—would constitute a real threat. However, the fictional scenario is not entirely without plausibility (see p. 73), and in view of the low level of political information most Americans possess, many respondents were probably unable to discount the possibility of a genuine threat with assurance.

realistic assessments of danger: 'When people are confronted with a group that violates the norms of proper, orderly behavior, the increased perceptions of threat lead them to respond with intolerance . . .' (p. 79).

It is difficult to disentangle specific moral principles from the range of personality and moral factors that are brought to bear in tolerance judgements. But the studies I have reviewed show problems in focusing on moral principles in isolation from other personality factors. Because tolerance principles are closely bound up with perceptions of threat, when many people make tolerance judgements, their democratic principles are qualified to allow exceptions for normative disruptions that are perceived as threatening, although they fall beyond concerns of public safety (or strong offence). According to the criteria presented in the previous section, the principles involved in such cases should be identified as weak rights principles, rather than strong.

The Marcus group's analysis of the psychology of threat perceptions is supported by studies of what has come to be called 'symbolic racism' (McConahay and Hough 1976). I will look at three studies. First, in order to analyse the role of racial threat in Los Angeles mayoral elections contested by white and black candidates, Donald Kinder and David Sears surveyed 198 white suburbanites after the 1969 election and 239 after the 1973 election (Kinder and Sears 1981; discussed by Marcus *et al.* 1995: 104). Both elections involved Tom Bradley, a black Democratic candidate. Kinder and Sears found that subjects' candidate preferences were essentially unaffected by opinions of the likelihood that threatening events would occur. They write: 'the political consequences of racial prejudice are carried by symbolic resentments, not by tangible threats' (1981: 427); 'the white public's political response to racial issues is based on moral and symbolic challenges to the racial status quo in society generally rather than on any direct, tangible challenge to their own personal lives' (p. 429).

Analysing anti-busing attitudes in Louisville, Kentucky, in 1976, John McConahay surveyed 1,049 people (879 whites), aged 18 and older (McConahay 1982). He recorded attitudes in reference to a school busing plan that had been implemented in 1975, which inspired protests, demonstrations, fire-bombings, and other resistance (p. 699). For purposes of this study, McConahay measured self-interest on the basis of a collection of factors, including having school-age children, owning a home, and expressing happiness with one's neighbourhood (pp. 703–4). He found, strikingly, that a self-interest analysis of respondents' attitudes towards the busing issue was 'untenable'. Measures of self-interest 'were virtually useless in discriminating degrees of support or opposition' (p. 714). Measures of racial attitudes, on the other hand, 'correlated strongly and consistently with the anti-busing position' (p. 714). In other words, attitudes towards blacks were a far stronger determinant of attitudes towards busing than the likelihood that one would be directly affected. According to McConahay, although not rooted in what would commonly be viewed as self-interest, the whites' attitudes can be viewed as rational or maximizing, but maximizing their values—'or in this instance, prejudices'—rather than other utilities, such as money, power, or status (p. 715).

Like that of Kinder and Sears, McConahay's study indicates that many people's attitudes towards threatening public policies are driven more by their values (or prejudices) than by realistic threat assessment. Further confirmation of this finding is provided by Kinder and Lynn Sanders' analysis of American's attitudes towards a range of issues concerned with race. Kinder and Sanders analysed data from National Election Studies between 1970 and 1992, especially 1986 (N = 2,176), which is an especially valuable source for racial attitudes, and 1992 (Kinder and Sanders 1996: 15). Their findings are consistent with 'the generally anemic effects of self-interest on public opinion' reported in many previous studies (p. 262).[16] In regard to the question of how people assess particular threats, Kinder and Sanders report 'a large divorce between perception and reality' (p. 265). The racial threats that whites perceived 'were almost entirely a consequence of the racial sentiments they felt' (p. 265). Kinder and Sanders cite additional instances of exaggerated racial threats, e.g. fear of urban riots during the 1960s (p. 265).

The symbolic racism studies do not involve curtailment of central democratic rights. All three concern issues of equal treatment and how different people viewed requirements of this sort. But what interests us are subjects' moralized perceptions of threats, which, as we have seen, closely resemble what the Marcus group observed in regard to tolerance judgements. Marcus and his colleagues note similarities between how subjects responded to cases of this sort and those involving civil liberties: 'Assessment of probability, the likelihood that a specific threat is imminent, did not seem to influence political tolerance judgments, racial beliefs, or candidate preferences' (Marcus *et al.* 1995: 104). According to all these studies, perceptions of danger are bound up with overall orientations towards the moral order and for many people extend beyond actual concerns of public safety. In other words, perceptions of threat are oftentimes conduits for a range of values held to be important.

Let us return to the analysis of tolerance judgements discussed above. As we have seen, faced with a threat, the subject, Jones, departs from professed commitment to a general principle and supports restricting the rights of some unpopular group. This broad scenario can be filled in in

---

[16] They note that, not surprisingly, self-interest works most when benefits or harms are clearly recognized, substantial, and virtually certain to come about (p. 262).

various ways. According to the studies we have seen, when the principle is set aside, what is often actually at work is the subject's perception of threat, based on his *values*, rather than the prospect of genuine danger. Once again, in cases such as this, the broad principle should be viewed as containing qualifications in regard to other values, perhaps a range of values, beyond concerns of safety. Because principles are set aside to take these into account, in many cases the broad principles should be identified as weak rather than strong.[17]

Somewhat schematically, I interpret the evidence along the following lines. (1) Jones supports value X in addition to concerns of public safety. (2) Therefore, Jones identifies policy P (which threatens X) as a threat (in some unqualified sense), and so believes that some right, R, should be restricted to deal with the threat. (3) The consequence is that R is restricted to accommodate concern for X. But rather than directly noting the need to balance the two values, Jones proceeds to this conclusion through perception of threat. For this reason, I view the principles underlying R as, in effect, a weak principle, tacitly qualified by concern for X. Further evidence presented below supports this account of the subject's reasoning.

5. BARS TO DEMOCRATIC CONSENSUS

The studies I have examined reveal a lack of consensus on strong rights principles in American society. As Prothro and Grigg noted almost forty years ago, although there is general agreement on democratic principles stated in the abstract, in regard to particular applications, consensus breaks down (Prothro and Grigg 1960: 286). However, as we have seen, the psychological mechanisms involved differ from what Prothro and Grigg imagined and rule out the possibility of general support for strong rights principles, which many members of society apply incorrectly.

Important implications are clear immediately. If consensus on central democratic rights is necessary for the smooth functioning of democratic

[17] It could be argued that what is at work in such cases are disagreements over factual matters as opposed to differences on abstract moral principles. As we have seen, different members of society disagree on applications of their moral principles, with these in turn mediated by disagreements about ostensibly factual questions, e.g. whether a given group constitutes a significant danger to society. But disagreement on this last question should not be characterized as empirical (certainly not strictly empirical). Rather, the views a given subject will take on such questions are bound up with—or 'constrained by' (see below, pp. 161–2)—basic aspects of their overall philosophical or world-views. Disagreements on these issues are unlikely to be resolved by empirical evidence. For further discussion, see the next section.

societies, the studies we have reviewed show how difficult it will be to achieve this. People bring quite different kinds of principles to bear, and so it is not surprising that they draw different conclusions. In regard to the quest for liberal consensus, this situation entails the need for some means to get supporters of different views of rights to agree on common principles, or, barring this, some means to adjudicate disputes between them.

Once we recognize that many members of society have qualified rights principles, we confront a host of problems. Because weak rights principles allow a range of exceptions, we must ask if these are legitimate, according to the liberal commitments discussed in Chapter 1. But we must also assess the legitimacy of exceptions to strong rights principles and difficulties in assessing possible exceptions in practice.

To some extent, assessing exceptions is clear. Since liberty is a great value, people should not be allowed to abridge the rights of unpopular minority groups because of prejudice, as opposed to threats of genuine harm.[18] Members of unpopular groups should not be prevented from disseminating their views, associating freely, being employed in various professions, e.g. as college teachers, without good reasons. But even if we postulate that only real threats justify abridgements, we have seen that people will disagree as to what constitutes genuine threats. Like other moral notions, this will be widely contested. As the studies I have examined show, people interpret threatening behaviour differently, on the basis of their overall points of view, including differences in how they perceive threats. For instance, Bob Altemeyer discusses a 'dangerous world orientation', a propensity to perceive the world as a dangerous place, populated by threatening groups (Altemeyer 1988, ch. 5). Because of the large number of people in contemporary society who see the world in this way, calls for greater tolerance would be widely viewed as courting danger and so to be resisted. Accordingly, in order for members of different groups with different perceptions of danger to live together amicably, they must have common criteria of justifiable threat, or means to adjudicate disputes about them.

Through application of criteria discussed in Chapter 1, a certain range of threats can be excluded. Because of the value of individual liberty, the burden of proof is on people who argue that a given threat justifies restricting others. The basic canons of justification in such matters have been discussed. The group in question must be shown to be a threat, on the basis of evidence that rests on (relatively) non-controversial grounds, common

---

[18] In order to keep matters simple throughout discussion here, I do not mention that liberal principles under discussion may also be restricted by concerns of strong offence and perhaps a minimal core of moralistic considerations, though this is assumed.

sense, principles of basic scientific reasoning, etc. Claims rooted in controversial religious beliefs or other comprehensive views cannot be appealed to in order to justify intolerance.

An example of an argument that rests on indefensible factual claims is presented by Lord Devlin, who argues for the state's right to suppress immoral conduct, especially homosexual behaviour. Devlin argues that the state's right to protect itself legitimizes punishment for crimes such as treason. But society is damaged by other sorts of conduct. Viewing public morality as a 'seamless web', Devlin asserts that safeguarding this is necessary for the preservation of society:

> society means a community of ideas; without shared ideas on politics, morals, and ethics, no society can exist. . . . For society is not something that is kept together physically; it is held by the invisible bonds of common thought. If the bonds were too far relaxed the members would drift apart. A common morality is part of the bondage. The bondage is part of the price of society; and mankind, which needs society, must pay its price. (Devlin 1965: 10)

Because public morality is undermined by conduct of which the majority disapproves, such conduct can be suppressed. Nothing less than the preservation of society is at stake.

Devlin's view would justify a great deal of government interference in people's rights. But his account depends on questionable factual premises. We should note that Devlin's claims are couched in terms of preventing harms—significant harms—to the community. To justify restricting individual liberties on the basis of preventing harm, it is not enough to show that homosexuality poses a danger to 'society'. One must demonstrate the prospect of real danger to actual individuals.[19] Devlin presents no credible evidence that homosexual conduct has anything like the consequences he suggests. In his response to Devlin, H. L. A. Hart likens Devlin's view to the Emperor Justinian's opinion that homosexual-

---

[19] There are complicating factors here, in that moralistic concerns could justify restrictions on certain homosexual activities. Complex issues of weighing competing values are involved here, full discussion of which would distract us from our main concerns. In any case, according to liberal consensus, such issues must be worked out politically. Briefly, it seems to me that community values could justify restriction on such things as same-sex marriage or adoption, without flagrantly violating liberal constraints. But the kind of wholesale violation of individual liberty and autonomy entailed by criminalizing consensual sexual activities would require stronger grounds than preserving community values. In the absence of significant harms to individuals, criminalizing such practices would likely require invocation of values associated with particular comprehensive views, which would be ruled out by liberal consensus. For discussion of different elements in community values as these weigh against concerns of autonomy, see Feinberg (1988: 81–123); for a contrary view, see George (1997).

ity causes earthquakes (Hart 1963: 50).[20] Accordingly, unless Devlin could demonstrate that homosexuality poses a genuine danger, his argument would not justify intolerance.[21]

Although Devlin's argument is difficult to maintain, it calls attention to troubling questions about the nature of genuine threats to public safety, and so the lengths to which society can go to protect itself from sources of danger. Although the harms invoked by Devlin are improbable, in other cases there is room for wide differences of opinion. Thus certain liberal societies place restrictions on rights to free speech and political expression.

The former West Germany is a clear example. In part, Article 5 of the West German Constitution reads as follows:

Everyone has the right to express his opinion freely in speech, writing, and picture, and to spread it, and to inform himself unhindered from universally accessible sources. Freedom of the press and freedom of presentation of views through film and broadcast are protected. Censorship does not take place. (Castberg 1960: 362)

But in view of German experience, Article 5 contains limitations. Freedom of expression can be limited 'for the protection of youth and in the right to personal dignity' (Article 5, Limitations Section (2); Castberg 1960: 365). In addition: speech must not clash with 'the constitutional order' (p. 366). There are boundaries for political debate. For example, Article 5(3) protects scientific teachers and researchers, but not when they contest the democratic order. A teacher who is a spokesperson for communist or neo-fascist ideas is not giving scientific instruction and is therefore not protected by Article 5 (p. 369). Article 8, Section 3(1) forbids 'the wearing in public or in an assembly of uniforms, articles of uniform, or similar articles of dress as the expression of a common political opinion'. Expressly mentioned are former national socialist organizations (p. 371). Article 9 provides rights to form unions and associations. But Section 2 forbids associations directed 'against the constitutional order', and against 'the idea of international understanding' (pp. 371–2).

Although one might suppose that the experience of Germany licenses unique exceptions to free speech, similar restrictions are in place in other liberal countries. In Canada, for example, James Keegstra, a high school teacher, was charged under the Criminal Code for 'willingly promoting hatred against an identifiable group, for making anti-Semitic statements to his class, which they were expected to reproduce in order to achieve

[20] For Devlin's unconvincing response on these points see Devlin (1965: 13 n. 1).
[21] On intolerance and homosexuality, see Gibson (1987) and Gibson and Tedin (1988); see below, Ch. 4 n. 15 and p. 233.

grades.'[22] Keegstra appealed to the Canadian Supreme Court, which found 4–3 against him, arguing on the basis of the need 'to restrict the content of expression by singling out particular meanings that are not to be conveyed' (p. 9787). Although the majority found that the kind of expression in which Keegstra engaged is covered by guaranteed freedom of expression in the Canadian Charter of Rights, they also found that in this case this guarantee could be justifiably restricted for the sake of 'the fundamental values and aspirations of Canadian society' (p. 9789). Promotion of a 'free and democratic society' justifies limiting forms of expression incompatible with these values. Hate speech not only can cause emotional damage to members of particular racial or religious groups, but threatens wider discord in society at large. The high value of 'freedom of expression in the abstract' does not support protection of hate propaganda' (p. 9791).[23]

To some extent, opinions about the extent to which particular forms of expression constitute real threats will be heavily influenced by different people's assessments of the amount of risk a society should be willing to bear for the sake of individual rights. Understandably, in view of their country's unfortunate history, many Germans have been willing to bear relatively little. Thus the Keegstra opinion is of interest, because Canada has had a less troubled history. But in a multicultural society such as Canada, strong arguments can be made for circumscribing various rights in order to protect the feelings of diverse groups. As these examples illustrate, questions of balancing rights against other values are not always clear-cut. Especially in a diverse society means must be devised to produce agreement on how to deal with significant risks among people who disagree about what constitutes risks and the point at which rights claims can be overridden by such concerns. To some extent, questions along these lines concern public policy issues rather than fundamental moral principles. But basic moral issues are also involved. Questions of balancing rights against other moral concerns would draw us into thorny issues concerning how rights are conceptualized and justified—kinds of issue that political liberalism (and liberal consensus) tries to avoid.

Questions of balancing rights against other values become even more complex when we move from public safety (perhaps less broadly construed) to what we have identified as moralistic concerns. The studies

[22] *Supreme Court of Canada Reports Service, Digest 1654*, 77 (Aug. 1991), 9786; for knowledge of this case, I am indebted to Sniderman *et al.* (1996: 63), where it is briefly discussed.

[23] For contrary balancing of values in this case, see the dissenting opinion of J. McLachlin, *Supreme Court of Canada Reports Service, Digest 1654*, 77 (Aug. 1991), 9793 ff.

discussed in the previous sections show that many people are willing to abridge others' rights on such grounds. A brief look at additional survey evidence confirms this finding.

Consider surveys directed by McClosky and Brill in the late 1970s. Two results are striking. First, high percentages of sampled populations were willing to curtail other people's rights on moralistic grounds. Secondly, confirmation that tolerance attitudes are deeply rooted in subjects' overall personalities and/or philosophical orientations is provided by connections between their attitudes towards rights and their political ideologies. Political liberals were found to be substantially and consistently more tolerant than conservatives.

McClosky and Brill employed two national surveys, each of which had separate mass and élite samples, and cumulatively involved some 3,000 general respondents and almost 5,000 élites (1983: 25–6). The latter category included 'ideological élites', whom McClosky and Brill describe as 'knowledgeable respondents who are active in, or associated with, ideological organizations which range in their political and philosophical outlooks across the ideological spectrum' (p. 277 n.). To cite a few examples, in the mass sample 68 per cent of strong conservatives (based on self-identification) responded that 'novels that describe explicit sex acts' 'have no place in a high school library and should be banned', but only 26 per cent of strong liberals would ban them. Sixty-five per cent of strong liberals responded that the novels 'should be permitted in the library if they are worthwhile literature', but only 25 per cent of strong conservatives would allow them. Of community leaders, 75 per cent of strong liberals would allow the books, but only 34 per cent of strong conservatives would; 17 per cent of strong liberals would ban them, but 58 per cent of strong conservatives would (p. 308). Of the mass sample, 85 per cent of strong conservatives responded that a person 'who publicly burns or spits on the flag' 'should be fined or punished in some way'. Fifty-four per cent of strong liberals agreed. Thirty-two per cent of strong liberals responded that the person 'may be behaving badly but should not be punished for it by law'; this view was shared by only 9 per cent of strong conservatives. Of the élite sample, 47 per cent of strong liberals would punish actions against the flag, while 42 per cent would not. Eighty-six per cent of strong conservatives would punish, and only 7 per cent would not' (p. 307). Of the mass sample, 61 per cent of strong conservatives responded that 'protesters who mock the President by wearing death masks at one of his public speeches' 'should be removed from the audience by the police'. This was the response of 47 per cent of strong liberals. Of the élites, 34 per cent of strong conservatives would remove the protesters, but only 18 per cent of strong liberals would (p. 307). In response to a question similar to one asked by

Stouffer, in the mass sample, 18 per cent of strong conservatives responded that 'The freedom of atheists to make fun of God and religion' 'should be legally protected no matter who might be offended', while this was the response of 41 per cent of strong liberals. Sixty-four per cent of strong conservatives and 41 per cent of strong liberals responded that the atheists 'should not be allowed in a public place where religious groups gather'. In the élite sample, 66 per cent of strong liberals and 33 per cent of strong conservatives would afford the atheists legal protection; 18 per cent of strong liberals and 50 per cent of strong conservatives would not allow them to mock religion (p. 309). Differences between liberal and conservative ideological élites were stark. To the statement 'When it comes to free speech', 94 per cent of left liberals responded that extremists 'should have the same rights as everyone else', and only 1 per cent that they 'should not be allowed to spread their propaganda'. Fifty-one per cent of 'conservative right' élites would allow the extremists to speak, while 29 per cent would not allow them to (p. 302). Eighty-two per cent of left liberals responded that 'censoring obscene books' 'is an old-fashioned idea that no longer makes sense', and only 4 per cent that this 'is necessary to protect community standards'. Eighty-five per cent of conservative right élites supported censorship, with only 7 per cent against (p. 302). In response to: 'How do you feel about movies that use foul language or show nudity and sexual acts on the screen?' Eighty-two per cent of left liberals responded that 'they have as much right to be shown as other films', and 5 per cent that 'they should be banned'. For the conservative right, the responses were almost precisely reversed: 85 per cent favoured banning, and 11 per cent allowing them to be shown (p. 303).

Similar findings could be multiplied, while the implications are clear. Large percentages of respondents in both élite and mass samples were willing to abrogate rights for what we have identified as moralistic considerations. Thus the principles to which these respondents subscribe can be characterized as weak. The fact that conservatives are consistently far more willing to abrogate rights than liberals tells strongly against the error view. It is far-fetched to believe that conservatives somehow consistently reason incorrectly in approaching particular cases, while liberals do not. It is much more plausible that liberals and conservatives have different views of rights—again, as parts of their overall philosophies. A conclusion along these lines is drawn by McClosky and Brill, whom I quote at some length:

Conservatives and liberals may differ in their attitudes towards tolerance partly because of an underlying disagreement about the nature of a *right*. Liberals are, in effect, more inclined than conservatives to believe that rights are *natural* and *inalienable*, that a person possesses them simply by virtue of being human. . . . Although some conservatives share this perspective, many tend to think of rights as contingent upon proper conduct—as benefits to be earned, won, or merited. Most conservatives do not appear to regard a right as inextinguishable. An individual who abuses it, or behaves outrageously, or fails to honor its purposes, may lose it. (McClosky and Brill 1983: 276–7)

It should be noted that these conclusions, drawn by McClosky and Brill from surveys conducted in the United States, are similar to those drawn by Sniderman and his associates from their large Canadian survey. As noted above (p. 53), Sniderman and his associates argue that the thesis of democratic élitism owes much of its plausibility to lumping together liberal and conservative élites. While democratic élitism claims that élites are generally more tolerant than the mass public, Sniderman and his associates found that élite tolerance is 'bimodal' rather than 'unimodal'. Conservative élites are markedly less supportive of civil liberties than liberal élites, differing little from conservative citizens (1996, ch. 2), For example, in response to the question 'Do you think that films that show sexually explicit acts should be allowed or should they be banned?' approximately 85 per cent of élites affiliated with the New Democrat Party opposed banning, but only 49 per cent of Progressive Conservatives opposed it; 48 per cent of the mass public opposed banning (pp. 73–4).

Taken in conjunction with the Sniderman study, the surveys discussed by McClosky and Brill afford powerful support for both widespread adherence to weak rights principles, and the claim that these are embedded in overall political views. Once again, let us return to the role of perceptions of threat in tolerance judgements. We have seen that in many cases such perceptions serve as conduits for other values. We can hypothesize that the relatively intolerant conservatives studied by McClosky and Brill, Sniderman, and other researchers perceive affronts to a wider range of moral values as threatening and so are willing to curtail rights in order to protect them. Once again, rather than errors in applying unqualified principles, what is at work in such cases are applications of qualified, weak principles that are highly integrated into overall world-views.

Confronted with such views, we could respond that their adherents are not liberals, and so their views should be ruled out of bounds. As we have seen, according to Feinberg, a liberal is willing to limit liberty only to prevent harm or strong offence. But from the point of view of liberal consensus, this approach will not work. Since our task is to find a measure of general agreement, we cannot set the views of significant portions of the population aside. Moreover, with views of rights contested, we cannot simply stipulate that Feinberg is correct. In a diverse society people with different comprehensive views will differ in how they weigh rights against other values. As long as some reasonable conception of rights is adhered to, we cannot exclude proponents of weak rights from liberal consensus.

In effect, weak rights are components of some of the disparate comprehensive views that constitute a diverse society. Evidence of connections between other moral/political principles and overall comprehensive views will be seen in subsequent chapters.

6. IMPLICATIONS

Throughout this chapter a number of claims have been established. First, general consensus on democratic rights stated in the abstract provides support for the basic commitments of liberal theory, as discussed in Chapter 1. There is almost unanimous acceptance of some conception of basic rights, though further inquiry casts doubt on exactly what this amounts to. Lack of consensus on specific cases shows that general principles are understood differently by different members of society, presumably on the basis of their overall values and views of the world. The evidence I have reviewed shows that many members of society subscribe to weak rights principles, which contain tacit qualifications. This of course entails that there is no general agreement on strong principles. The evidence does not suggest general agreement on weak principles either. Rather, there seems to be considerable disagreement on democratic rights.[24] Accordingly, granted disagreement about the weight and scope of democratic rights, if people are to live together co-operatively, liberal societies require means to adjudicate their disputes.

It is possible that, to some extent, these disagreements can be alleviated through increased education. The studies I have examined repeatedly show that increased education brings increased tolerance. With better-educated respondents, there is less slippage between adherence to abstract principles and specific applications. Education apparently strengthens commitment to principles, while the principles themselves become more general, admitting fewer qualifications. Education does not significantly affect acceptance levels in regard to abstract rights statements, which are accepted almost unanimously by less educated as well as better-educated subjects. But the fact that better-educated subjects have been found not to have to be reminded of rights principles to provide tolerant responses (above, p. 66) as well as their increased ability to 'counter-argue' conflict-

[24] In Ch. 7 I will consider a somewhat different line of argument that attempts to show that, in spite of appearances to the contrary, liberal citizens are committed to strong principles. This is Rawls's argument for the priority of liberty, in *Political Liberalism*. I do not believe this argument succeeds, and we can postpone discussion until Ch. 7.

ing values indicates their stronger commitment. Once again, as Chong notes, better-educated respondents were more likely to assess situations 'in terms of underlying norms and principles' and to 'deflect contrary arguments that were brought to mind concerning the nature of the groups in the middle of the controversies' (Chong 1993: 889, 892; above, p. 65; also Marcus *et al.* 1995: 223, 145; above, p. 66). The ability to deflect contrary considerations indicates less susceptibility to having views influenced by possible threats, and so, by implication, commitment to strong rights principles, which admit relatively few qualifications.[25]

The argument between Devlin and Hart suggest an additional important role for increased education. Not only can it strengthen adherence to democratic principles, but it can help people differentiate between different sorts of threat. If public education could increase people's awareness of the difference between genuine threats that require suppression and merely (what can be viewed as) distasteful or obnoxious behaviour, which should be tolerated, this would represent a significant advance.[26] To some extent, this could be accomplished through greater public awareness of means of reasoning to be used in assessing threats. However, we have also seen that perceptions of threat are bound up with subjects' overall values and views of the world. As people feel more threatened, they become increasingly willing to abrogate rights. In effect, increased perception of threat is psychologically tied to a weaker conception of rights. Connections along these lines will be returned to in the following chapter.

As a practical matter, we must recognize that different members of society are likely to accept widely different rights principles well into the future. Public education has an important role in increasing understanding of and appreciation for democratic principles and helping people to assess threats accurately. But to the extent that the threats people perceive actually amount to perceived violations of norms, more discriminating assessment of actual dangers would have limited effects. To bring about consensus, strong measures would be needed. To the extent that

[25] Sullivan *et al.* (1982) argue that the content bias of previous studies exaggerated the effects of education on tolerance. Their studies indicate that highly educated people choose right-wing groups as 'least liked', while less educated respondents tend to choose left-wing groups. Beyond this, 'although there remains some tendency for the highly educated to be more tolerant, this tendency is not as strong as prior research has suggested' (Sullivan *et al.* 1982: 119; see 1982, ch. 5). Other studies that question the effect of education include Lawrence (1976) and Mary R. Jackman (1973, 1978). On effects of education, see also, Altemeyer (1988: 91 ff.), discussed below, p. 112.

[26] This is related to, though quite different from, the call for greater logical sophistication made by Prothro and Grigg (1960). The demand here is for psychological sophistication, for the ability to discriminate between objects that pose a genuine threat and others that are merely distasteful, although the 'symbolic' politics studies noted above indicate how difficult this will be in practice.

perception of threat stems from deep-seated comprehensive views, especially religious views, extensive and intrusive public education would be required. But this would likely be resisted as undermining religion, and so important rights.

Barring agreement on principles, means must be found to bring about a measure of consensus in spite of these disagreements. A major theme of this work is that this task can be accomplished by democratic procedures and institutions, which liberal citizens support overwhelmingly. But in order fully to appreciate the significance of support for democracy, we must broaden the scope of our inquiry into the problem democratic procedures must address. We have seen that differences in how people perceive threats to their core values—and differences in the values that are threatened—are bound up with deep-seated, comprehensive views. Further light is cast on these connections by examining one major source of intolerance and other anti-democratic attitudes in modern liberal societies, religion. As we will see, at least certain religious orientations, subscribed to by large percentages of the American population, have been found to be strongly connected to anti-democratic attitudes and are also bound up with distinctive ways of addressing moral issues. It is to these subjects that I now turn.

4

Religion and Democratic Values

In the last chapter I explored widespread non-democratic beliefs of democratic citizens and bars to consensus on strong rights principles. Studies I have reviewed repeatedly note connections between religion and intolerance. In this chapter my first concern is to determine what it is about religion that tends to conflict with strong democratic rights. I will examine numerous studies of the relationship between religion and other anti-democratic sentiments, especially prejudice.[1] The evidence is, if anything, over-abundant and points in different directions. But certain relationships emerge clearly, especially between prejudice and a particular cognitive style, which has been referred to as 'authority-mindedness'. This cognitive style is most apparent in religious fundamentalists, while fundamentalism in turn has been closely associated with prejudice and other anti-democratic attitudes, including 'right-wing authoritarianism'.

My second main concern is the prevalence of the anti-democratic aspects of religion. Obviously, the seriousness of the problems religious intolerance raises for liberal consensus depends on how widespread it is. Given the elusiveness of the underlying cognitive causes I will identify, we will see that it is difficult to determine this with precision. But, by all indications, the cognitive factors are widespread and so constitute a significant problem. In the concluding section I will briefly discuss the potential of education to overcome this.

1. INTOLERANCE AND RELIGION

Many studies examined in the last chapter note strong relationships between intolerance and religion, a connection first reported by Stouffer. Stouffer noted markedly lower tolerance levels among churchgoers than non-churchgoers (Stouffer 1955: 142). In comparison to 36 per cent of his

[1] On the relationship between intolerance and prejudice, see below, pp. 86–8.

national sample classified as 'more tolerant', 28 per cent of respondents who reported having attended church in the last month fell into this category. To some extent, this could be expected, since two of Stouffer's tolerance items referred to granting liberties to atheists, but the finding held on other questions as well. For instance, in regard to granting a supporter of government ownership of big business and the railroads rights to free speech, 67 per cent of the general sample responded positively, but only 60 per cent of churchgoers did the same (p. 142). Stouffer notes similar findings in regard to his sample of civic leaders, with 73 per cent of non-churchgoers and 62 per cent of churchgoers described as 'relatively tolerant' (p. 151). One other of Stouffer's findings worth noting is that his small sample of Jewish respondents, both male and female, were much more tolerant of nonconformists than either Catholics or Protestants (p. 143).

In keeping with the overall increase in levels of tolerance they observed since the time of Stouffer's study, Nunn and his colleagues recorded increased levels of tolerance in a range of religious groups, for both general respondents and civic leaders. The Nunn group surveyed religion in some depth, from a variety of perspectives. They too noted significant gaps between non-religious (87 per cent tolerant) and Jewish respondents (88 per cent tolerant) and Catholics (59 per cent tolerant), Protestants (46 per cent), and 'Other' (60 per cent). The pattern Stouffer noted among church attenders and non-attenders also held (Nunn *et al.* 1978: 129–30). In addition to these relationships, Nunn and his colleagues examined connections between tolerance and a scale of religious beliefs. Important items concerned belief in the existence of God and in the Devil. High percentages of respondents reported believing in God (69 per cent absolutely certain, 19 per cent some doubt) and in the Devil (50 per cent completely true, 21 per cent probably true) (p. 132). The Nunn group found a strong relationship between active participation in religious services and certainty that the Devil exists (p. 132).

Particular aspects of religion strongly affected tolerance judgements. Nunn and his colleagues report high correlations between belief in the Devil and lack of tolerance. Seventy-three per cent of respondents who were classified as 'less tolerant' claimed certainty that the Devil exists; another 14 per cent of the less tolerant thought the Devil probably exists. Of respondents classified as 'more tolerant', 35 per cent were certain of the Devil's existence, and 24 per cent thought this was probably true. Nunn and his colleagues hypothesize that belief in the Devil fosters intolerance because of the belief that the Devil does not work directly in the world, but through human agents, especially nonconformists (p. 139). The Nunn group also found that factors connected to high religiosity, including relatively low education and relatively high perceptions of threats to our way of life from communists and revolutionaries, correlated strongly with intolerance (pp. 134–5).

Numerous studies support the relationship between religion and intolerance, including those by Sullivan and his colleagues and McClosky and Brill, discussed in the previous chapter.[2] The overall relationship is refined in important ways in three studies, by Kathleen Beatty and Oliver Walter (1984), Clyde Wilcox and Ted Jelen (1990), and John Green, James Guth, Lyman Kellstedt, and Corwin Smidt (1994). Beatty and Walter analysed intolerance of different religious groups. Most earlier studies had looked at relatively broad religious denominations, especially Protestants in general. On the basis of General Social Survey data, from the years 1976, 1977, and 1980, Beatty and Walter distinguished sixteen Protestant denominations, Jews, Catholics, and non-affiliates, and further distinguished these groups according to levels of religiosity, although these distinctions were incomplete (as they note: 1984: 321). Beatty and Walter's data did not allow them to distinguish between different branches of Baptists, although other studies had shown Southern Baptists to be considerably more orthodox than American Baptists. The same could be said of Missouri Synod Lutherans, who are more orthodox than American Lutherans (on doctrinal orthodoxy, see below).

Beatty and Walter measured political tolerance through standard questions concerning allowing members of nonconformist groups to make speeches 'against churches and religion', to teach in a college or university, and not have books they had written against churches and religion removed from the public library (p. 328). The groups in question were: atheists, communists, homosexuals, militarists, and racists, a range spanning the ideological spectrum. Jews and people with no religious affiliation were found to be least intolerant (p. 323). Although there was some variation among the tolerance levels of different Protestant denominations, members of denominations generally characterized as 'fundamentalist' (Church of Christ, Seventh-Day Adventist, Baptist, Assembly of God, Pentecostal, Church of God) were found to be the least tolerant (pp. 322–3). Beatty and Walter measured religiosity according to frequency of church attendance, and noted correlations between increased religiosity and increased intolerance. For every denomination examined, 'those who attend more frequently are also the more intolerant. In addition, attendance seems to have a greater impact . . . on the tolerance of the less tolerant groups' (p. 325).

[2] These researchers use different measures of religion and religiosity; see e.g. Sullivan *et al.* (1982: 137–9), McClosky and Brill (1983: 404–6), Nunn *et al.* (1978, ch. 8).

Questions naturally arise as to why members of some denominations are less tolerant than others, and about the connection between increased attendance at religious services and intolerance. Beatty and Walter hypothesize as follows: 'We suspect that religious theology, intolerant leadership cues, and a history of persecution for religious beliefs may interact to create distinctive denominational patterns of tolerance' (p. 328).

Wilcox and Jelen inquired into the widely reported finding that evangelical Christians are more intolerant than others. They used data from both the study by Nunn and his colleagues and General Social Surveys data from 1972 and subsequent years. Both bodies of data concern responses to standard questions about granting rights to unpopular groups. The mass sample data from the Nunn survey showed evangelical Christians to be 'significantly more intolerant than other Americans', at the 0.01 level in each case. Evangelicals were also more intolerant in Nunn's élite samples, though the differences were smaller (though still significant at the 0.01 level) (Wilcox and Jelen 1990: 30–1). Similarly, Wilcox and Jelen constructed a 'doctrinal orthodoxy index', based on questions concerning the existence of God, of the Devil, of miracles, and of Jesus Christ (p. 30). Groups with high orthodoxy scores were found to be more intolerant than others, towards all four object groups in the sample (communists, suspected communists, socialists, and atheists). Doctrinal orthodoxy was found to be 'a significant predictor of intolerance, even among members of the elite sample' (p. 31).

To some extent the greater intolerance of evangelicals can be accounted for by their lower levels of education. But this does not eliminate the strong effects of religious factors. Among the mass sample, doctrinal orthodoxy was found to have a significant effect on intolerance, even with education controlled (p. 33). These overall results were confirmed by Wilcox and Jelen's analysis of General Social Survey data. Of the denominational categories distinguished—no religious preference, Jews, Catholics, mainstream Protestants, pentecostals, evangelicals, fundamentalists—the last three were found to be the most intolerant, with pentecostals significantly less tolerant than evangelicals and fundamentalists, findings that also held with demographic factors and religiosity controlled (pp. 38–40).

I have noted that a portion of evangelicals' greater intolerance can be attributed to their lower levels of education. Similarly, since increased religiosity is associated with increased intolerance, a measure of evangelicals' intolerance was due to their greater religiosity. But because evangelicals continued to be more intolerant, even with these factors controlled, Wilcox and Jelen concluded that 'evangelical doctrine has an independent effect on political intolerance' (pp. 42–3). The exact nature of this effect is a subject I will explore throughout this chapter. Wilcox and Jelen offer two hypotheses. First, evangelicals' commitment to an inerrant Bible may make them doubt the value of free thought and expression. Alternatively, belief in a literal Devil may contribute to intolerance, since the Devil is thought to work in the world through human agency—perhaps through the unconventional groups about whose rights subjects are asked (p. 43).

The study by Green and his colleagues provides additional evidence on the relationship between fundamentalism and intolerance (Green *et al.* 1994). Green and his colleagues conducted a national mail survey of religious activists, in 1990–1, receiving 4,995 usable responses. Attitudes towards civil liberties were measured through a variant of Sullivan's two-step procedure. Respondents were asked to identify 'The political organization that you regard as most dangerous to the country right now'. Once a group had been named, subjects were asked standard questions about such things as allowing the group to make public speeches, run candidates for public office, demonstrate, and teach in public schools (p. 31).

On the whole, activists were reasonably tolerant: 65.5 per cent would allow the most dangerous group to make a public speech; 63.5 per cent would prohibit government from tapping their telephones. Other responses were similar, though only 20.9 per cent would allow a group member to teach in the public schools. On a tolerance scale, 49.8 per cent were classified as highly tolerant, as compared to 17.3 per cent highly intolerant (p. 32). Green and his colleagues note that, as a group, the religious activists compare favourably with other national samples (p. 32). Target group selection, however, shows that respondents identifying left-wing, feminist, and secularist groups as most dangerous were considerably less tolerant than those naming right-wing groups (pp. 33–4).

In general, respondents identified as fundamentalists were least tolerant ($r = -0.29$, $p < 0.05$), and fundamentalism made the strongest contribution to intolerance (with tolerance as dependent variable, Beta = -0.29, $p < 0.05$). Other religious variables (e.g. orthodoxy, piety, religious involvement) made smaller contributions to intolerance, although charismatic religion made a substantial contribution (Beta = -0.10, $p < 0.05$). Christian militancy, a scale made up of religious–political attitudes (see p. 38), made a stronger contribution (Beta = -0.24, $p < 0.05$) (p. 37). Among other contributing factors worth noting, education had a significant effect (Beta = 0.25, $p < 0.05$), while education and fundamentalism were 'strongly and negatively related to one another' (p. 41). Green and his colleagues conclude:

Fundamentalists are indeed less supportive of civil liberties than other religious activists, though not perhaps as severely intolerant as some observers suppose. Their special worldview reduces support for civil liberties directly, but it also helps generate a higher level of perceived threat, an aggressive distrust of the political process, and intense concern about moral decay, all of which reduce tolerance. (p. 43)

Connections between particular aspects of religion and anti-democratic views are important for this analysis and will be explored in detail. Thus it bears mention that, in their study, McClosky and Brill call attention to similar aspects of religious doctrine. The overall findings of their analysis are in accord with what we have seen. Jews and subjects who claimed no religion were found to be relatively tolerant. Baptists, a category that included many fundamentalists, scored lowest on McClosky and Brill's civil liberties scale (McClosky and Brill 1983: 404). Similarly, 'religiosity' was measured through a number of different scales. But its effects were clear: 'as religiosity increases, support for civil liberties declines' (p. 406). To account for these findings, McClosky and Brill too appeal to a central feature of religious doctrine:

Because religious 'true believers' have embraced a body of received doctrines or dogmas, they have difficulty processing . . . 'inconvenient facts.' Entertaining facts that do not fit with their theological convictions might shatter their religious belief structure or might require them, at a minimum, to reconcile a number of diverse and incompatible ideas, some of which they could not bear to renounce, even in the face of contradictory evidence. (p. 411)

Because they view important truths as received or revealed, the highly religious are not attuned to the beneficial effects of the free flow of ideas, which could well lead people away from truth into error (pp. 413–14).

In the tolerance literature, then, religion is consistently associated with intolerance. The six different studies discussed in this section agree on several major points. Greater religiosity is associated with increased intolerance, while evangelical and fundamentalist denominations are generally identified as especially intolerant. In order to explain these findings, researchers posit connections between evangelical and fundamentalist doctrines and closed-mindedness. Belief in biblical truth fosters intellectual rigidity, which is readily associated with other forms of intolerance. This set of connections will be pursued in greater detail.

2. RELIGION AND PREJUDICE

Much of the literature I will examine in the following sections centres on *prejudice* towards various out-groups rather than *intolerance*. Though closely related, the two notions are distinguishable. Briefly, 'prejudice' is generally defined as a negative attitude towards groups of people that is not grounded in adequate reasons. Gordon Allport's brief definition is 'thinking ill of others without sufficient warrant'. As Allport notes, two ingredients are included here: a negative feeling or attitude, and a failure of rationality (Allport 1954: 6–7; italics omitted). But more than this is involved.[3] In general, the negative feeling is focused on individuals because of characteristics they share, or are believed to share, with other members of their group—the group with which they are associated by the bearer of prejudice. A common mechanism is stereotyping, attributing (generally derogatory) characteristics to some group as a whole. According to Allport, a fuller definition of prejudice is 'an aversive or hostile attitude toward a person who belongs to a group, simply because he belongs to that group, and is therefore presumed to have the objectionable qualities ascribed to the group' (p. 7). Throughout this discussion, I will be concerned primarily with cognitive aspects of prejudice, as opposed to affective aspects, though, in practice, these cannot always be separated. I will explore the kinds of beliefs that contribute to prejudice and the distinctive way people hold them.

Prejudice is clearly different from intolerance in central respects. As noted in the last chapter, tolerance implies a willingness to 'put up with' things one rejects or opposes (Sullivan *et al.* 1982: 2; see above, p. 43). Thus, in regard to matters of religion, one can be both prejudiced and tolerant. One can have negative attitudes towards members of some religious group but still not support measures to suppress their rights to practice their religion (Smidt and Penning 1982: 232–3). Because it moves beyond attitudes people hold to encompass concerns such as rights to free speech and free association, tolerance and intolerance have direct political implications and have, as we have seen, received considerable attention from political scientists. Prejudice has been less studied by political scientists. However, social psychologists have examined it in detail, while the relationship between prejudice and religion has received enormous attention. The resulting literature is far too vast to be reviewed here. But I will explore important studies and central findings. My general rule of thumb is that, because of the close relationship between prejudice and intolerance, results in regard to the former attitude can be presumed to hold in regard to the latter as well. If Smith is prejudiced against group X, we can assume that she will probably be willing to abrogate the rights of its members. It is important to bear in mind that this is only a presumption, and not a strong one at that. In spite of the close relationship between prejudice and intolerance and the fact that many authors construe 'prejudice'

---

[3] Allport notes the possibility of favourable prejudice (Allport 1954: 6), a subject I will not discuss.

widely, I will generally keep the two notions distinct. But in certain contexts I will combine them (perhaps along with other attitudes as well)
under the general category of 'anti-democratic sentiments'.

The connection between religion and prejudice is immediately paradoxical. Most religions, including Christianity, preach goodwill and understanding, that people should love their neighbours and refrain from
judging them. But religion has been linked to anti-Semitism and other
forms of prejudice and to authoritarianism, as well as intolerance for civil
liberties. Most of the studies I will examine were conducted in the United
States, focusing on Christianity, and using white adults, frequently college
students, as subjects. And so the extent to which their findings can be gen-
eralized is open to question.[4] But even with these limitations, this body of
research suggests strong conclusions about American democracy, which
have important implications for democratic theory.

Connections between religion and anti-democratic sentiments first
became a subject of intense interest to social scientists after the Second
World War, when the nature of Nazi atrocities became fully known. In *The
Authoritarian Personality* Theodor Adorno and his associates established
links between religion and the so-called 'authoritarian personality'.
Adorno and his associates found that both authoritarianism and ethnocentrism were higher among church attenders than among non-attenders.
They defined ethnocentrism as thinking based on a 'pervasive and rigid'
distinction between in-groups and out-groups, with submissive attitudes
and positive attitudes towards the former and negative stereotypes and
hostility towards the latter (Adorno *et al.* 1950: 145–50). Along similar
lines, Else Frenkel-Brunswick and R. Nevitt Sanford explored 'personality factors' in anti-Semitism, from a psychoanalytic perspective, noting the
role of a certain kind of religion, among other factors (Frenkel-Brunswick
and Sanford 1945; see pp. 279–80). Allport and other researchers studied
the connections between religion and prejudice more generally. They
found that Catholic and Protestant students were more likely than those
with no religious affiliation to be prejudiced against blacks (Allport 1954:
27). Charles Glock and Rodney Stark argued for a direct connection
between Christian orthodoxy and anti-Semitism, rooted in Christianity's
claim to exclusive possession of religious truth (Glock and Stark 1966).
An enormous literature has arisen on these and related topics. Studies of
the relationship between religion and different anti-social attitudes is

---

[4] Notable studies in other countries are Perkins (1983, 1985) in England; Eisinga *et
al.* (1990, 1995) in the Netherlands; and Ponton and Gorsuch (1988) in Venezuela.
Griffin *et al.* (1987) argue against being able to generalize about religion and prejudice
across countries. They hold that the specific ways in which phenomena work themselves out depend on particular features of the culture of the country involved.

probably the most extensively studied topic in the psychology of religion (Batson and Ventnis 1982: 255). In an important review of the literature published in 1974 Richard Gorsuch and Daniel Aleshire discuss over a hundred studies,[5] while considerable additional research has been conducted in subsequent years.

Many details of these studies, both substantive and methodological, are still in dispute, while complete consensus is unlikely ever to arise. For instance, there is disagreement on the most basic subject: what we mean by religion. C. Daniel Batson and W. Larry Ventnis note a catalogue of forty-eight different definitions of religion that have appeared in the literature (Batson and Ventnis 1982: 5). The nature of a person's religion can be assessed according to at least eight different measures: denomination one belongs to; degree of doctrinal orthodoxy; religious practice (e.g. prayer, table grace, etc.); religious knowledge; degree of association with co-religionists; active involvement in religious organizations; attendance at religious services; or some combination of these measures (Wuthnow 1973: 119–20). Scholars disagree as to which is the proper measure, while results of many studies will vary according to which is employed. Something similar could be said in regard to prejudice. Is this directed at particular racial or religious minorities, or against minorities in general? Thorny methodological issues are encountered. Different aspects of religion are investigated through the use of sets of questions, or scales. For virtually any concept, scholars argue about the most appropriate scale, about what a given scale actually measures, and about numerous technical issues. On a more general level, one can question the validity of using questionnaires. As we will see, it is not clear that responses to questionnaires adequately reflect subjects' prejudice. In addition, the findings yielded by questionnaires are generally correlational rather than causal. More than 90 per cent of recent studies in psychology of religion have been correlational (Batson and Ventnis 1982: 316). However, although it is not easy to infer causation from correlations, the consistency of the correlations through numerous studies clearly indicates the importance of the factors under discussion.[6] Issues such as these, and others like them, have important consequences for our understanding of the psychology of religion, and for religion itself. But without wishing to minimize the significance of such problems, for obvious reasons I will attempt to avoid them as much as possible. In regard to this subject, as with discussion of tolerance in the previous chapter, this is possible, because important findings have been clearly

[5] For Batson and Ventnis's table, listing forty-four different findings, see (1982: 258–63).

[6] For brief discussion of the advantages and disadvantages of correlational studies, see Batson and Ventnis (1982: 316–18).

established. Issues that remain deeply controversial will be so identified as we come to them.

Although many issues remain controversial, a large number of scholars with different interests and different religious orientations agree on central points. For instance, of forty-four findings from previous studies that Batson and Ventnis discuss, thirty-four show a positive relationship between amount of prejudice and degree of interest in, or adherence to, religion. Eight findings do not present clear relationships, while only two show a negative relationship—both of which tested adolescents or children. Batson and Ventnis conclude: 'Comparing the different columns and rows in [their table], one can see that the pattern of results is highly consistent, regardless of how prejudice or religion is measured' (1982: 257). Along similar lines, in a well-known textbook on psychology of religion, David Wulff writes as follows:

Using a variety of measures of piety—religious affiliation, church attendance, doctrinal orthodoxy, rated importance of religion and so on—researchers have consistently found positive correlations with ETHNOCENTRISM, AUTHORITARIAN-ISM, dogmatism, social distance, rigidity, intolerance of ambiguity, and specific forms of prejudice, especially against Jews and blacks. (Wulff 1991: 220–1)

It is important to note, however, that relationships between prejudice and religion are not straightforward. Many scholars argue that they are not directly correlational but curvilinear. Very simply, with increases in religion, people tend to be more prejudiced, but beyond a certain point, this association is reversed. People who are identified as more religious appear to become less prejudiced. This finding is reported by Gorsuch and Aleshire, in their review of the literature (up to 1974). They note that in studies that use church membership as the only measure of religious commitment, the relationship is clear and consistent: church members are more prejudiced than non-members (p. 283). However, they believe it is overly simple to group together all people who profess church membership. When additional measures are employed, a more complex pattern emerges. Analysis of twenty-five studies that focus on religious activity (based on church attendance) reveals the curvilinearity of the relationship. Twenty studies indicate that marginal church members are more prejudiced than both the non-active and the most active. But prejudice among the most active is seen to decline; unusually active church members are unusually tolerant, while there is little difference between the prejudice levels of the highly religious and the non-religious (p. 285).[7]

---

[7] See Wulff (1991: 221–4), Allport and Ross (1967: 433–4), Bock and Warren (1972). The claim that the relationship between religion and prejudice is curvilinear is contested by influential scholars; see e.g. Altemeyer and Hunsberger (1992) and Hunsberger (1995: 116); see also below.

If the relationship between religion and prejudice is curvilinear, then something other than religion *per se* is at work. As Allport says: 'The role of religion is paradoxical. It makes prejudice and it unmakes prejudice. . . . Some people say the only cure for prejudice is more religion; some say the only cure is to abolish religion' (Allport 1954: 444), Accordingly, researchers have sought to identify specific factors in religion responsible for anti-democratic attitudes. In *The Authoritarian Personality* Adorno and his associates discuss a form of 'neutralized' religion, which is shorn of true belief and subscribed to for other than religious reasons, as a means to other ends rather than an end in itself. This form of religion functions as 'an agency of social conformity'; it promotes rigidity, submissiveness, and intolerance (Adorno *et al.* 1950: 729–33). Along similar lines, Russell Allen and Bernard Spilka distinguish different ways in which 'the individual himself formulates or structures his religious beliefs' (Allen and Spilka 1967: 194). They distinguish 'consensual' and 'committed' styles of religion, and associate prejudice with the former but not the latter.

The most influential analysis of religious sources of prejudice was presented by Allport, who also distinguished different ways of being religious. Allport's distinction between 'intrinsic' and 'extrinsic' orientations to religion has been described as 'perhaps the most frequently-used measure of religiousness aside from church attendance' (Donahue 1985*a*: 422). In a classic 1967 paper, co-authored with Michael Ross, Allport states: 'the extrinsically motivated person *uses* his religion, whereas the intrinsically motivated *lives* his religion' (Allport and Ross 1967: 434). Briefly, people with extrinsic orientations find religion valuable in a range of different ways, 'to provide security and solace, sociability and distractions, status and self-justification'. The accepted creed is shaped to meet these other ends: 'In theological terms the extrinsic type turns to God but without turning away from self' (p. 434). To give a mundane example, an extrinsic person might belong to a church because of social, or even business, benefits of membership, rather than because the religion in question is deeply meaningful to him. In contrast, people with intrinsic orientations 'find their master motive in religion'. For them, religion is an end, not a means; having embraced a creed, they try to live according to its ideals (p. 434).[8] Although the two orientations are clearly distinguishable, it is important to note that they are not opposite poles of a unidimensional continuum. They have been found to measure different aspects of being religious, both of which often exist together in the same subject (Hood 1971).

---

[8] For the scales used to identify intrinsic and extrinsic orientations, see Feagin (1964) and Wulff (1991: 230, 145).

Numerous studies have shown that people who are intrinsically oriented are significantly less prejudiced than those extrinsically oriented.[9] The results of Allport and Ross's study of 303 churchgoers of different orientations support this claim. Allport and Ross argue that a person of extrinsic orientation uses his religion to further other ends: security, status, etc. Prejudice fits neatly with such a person's character, because it too can serve other ends. Prejudice 'is a "useful" formulation; it too provides security, comfort, status, and social support' (1967: 441). In other words, these two psychological tendencies could well suit similar personalities and be mutually reinforcing. In internalizing his religion, in contrast, someone with intrinsic orientation also internalizes its values of compassion and love for one's neighbours (p. 441). If a significant proportion of subjects classified as more religious are intrinsic in orientation, this could help explain the curvilinear relationship between religion and prejudice. Indeed, Allport argues that in order to lessen the amount of prejudice in society, 'we need to enlarge the population of intrinsically religious people' (1966: 457).

However, strong evidence against the causal role of the intrinsic–extrinsic distinction has been brought forth. An important line of criticism has been developed by Batson and different associates, who argue that intrinsic and extrinsic categories alone do not capture central aspects of the religious experience. Batson and Ventnis propose a 'functional' definition of religion, one that 'allows for the uniqueness, complexity, and diversity of the religious experience': 'We shall define religion as whatever we as individuals do to come to grips personally with the questions that confront us because we are aware that we and others like us are alive and that we will die' (Batson and Ventnis 1982: 7; italics omitted). Batson and Ventnis refer to such questions as 'existential' questions. In order to examine this aspect of the religious experience, they postulate an additional orientation to religion, 'an open-ended, questioning orientation', to which they refer as *'religion as a quest'* (p. 150).[10] Questions intended to measure

---

[9] Allport and Ross's results were complicated by their identification of a further orientation, the 'indiscriminately proreligious', who are the most prejudiced of all. This group has received relatively little attention from subsequent researchers, and I will not discuss it here. It is worth noting that Hoge and Carroll argue that it is a mask for dogmatism (1973: 195); for references for studies of this orientation, see Donahue (1985*a*: 420–1) and Wulff (1991: 232–3). For discussion of the indiscriminately antireligious orientation, see Thompson (1974).

[10] Consideration of the quest orientation forces reformulation of other categories. Batson and Ventnis propose a three-part classification: religion as 'means', as 'end', and as quest (see 1982, ch. 5). However, though there are significant differences between the first two of these and extrinsic and intrinsic orientations, there is sufficient overlap to allow us to retain the latter terms, which have become entrenched in the literature.

the quest orientation include the following (Batson and Ventnis 1982: 153; the 'interactional' scale):

1. It might be said that I value my religious doubts and uncertainties.
2. I do not expect my religious convictions to change in the next few years. (reversed in scoring)
5. God wasn't very important to me until I began to ask questions about the meaning of my own life.
6. Questions are far more central to my religious experience than are answers.

Batson and his colleagues contend that this scale captures something important in religion that other measures miss. Batson and Lynn Raynor-Prince (1983) argue that, in keeping with the critical, open-ended attitude central to the quest orientation, it also correlates with higher levels of cognitive complexity in the religious domain than other orientations.[11]

Not unexpectedly, Batson's analysis of the quest factor has received criticism. For instance, his reliance on undergraduate students as his primary research subjects has been questioned, since it is well known that the college years frequently involve significant religious questioning (Donahue 1985*b*, 414). In addition, the quest scale has consistently failed to correlate with other measures of religiousness. It has been proposed that, rather than addressing an aspect of religion, quest actually identifies agnosticism (see Donahue 1985*b*: 413; but cf. Batson 1976: 32; for further criticisms, see Wulff 1991: 237–42). However, whether or not the quest orientation is described as a 'religious' outlook or something else, it has been found to bear a strong negative relationship to prejudice.

In an important study Batson and colleagues questioned the conventional wisdom concerning the relationship between intrinsic orientation and prejudice, contending as well that the quest orientation bears a stronger negative relationship to racial prejudice. Batson and his colleagues argued that other studies are infected with a form of measurement error. Responses to questionnaires by intrinsic subjects can indicate desires not to *appear* prejudiced, rather than actual lower levels of prejudice (Batson *et al.* 1986: 176). In order to test this hypothesis, Batson and his colleagues devised a means to distinguish between 'overt' and 'covert' prejudice. Briefly, their subjects, forty-four white introductory psychology students at the University of Kansas, were given the opportunity to watch a movie in different theatres, which would entail sitting next to either a black or a white student, both of whom were clearly visible. The hypotheses were confirmed. Under conditions in which the desire not to appear prejudiced was presumed no longer to be in effect, intrinsic orientation 'seemed to lose its power as a predictor for or against racial prejudice'. But

---

[11] See also Sapp and Jones (1986); compare Hunsberger *et al.* (1994).

the quest factor continued to operate; scores on quest scales were the only reliable predictors of lack of prejudice (pp. 179–80). In their conclusion Batson and his colleagues note 'growing evidence . . . that a quest orientation to religion is related to a true reduction in prejudice' (p. 181)[12]

Researchers other than Batson have presented similar findings. In a study of different religious orientations and prejudice Sam McFarland analysed discriminatory attitudes towards blacks, women, homosexuals, and communists. The quest orientation was included, along with fundamentalism, as well as intrinsic and extrinsic orientations. McFarland reasoned that the different discriminatory attitudes should correlate highly as a general tendency to discriminate. Because prejudice is associated with dogmatic certainty (on which, more below), subjects high in quest orientation should be low in discriminatory attitudes, and subjects high in fundamentalism should be high in discrimination (McFarland 1989: 327).

Subjects were 247 undergraduates at Western Kentucky University. As predicted, quest correlated negatively and fundamentalism positively with all discriminatory attitudes. The pattern was more complex for intrinsic and extrinsic orientations. The former correlated, though weakly, with discrimination against communists and homosexuals, but not against blacks or women (p. 330). Extrinsic orientation correlated with discrimination against blacks, with strong differences between the attitudes of males and females, with males more discriminatory than females. Taking all factors into account, McFarland describes the result as a 'complex mapping' of relations between religions orientation and discrimination (p. 333). But central findings are clear. Fundamentalism correlated positively with discrimination against each target group and with the general tendency to discriminate. McFarland suggests that fundamentalism 'cloaks a general closed-minded, ethnocentric mindset', which is manifested in a general tendency to discriminate. Quest seemed to be associated with a general anti-discriminatory attitude, although without favourable attitudes to any of the groups in question (p. 333).[13]

On the basis of the studies of Batson and McFarland, along with the intolerance studies discussed in Section 1, we can postulate an alternative account of prejudice. The main point is that prejudice and other anti-democratic sentiments are not associated with religion *per se*, but with certain aspects of religion that are bound up with intellectual rigidity, closed-mindedness, and social conformity. In contrast, the quest orientation, which is by definition an attitude of openness, generally stands

---

[12] See also Batson *et al.* (1978) and Herek (1987); for discussion, see below, n. 15.

[13] In a study of 275 university students in Venezuela, Ponton and Gorsuch (1988) found that extrinsic orientation correlated positively with prejudice, intrinsic orientation negatively, and quest did not correlate in either direction.

opposed to these sources of rigidity and so correlates negatively with prejudice. This line of argument does not rule out the existence of factors other than sources of rigidity in religion's contribution to anti-democratic attitudes. But regardless of the extent to which other factors contribute and the manner in which they are related to moral and intellectual rigidity, the latter characteristics can be seen to contribute significantly to anti-democratic attitudes.

This line of argument receives confirmation from Robert Altemeyer's studies of 'right-wing authoritarianism' (RWA). RWA is basically a more sophisticated and carefully documented version of the 'authoritarian personality' originally postulated by Adorno and his associates. Altemeyer has established that RWA can be defined as a combination of three attitudes—authoritarian submission, authoritarian aggression, and conventionalism—and that this confluence of attitudes can be identified by the RWA scale he has developed.[14] He has established strong connections between RWA and religion. People scoring high in RWA (the upper 25 per cent of respondents) report that their religious training taught them to submit to authority more, imposed stricter rules of proper conduct, and taught them to be more hostile to 'outsiders' than people with lower RWA scores. High RWAs are unusually accepting of illegal and unjust acts committed by their government. They are much more likely than low RWAs to believe that democracy gives people too much freedom, and that the Bill of Rights should be repealed. While most people express unwillingness 'to locate and arrest homosexuals, or communists, or members of "religious cults" and have them tortured and even executed', people with high RWA scores are more equivocal (Altemeyer and Hunsberger 1992: 115; for Altemeyer's 'posse' scale, see below, p. 103). Thus Altemeyer has gone beyond examining prejudice towards outsider groups to ask his subjects about other forms of 'authoritarian aggression'.

In the particular series of studies I will examine here, Altemeyer and Bruce Hunsberger surveyed Manitoba University students and their parents in 1990 and 1991. More than 700 students and 700 parents in all were involved. Altemeyer and Hunsberger examined relationships between the quest orientation, religious fundamentalism, and RWA, to one another and to a range of anti-social attitudes. They hypothesized that religious fundamentalism would correlate more closely with authoritarianism than the quest orientation, and more closely than would widespread measures of doctrinal beliefs, such as the Christian orthodoxy scale (see below, p. 108). They describe religious fundamentalism as a specific attitude towards religion:

[14] Altemeyer (1981); see below; for the 1990 version of the RWA scale, see Altemeyer and Hunsberger (1992, app. A, pp. 129–30).

By 'fundamentalism' we mean the belief that there is one set of religious teachings that clearly contains the basic, intrinsic, essential, inerrant truth about humanity and deity; that this essential truth is fundamentally opposed by forces of evil which must be vigorously fought; that this truth must be followed today according to the fundamental, unchangeable practices of the past; and that those who believe and follow these fundamental teachings have a special relationship with the deity. (Altemeyer and Hunsberger 1992: 118)

A great advantage of this formulation is that it is not tied to specifically Christian aspects of fundamentalism. (For sample items of the twenty opinion statements that comprise Altemeyer and Hunsberger's religious fundamentalism scale, see below, p. 100).

The results of Altemeyer and Hunsberger's studies are striking. They observed strong correlations between religious fundamentalism and RWA (0.68) and a similarly strong negative correlation between the quest orientation and RWA (–0.67). The correlation between quest and fundamentalism was –0.79. (All correlations were significant at the 0.01 level.) There were also uniformly positive correlations between fundamentalism and various forms of prejudice and aggression, and negative relationships between the quest orientation and prejudice (Altemeyer and Hunsberger 1992: 122–3).

The relationships between RWA, fundamentalism, quest scales, various measure of prejudice, and different religious denominations established by Altemeyer and Hunsberger were in several respects consistent with earlier studies. Jews and people with no affiliation generally scored lowest on measures of authoritarianism and fundamentalism, and highest on quest, while the reverse was generally true of Mennonites and 'fundamentalists' (mainly Baptists, but also evangelicals, pentecostals, and some other groups) (1992: 124–5).

Although this study was preliminary in various ways and requires further research, Altemeyer and Hunsberger's findings strongly support the hypothesized connections I have noted. Their analysis indicates that RWA and fundamentalism share a kind of cognitive rigidity that leads directly to prejudice. Because of its relative lack of rigidity, the quest orientation avoids prejudice. Altemeyer and Hunsberger report that different religious observances correlated positively with RWA and fundamentalism, but negatively with quest orientation (church attendance: 0.43, 0.65, –0.56, respectively; frequency of reading scripture outside church: 0.28, 0.51, –0.36, respectively) (p. 123). These results once again call into question whether the quest orientation should be described as 'religious'. But they also confirm that between quest and fundamentalism quite different cognitive orientations are at work. Powerful support for this claim is Altemeyer and Hunsberger's finding that not a single one of the 491 parents in their February 1991 study was rated in the top quartile in both fundamentalism and quest, or in the bottom quartile of both (p. 126).

As the open, questioning attitude of the quest orientation does not easily foster prejudice, so the closed mindset of fundamentalism lends itself to prejudice and authoritarianism. In previous studies Altemeyer found that authoritarians 'reduce guilt over their misdeeds almost completely through religion' (Altemeyer and Hunsberger 1992: 127; Altemeyer 1988: 189–90). The structure of fundamentalism is well suited for this purpose. Adherents of fundamentalism believe: 'Doubt itself is wrong; faith must conquer all.' 'Clever arguments' against their beliefs only make their beliefs even stronger. 'Becoming too open-minded about religion easily can lead to "missing the truth" ' (1992: 127). According to Altemeyer, people trained to think in this way 'would tend to accept, uncritically, the stereotypes about minorities that abound in our culture and would be relatively willing to do whatever the authorities said had to be done to such a minority' (p. 127).[15]

3. INTELLECTUAL RIGIDITY AND ANTI-DEMOCRATIC ATTITUDES

The studies discussed in the previous section indicate that, rather than a direct association between religion and anti-democratic attitudes, certain factors associated with religion are actually at work. The nature of the intellectual rigidity to which these factors contribute remains to be explored, while we must hold open the possibility that other—and perhaps quite different—sources of anti-democratic attitudes function in the cases

---

[15] The evidence suggests that the negative association between intrinsic orientation and prejudice is misleading. Rather than being without prejudice, intrinsics desire to *appear* to be so. In studies by Batson and his colleagues the negative associations that were observed with overt measures disappeared when covert measures were used. In contrast, negative associations between the quest orientation and prejudice were observed with both overt and covert measures. See Batson *et al.* (1978, 1986). Along similar lines, Gregory Herek argues that intrinsics' reported lack of prejudice is due to conformity with the dictates of their religious groups. Their observed lack of prejudice against blacks can be attributed to the fact that most religions strongly condemn racial prejudice. But in regard to lesbians and gay men, prejudice against whom is not condemned by many religious denominations, intrinsics were found to be prejudiced (see Herek 1987). On intrinsic orientation and social desirability, see Watson *et al.* (1986) and Leak and Fish (1989). I should note that theorists argue that prejudice against homosexual men and women is not necessarily prejudice, since the conduct in question is arguably morally wrong. See Gorsuch (1993) and the response by Altemeyer and Hunsberger (1993).

we have seen. The evidence bearing on questions that interest us is not always precise, and many findings are not firmly established, although the overall thrust of the evidence is clear.

One problem I must address before proceeding is that certain findings in the tolerance literature are not consistent with those so far examined in psychology of religion. Stouffer's initial finding that people who attended religious services regularly were less tolerant than those who did not (1955: 155–6) has not been contravened. But such a conclusion depends on grouping together very different kinds of church member. Had Stouffer distinguished different levels of attendance, presumably, he would have discovered corresponding differences in tolerance levels, that the relationship between intolerance and religion is curvilinear. However, Beatty and Walter found a direct correspondence between levels of attendance at religious services and intolerance: 'those who attend more frequently are also the more intolerant' (Beatty and Walter 1984: 325). McClosky and Brill report a similar finding: 'as religiosity increases, support for civil liberties declines' (McClosky and Brill 1983: 406; also Altemeyer and Hunsberger 1993: 34; see above, Section 1). These findings conflict with the large body of research indicating a curvilinear relationship between religion and prejudice, and it is not clear how this inconsistency can be resolved. It is possible that more sophisticated versions of the intolerance studies, especially ones employing finer distinctions between different kinds of religiosity, would have provided different results. It is also possible that differences between prejudice and intolerance are at work here, that religiosity's relationship with the former but not the latter is curvilinear. But again, the conflicts remain puzzling. In spite of this difficulty, we should note that other findings in the intolerance studies are consistent with the bulk of research. For instance, Stouffer, Beatty and Walter, Nunn and his colleagues, and McClosky and Brill all found that non-religious people and Jews tend to be less prejudiced than people of other religious affiliations. Findings along these lines have been confirmed consistently for many years (see above, Section 1). In addition, Beatty and Walter's ranking of the different intolerance levels of different religions and denominations, with fundamentalism as least tolerant, is consistent with the findings of Wilcox and Jelen, and Green and his colleagues, and is supported by numerous subsequent researchers, including McClosky and Brill (1983: 404–5; see above, Section 1).

The direction of these findings is clear: members of denominations that can be characterized as 'fundamentalist' are more intolerant and more prejudiced than others. Although all anti-democratic attitudes that stem from religion might not result from fundamentalism, it is clearly an important factor. In seeking out the elements in fundamentalism responsible for anti-democratic sentiments, we should note consistent negative correlations between the quest orientation and prejudice, which strongly suggest that intellectual openness is inimical to prejudice, while the rigid mindset apparent in religious fundamentalism is an important source.

The nature of the evidence makes it difficult to identify the relevant cognitive orientation with precision. But indications are that many fundamentalists hold views along the lines of the 'dogmatic' mindset classically described by Milton Rokeach. Rokeach argues that 'dogmatic' thinking refers to 'a total configuration of ideas and beliefs organized into a relatively closed system'. In contrast to 'rigid' thinking, which can refer to the resistance to change of single beliefs, dogmatism is characterized by a systemic relationship between the relevant ideas. To the extent that a person is dogmatic or 'closed in his thinking', when he is questioned 'the preservation of his total belief system will be at stake rather than the preservation of a particular belief in his system' (Rokeach 1960: 183).[16]

The way a person's beliefs are held is obviously affected by the nature of the beliefs themselves. Certain beliefs lend themselves more easily to dogmatic thinking than others. This is true of beliefs rooted in authority, which are held on the basis of authoritative status attributed to certain central or core beliefs, from which other beliefs are derived. As Lee Kirkpatrick, Ralph Hood, and Gary Hartz argue, fundamentalist religion is prototypical of centralized belief systems, with the ultimate authoritative status assigned to scripture, which is accepted as the word of God, completely and literally true (Kirkpatrick *et al.* 1991: 170–2). Kirkpatrick and his colleagues argue that the authoritative status of scripture is what defines fundamentalism.[17]

Discussion of fundamentalism is complicated by different interpretations of exactly what this is and how it can be identified. As we have seen, some scholars view fundamentalism as a kind of psychological outlook. For others it is a set of beliefs or doctrines that have particular characteristics. Other researchers examine people identified as fundamentalists, either historically or as members of particular religious denominations. Because 'fundamentalism' extends beyond particular Christian denominations, it is necessary to study it through measurement scales that are not tied to Christian beliefs. Kirkpatrick, Hood, and Hartz argue that scales frequently used to assess fundamentalism actually measure Christian orthodoxy. In contrast, they view fundamentalism as a way of holding beliefs, a dogmatic cognitive style (Kirkpatrick *et al.* 1991; Rokeach 1960).

[16] On more recent research findings on dogmatic thinking and how it relates to 'right-wing authoritarianism', see Altemeyer (1996, ch. 8).

[17] For different ways in which the Bible can be interpreted 'literally', see Hogge and Friedman (1967) and Jelen (1989).

To get an idea of the kinds of belief held by religious fundamentalists, we can look at representative items from the twenty-item religious fundamentalism scale developed by Altemeyer and Hunsberger (Altemeyer and Hunsberger 1992, app. B, pp. 130–1). Altemeyer and Hunsberger distinguish this scale from an index of Christian orthodoxy. It is intended to measure religious fundamentalism in a broader sense.[18]

1. God has given mankind a complete, unfailing guide to happiness and salvation, which must be totally followed.
3. Of all the people on this earth, one group has a special relationship with God because it believes the most in his revealed truths and tries the hardest to follow his laws. . . .
7. Different religions and philosophies have different versions of the truth, and may be equally right in their own way. (scored negatively)
8. The basic cause of evil in this world is Satan, who is constantly and ferociously fighting against God.
9. It is more important to be a good person than to believe in God and the right religion. (scored negatively) . . .
14. God's true followers must remember that he requires them to *constantly* fight Satan and Satan's allies on this earth. . . .
18. Whenever science and sacred scripture conflict, science must be wrong. . . .
20. To lead the best, most meaningful life, one must belong to the one, true religion.

This set of beliefs constitutes a tightly interlocked system. Altemeyer and Hunsberger record its high psychometric properties (1992: 118–19).[19]

Christian fundamentalists subscribe to beliefs such as these. In their eyes, God's unfailing guide is scripture, which contains not only the truth but complete truth. Whenever science clashes with this, the former must be set aside. The stakes for adhering to the true faith could not be higher. The Devil exists and tempts us; God's true followers must combat Satan and his allies. Belief in the right religion, rather than how one behaves towards others, determines salvation. Survey evidence for the prevalence of beliefs along these lines in different denominations will be presented in the following section.

In the last chapter I noted connections between intolerance judgements and sense of threat. Thus it is important to note that fundamentalists' emphasis on the Devil and the need to combat his works can give rise to a

[18] Compare the items that constitute the 'Christian orthodoxy' scale (Hunsberger 1989; Fullerton and Hunsberger 1982). See Altemeyer (1996: 164–5) on preliminary research applying this measure of fundamentalism to non-Christian fundamentalists: Muslim, Jewish, Hindu.

[19] Compare the Christian orthodoxy scale developed by Stark and Glock (1968, ch. 2); for beliefs of denominations generally regarded as fundamentalist, see below, Section 4.

heightened sense of threat. Belief in biblical authority also works in this direction. The Bible is of course apocalyptic, especially in the book of Daniel in the Old Testament, and Revelation in the New. At the core of Christian fundamentalists' faith, along with biblical inerrancy and conviction that they are saved, is belief in the coming millennium. Scholars disagree about the importance of core beliefs of Christian fundamentalism, but acceptance of the millennium is central to all variants of Christian fundamentalism.[20] Acceptance of fundamentalist doctrines and belief in a dangerous world are mutually reinforcing. Fear sends people to their Bibles for comfort, but, again, central to biblical prophecy is the imminent end of days. One common result is a strong tendency to look for signs of social, political, and cultural decay, which portend the coming end.

A helpful analysis of the fundamentalist mindset is offered by Kenneth Wald, Dennis Owen, and Samuel Hill (1989). Although personality characteristics of fundamentalists have been analysed in terms of pathology—most notably in association with the 'authoritarian personality' (see Kirkpatrick *et al.* 1991)—Wald and his associates move away from discussion of personality types to 'authority-mindedness', which they view as a normative stance: 'To put it simply, authority-mindedness is an ideological commitment that values authoritativeness and obedience as a matter of principle rather than the outgrowth of a personality disorder' (Wald *et al.* 1989: 95). This position is seen in acceptance of biblical inerrancy and church practice. It is also apparent in aspects of life not directly associated with religion, such as child-rearing practices, in which discipline and

---

[20] According to Ernest Sandeen, a central impetus of the fundamentalist movement was a particular form of millenarianism, 'dispensational pre-millenarianism'. Premillenarianism is the idea that Jesus's return—the second coming—will precede his thousand-year reign on earth, while for many fundamentalists, the appointed day could be any time. Dispensationalism refers to a view of history as unfolding in stages, in accordance with which God's truth is revealed—or dispensed—and through awareness of which the Bible must be read (Sandeen 1970: 68). 'Post-millennialists', who see Christ coming at the end of the current historical era, after the Holy Spirit and the gospel have spread throughout the world, tend to be 'optimistic about the spiritual progress of the culture' (Marsden 1980: 49). Pre-millenarians are less optimistic, viewing the advent of Christ as 'totally supernatural in origin and discontinuous with the history of this era' (Marsden 1980: 51). The view that the state of the world will worsen over time goes hand in hand with the search for signs of the coming end in contemporary events (see Strozier 1994). Although Sandeen's claims are probably overly narrow, there is little doubt that millenarianism in different forms has been a major factor in Christian fundamentalism since its inception (see Marsden 1971, 1980: 5; Sandeen 1971; Moore 1968). It is difficult to assess the relationship between fundamentalism—as measured on different scales—and views about the world's dangers with quantitative precision. But it bears mention that Altemeyer has established an association between RWA scores and scores on a six-item 'dangerous world' measure (1988, ch. 5; see pp. 168–9).

obedience receive greater attention than creativity and self-expression
(Wald *et al.* 1989). Nancy Ammerman describes authoritative relationships as central to the preaching situation, with the 'unquestioned and
respected leadership' provided by a 'biblically legitimized expert'
(Ammerman, quoted by Wald *et al.* 1989: 96). According to Wald and his
associates: 'The result is an epistemology that consists almost entirely of
arguments from authority' (p. 96), The epistemological stance of fundamentalists, based on constant invocations of authority, is described by
Wald and his colleagues as 'the single most distinctive quality of fundamentalist Protestantism' (p. 96).

Connections between fundamentalism and authority-mindedness
receive indirect confirmation from the close relationship between fundamentalism and right-wing authoritarianism (RWA) established by
Altemeyer (see above, p. 96).[21] As noted above, Altemeyer's conception of
RWA is comprised of three attitudes—authoritarian aggression, authoritarian submission, and conventionalism. These have been consistently
seen to covary, and to be associated with a range of other personality characteristics and behaviours (Altemeyer 1981: 1988).

Altemeyer's 1992 article 'Authoritarianism, Religious Fundamentalism,
Quest, and Prejudice', written with Hunsberger also discussed above, pp.
95–7), explores distinctive aspects of this relationship. In their 1990 study
of almost 700 students and their parents, Altemeyer and Hunsberger
found that religious fundamentalism correlated far more closely with
right-wing authoritarianism than did a measure of Christian orthodoxy
(0.60 as compared to 0.43), and that different measures of prejudice correlated significantly with religious fundamentalism, though less significantly than with right-wing authoritarianism (p. 119). Hunsberger argues
that the close association between religious fundamentalism and right-
wing authoritarianism is readily understandable: 'both religious fundamentalism and authoritarianism encourage obedience to authority,
conventionalism, self-righteousness, and feelings of superiority'
(Hunsberger 1995: 121).

To some extent, the anti-democratic attitudes of religious fundamentalists can be traced back to fundamentalists' specific beliefs. For instance, as
we have seen, belief in the Devil and that he works in the world through
human agents can lead to intolerance (Section 1). It has long been recognized that particular religious beliefs can encourage ethnocentrism, hostility towards members of groups other than one's own (see above, p. 88).
The study by Green and his colleagues presents striking correlations

---

[21] Compare Wald *et al.* (1989: 101–2) on differences between authoritarianism and
authority-mindedness.

between different specific fundamentalist beliefs and intolerance. Of these items, 'religious separatism', belief that true Christians remain separate from the 'world', showed the single largest bivariate correlation with tolerance ($r = -0.27$). The correlation with biblical literalism was -0.26, and with belief in the 'rapture' of the church, -0.23. The correlations with belief in biblical prophecy was -0.21, and with a pre-millennial view of scripture -0.17 (Green *et al.* 1994: 35–6; see above, n. 20). Green and his colleagues note that respondents who reject these doctrines, and so are placed at the opposite end of the fundamentalism scale, 'are strikingly more tolerant' (p. 36).

Along similar lines, in a well-known study, Glock and Stark recorded a strong association between Christian orthodoxy and anti-Semitism, based on the belief that the Jews were responsible for Jesus's death. They found that the more strongly subjects subscribed to orthodox views, the more likely they were to be anti-Semitic (Glock and Stark 1966).

In view of the close association between religious fundamentalism and right-wing authoritarianism, we should note the relationship established by Altemeyer between right-wing authoritarianism and high scores on his so-called 'posse' scale. The items on the posse scale are preceded by a brief paragraph presenting the supposition that the Canadian government has passed a law outlawing the Communist Party in Canada and that every Canadian has been asked to help enforce this at the local level. The statements with which respondents are asked to agree or disagree are as follows (Altemeyer 1988: 115–16):

1. I would tell my friends and neighbors it was a good law.
2. I would tell the police about any Communists I knew.
3. If asked by the police, I would help hunt down and arrest Communists.
4. I would participate in attacks on Communist headquarters organized by the proper authorities.
5. I would support the use of physical force to make Communists reveal the identity of other Communists.
6. I would support the execution of Communist leaders if the government insisted it was necessary to protect Canada.

In their 1991 survey Altemeyer and Hunsberger substituted 'radical' and 'extremist' political movements for 'Communists' in posse items (Altemeyer and Hunsberger 1992: 121).

As noted above, Altemeyer found that respondents who score high on the right-wing authoritarianism (RWA) scale—to whom I will refer as RWAs—are significantly more willing to engage in 'posse' activities than are other respondents (Altemeyer 1988: 116–17). The same is true, although at a lower level, of religious fundamentalists. The comparative correlations are: posse and fundamentalists, 0.34; posse and RWA, 0.51.

Compare the –0.34 correlation between the posse and quest scales (Altemeyer and Hunsberger 1992: 122).

The implications of this particular study are ominous. Throughout this and the preceding chapters I have discussed intolerance and prejudice, anti-democratic sentiments. But if responses to the posse questions are to be believed, then significant numbers of citizens are willing to put their anti-democratic beliefs into practice (see also Altemeyer 1981: 274–6).

In addition to its connections with anti-democratic sentiments, the cognitive underpinning of fundamentalism represents a problem for liberal consensus. As we saw in the first chapter, a central tenet of liberal theory is that people must assent to the principles by which they are governed. But fundamentalists' distinctive cognitive style (and less extreme versions of it throughout society) entail(s) standards of argument and justification quite different from those of many other citizens. Because it is generally accepted that democratic citizens require some measure of common values, beliefs, and cognitive capacities, the United States and other democratic countries have made education mandatory up to a certain age. However, the possible effects of non-religious public school education on children's religious beliefs raise troublesome issues. On the one hand, there is the publicly recognized need for education. But this can run counter to important values of religious freedom concerning parent's rights to pass their religion on to their children (on which, more below). Given profound differences between overall outlooks of different participants in debates about such issues, standards of evidence and argument to be employed are themselves controversial.[22]

I do not wish to suggest that beliefs of religious fundamentalists concerning such matters as biblical authority should be accepted in public debate. Beliefs along these lines are obviously rooted in particular comprehensive views and so are excluded by the ground rules of public reason. But even if we grant this important point, the practical problems remain of developing democratic principles to which fundamentalists could subscribe and arguments they would find convincing. This of course is not solely a practical problem. Unless suitable principles can be found, a high percentage of the American population will be governed by principles they cannot accept (see below, p. 97).

---

[22] For discussions of the place of religion in public reason, see Rawls (1997: 783–7), Minow *et al.* (1995), Audi (1989), Weithman (1991), Quinn (1995), George (1997).

4. RELIGIOUS PLURALISM IN AMERICA

If a central task of liberal consensus is outlining a basis for agreement on acceptable principles, the severity of the problem posed by the cognitive style I have examined depends heavily on the numbers of people involved. Thus we must attempt to determine rough percentages of the American population that should be described as 'fundamentalist' in intellectual orientation. Although this way of thinking is most closely associated with religious fundamentalists, it may well be held by devotees of various non-religious creeds. It is difficult to find precise evidence about something as elusive as a particular cognitive style. Similarly, it is not clear how many members of modern societies should be classified as 'fundamentalists'. As I have noted, scholars differ about exactly what constitutes a 'fundamentalist', while research results are influenced by the measure one chooses (Kellstedt and Smidt 1991). The main evidence available is in regard to Protestant evangelicals, and I will examine some of this. Because my focus is on cognitive style, I will also explore certain well-documented beliefs associated with different denominations.

As the term is generally used in the United States, 'fundamentalism' is an offshoot of Protestantism. As has been noted, it is characterized by a regard for the Bible as the final authority in all matters of faith and emphasis on personal salvation through Jesus Christ. Evangelicalism, in various manifestations, was the dominant form of American Protestantism throughout the nineteenth century, though, in response to increasingly widespread industrialization and urbanization towards the end of the century, different branches of evangelicalism developed, advocating different levels of accommodation to social change. During the 1910s and 1920s the term 'fundamentalism' came to be used to designate groups of conservative evangelicals who resisted modernism and associated tendencies towards theological liberalization. Influential scholars identify militant opposition to different forms of modernization as the core of fundamentalism during the period of its inception (see Marsden 1980).

Since the movement's origins, fundamentalists have differed from evangelicals less in terms of religious doctrine than in attitude. Fundamentalists generally possess a more aggressive, oppositional orientation. This can lead to strong separatist tendencies from other denominations and an unwillingness to associate with non-fundamentalists. According to Ammerman: 'The ultimate characteristic that has distinguished fundamentalists from other evangelicals has been their insistence that there *can be* tests of faith. Fundamentalists insist on uniformity of belief within the ranks and separation for others whose beliefs and lives are suspect' (Ammerman 1991: 7–8). It should be noted, however, that these are only tendencies. With frequent splintering of denominations throughout Protestantism, dividing lines have been blurred.[23]

Because the cognitive characteristics that interest us are present in many evangelicals—though probably to a lesser degree than fundamentalists—we can focus on these. Once again, in trying to document something as elusive as a particular cognitive style, real precision is difficult. But for our purposes, it should suffice to work out a rough idea of the prevalence of the relevant cognitive characteristics, in order to outline the nature of the problem this causes for liberal consensus.

As with fundamentalists, different means have been used to identify evangelicals (Wilcox 1992: 42–5; Kellstedt 1989). Most common have been denominational and doctrinal measures, identifying evangelicals according to the churches they attend, or the religious doctrines they accept. Specific doctrines that are commonly proposed are belief in the divinity of Christ, that eternal salvation can be attained only through acceptance of Christ, belief that the Bible is inerrant, and commitment to spreading the gospel (Kellstedt 1989: 4–5). To get some idea of the nature and prevalence of evangelical beliefs in the United States, I will look briefly at national surveys that span a thirty-year period, and at National Election Studies of religion among American voters.

We can begin with a recent survey directed by James Hunter and Carl Bowman, conducted by the Gallup Organization, in which 2,047 American adults were interviewed in depth in early 1996. Hunter and Bowman define evangelicals as follows:

An Evangelical, for the purposes of this survey, was defined as someone who: (1) Believes in God; (2) Does not describe his or her *religious beliefs* as liberal; and (3) Meets at least two of the following criteria—has a 'personal relationship' with God, believes scripture should be taken literally word for word, and prays daily. (Hunter and Bowman 1996: i. 98 n. 13)

According to Hunter and Bowman, this group comprises between 20 and 25 per cent of the American population (1996: i. 52). But it is important to bear in mind that evangelical Protestants are not the only members of modern society with such a distinctive view of the world. As Hunter argues in *Culture Wars*, common points of view are encountered across the orthodox wings of Protestantism, Catholicism, and Judaism (Hunter 1990: 47).

For example, in their survey, Hunter and Bowman distinguish orthodox and progressive Catholics, with the former comprising 12 per cent of their

---

[23] For dividing-lines, see Smidt (1988) and Beatty and Walter (1988).

sample (as opposed to the latter, 20 per cent) (1996, vol. ii, sect. ii). Orthodox Catholics share many religious attributes with evangelicals. They were identified as Catholics

(1) who believed that 'there is a God,' (2) who did not describe their religious outlook as 'liberal,' and (3) who met two of these three conditions: (*a*) reported that they had a 'personal relationship' with God, (*b*) believed the Bible is the actual word of God and is to be taken literally, and (*c*) reported that they pray daily. (Hunter 1994: 267 n. 27)[24]

Hunter and Bowman asked their respondents a number of questions about specific religious beliefs. Of evangelical respondents, 100 per cent believed there is a God, and 99 per cent that they have a personal relationship with God (1996, tables 88 and 89; all tables are in vol. ii). In regard to the Bible, 66 per cent of evangelicals agreed with the following statement: 'The Bible is the word of God, not mistaken in its statements and teaching, and is to be taken literally, word for word.' Another 21 per cent agreed: 'The Bible is the inspired word of God, not mistaken in its teachings, but is not always to be taken literally, word for word' (table 90). Orthodox Catholics were close on all these questions: 100 per cent reported believing in God; 99 per cent reported a personal relationship with God; on the Bible question, 45 per cent and 33 per cent reported agreeing with the first and second statements, respectively (tables 88–90). If we place authoritative status of scripture at the heart of the cognitive orientation that interests us, we can say that these figures suggest that in 1996 at least a quarter of the American population subscribed to some variant of that cognitive orientation.[25]

In *The People's Religion*, published in 1989, George Gallup and Jim Castelli reported on many aspects of American's religious beliefs, on the basis of extensive polling (Gallup and Castelli 1989, p. xvi; information on polls to support specific findings is in the notes, pp. 267–72). Gallup and Castelli identified respondents as evangelicals if they had a 'born again' experience, 'had a literal interpretation of the Bible (or believed the Bible to be without error in its teachings)', and had tried to encourage other people to accept Jesus Christ as saviour. They estimated that approximately 20 per cent of Americans fell into this category (p. 13). Among other details worth noting, 64 per cent of evangelicals reported that God had spoken to them directly, while 71 per cent reported that God speaks

---

[24] I am grateful to Carl Bowman, in private correspondence, for information on criteria of 'orthodox Catholics' used in Hunter and Bowman (1996).

[25] I should note that Hunter and Bowman's survey does not allow us to identify members of other religious groups with similar beliefs.

through the Bible (pp. 72–3). Ninety-six per cent of evangelicals agreed that 'God has a plan for their lives' (p. 73).

Surveys of American voters are conducted for the National Election Studies every two years. Topics addressed include religion.[26] For more than the last three decades the percentage of voters identifying themselves as evangelical Protestants has been approximately 30 per cent (ranging between a low of 28 per cent in 1978 and 1994, and a high of 32 per cent in 1970, 1986, and 1992). When given four choices to describe their opinions about the accuracy of the Bible, about half of all respondents chose the most literal, that 'The Bible is God's word and all it says is true'. Between 1964 and 1990 the low percentage choosing this option was 46 per cent in 1980; the high was 52 per cent in 1968. In 1990 the wording of the question about biblical accuracy was altered slightly. In 1990 45 per cent, in 1992 39 per cent, and in 1994 38 per cent of respondents chose: 'The Bible is the actual Word of God and is to be taken literally, word for word'.

An indication of the beliefs of different Christian denominations is provided by Stark and Glock, on the basis of polls of 3,000 church members in northern California and a national sample of 1,976 adults, conducted in 1963–4 (Stark and Glock 1968: 6–7). Table 4.1 has been constructed using several of their questions. The four questions Stark and Glock used to construct their 'orthodoxy index' concern belief in the existence of a personal God, the divinity of Jesus Christ, the authenticity of biblical miracles, and the existence of the Devil (pp. 58–9). They did not ask a specific question about belief in biblical inerrancy, but it is likely that scores would correlate with the other indicators of doctrinal orthodoxy presented.

These figures support what we have seen in the polls reviewed throughout this chapter. The denominations in the first three columns are three that scored highest in orthodoxy. There was considerable range among Protestant denominations; for example, 4 per cent of the Congregationalist sample scored high on the orthodoxy scale; and 10 per cent of Methodists. The last two columns provide general figures for Protestants and Catholics, as a basis for comparison.

Additional evidence of the importance of biblical faith to many adherents is that it is widely viewed as more important to personal salvation than good conduct or deeds. Stark and Glock note that members of the three denominations responded disproportionately in this direction. Consider Table 4.2.

[26] The National Election Studies are conducted by the Center for Political Studies at the University of Michigan's Institute for Social Research. Results are available on the internet at the following address: http://www.umich.edu:80/~nes/nesguide/nes guide.htm (retrieved 1998).

TABLE 4.1. *Beliefs of Christian denominations* %

Question	Missouri Lutheran	Southern Baptist	Sects[a]	Total Protestant	Roman Catholic
'No doubts' about existence of God	81	99	99	71	81
'No doubts' about divinity of Jesus	93	99	97	69	86
'Completely true' that Jesus born of a virgin	92	99	96	57	81
Believe in life beyond death	84	97	94	65	75
Believe the Devil exists	77	92	90	38	66
Believe that holding Bible to be 'God's truth' is required for salvation	80	61	89	52	38
General orthodoxy: 4 on scale of 4	66	88	86	33	62
General orthodoxy: 3 on scale of 4	21	9	10	21	19

Source: Stark and Glock (1968, chs. 1–3).

Note: Figures in columns relate to the percentage who agree. These figures are for the sample of church members; figures for the national sample were somewhat lower. For example, belief in God: Missouri Lutherans 70%; Southern Baptists 93%; sects 90%; total Protestants 79%; Roman Catholics 85% (p. 30).

a Incl.: Assemblies of God, Church of God, Church of Christ, Church of the Nazarene, Foursquare Gospel Church, and one independent tabernacle (Stark and Glock 1968, table 2). For the national sample, the list is similar though slightly different (table 3).

A striking depiction of the cognitive divide in American society is provided by Hunter, in *Culture Wars* (Hunter 1990). Hunter is concerned with how intellectual differences between religious and non-religious groups in American society contribute to the intractability of a range of public issues, e.g. abortion, gay rights, the place of religion in education. Defining a cultural conflict as 'political and social hostility rooted in different systems of moral understanding' (pp. 42), Hunter argues that these are exacerbated in contemporary American society by conflicting impulses towards 'orthodoxy' and 'progressivism'. Hunter's accounts of the two impulses function as ideal types, which are differentiated according to 'formal properties' of the respective belief systems. The former is characterized by 'commitment on the part of adherents to an external, definable,

TABLE 4.2. *Further beliefs of Christian denominations* (%)

Question	Missouri Lutheran	Southern Baptist	Sects	Total Protestant	Roman Catholic
'Belief in Jesus Christ as Savior' is necessary for salvation	97	97	96	65	51
Believe that 'Holding the Bible to be God's truth' is necessary for salvation	80	61	89	52	38
Believe that 'Doing good for others' is necessary for salvation	38	29	61	52	57
Believe that 'Discriminating against other races' would prevent salvation	22	16	29	25	24
Believe that 'Being anti-Semitic' would prevent salvation	22	10	26	21	20

Source: Stark and Glock (1968, ch. 2).

and transcendent authority': 'Such objective and transcendent authority defines, at least in the abstract, a consistent, unchangeable measure of value, purpose, goodness, and identity, both personal and collective' (p. 44). Cultural progressivism, in contrast, 'tends to be defined by the spirit of the modern age, a spirit of rationalism and subjectivism'. Its sources of moral authority are found in 'personal experience or scientific rationality' (pp. 44–5). As noted, Hunter believes that the two orientations span traditional religious divides. People with different religious affiliations can be orthodox or progressive, depending on how they see the world. Thus, for example, evangelical Protestants are found in alliance with devout Catholics and Orthodox Jews in the struggle against abortion (p. 47).

Hunter provides a vivid depiction of the orthodox world-view, which centres upon specific beliefs about the source of moral authority: 'Within communities that hold orthodox views, moral authority arises from a common commitment to transcendence, by which I mean a dynamic reality that is independent of, prior to, and more powerful than human experience' (p. 120). Common sources of transcendent moral authority include the Bible and other similar, inerrant texts, which ground 'certain non-negotiable moral "truths"' (pp. 120–2). One of Hunter's orthodox subjects described his conception of moral truth as follows:

. . . God tells me what's right and what's wrong. I may attempt in a limited capacity to try to understand that, but I have to start off from the point that I am surrendering my personal intellect to God. If something doesn't make sense to me, that has no bearing on the reality of it or my obligation to respond to it. (p. 121)

The close relationship between the view expressed here and what Wald and his colleagues characterize as 'authority-mindedness' is apparent. It should be similarly clear how beliefs such as those held by evangelicals and the more specific denominations noted above would contribute to a similar orientation.

Once again, the religious cognitive style discussed here is something of an ideal type, and it is difficult to say exactly how widespread this conception of moral authority is. But the evidence presented in this section, along with additional surveys that could be cited, suggests that views Hunter would characterize as 'orthodox' are subscribed to by at least 20–5 per cent of the American population.

5. IMPLICATIONS

If the aim of liberal consensus is to derive a set of principles that can be generally accepted throughout society, then the anti-democratic beliefs discussed in this chapter compound the difficulties discussed in the last. Though people may profess adherence to strong democratic principles, their actual beliefs fall short. In practice, substantial numbers, perhaps a majority, of democratic citizens are willing to abrogate the rights of unpopular minorities. Because of the general consensus on abstract democratic principles seen in the last chapter, we can assume that subjects discussed in this chapter also accept them. But many would be willing to set them aside in particular cases. The reasons they would invoke identify their rights principles as weak.

Further complicating matters is the fact that many religious members of society subscribe to principles of moral reasoning that are inimical to public reason and its spirit of open inquiry. Authority-mindedness, belief in transcendent truth, and reasoning from sacred texts are foundational cognitive principles of the religiously orthodox, not only Protestant evangelicals and fundamentalists, but adherents of a range of religions. Such people could well participate in public deliberations, using acceptable modes of argument. But they would doubtless have more difficulty doing so than others who are less authority-minded.

Difficulties in bringing people with authoritative epistemologies into democratic consensus are obviously formidable. Because the ground rules of public reason exclude arguments from sacred texts, we could perhaps rule the views of religious adherents out of bounds and formulate democratic principles without reference to the them. As noted in Chapter 1, political liberalism does not recognize the need to truck with fanatics.

However, given the high percentage of the population with the views in question, for both normative and practical reasons liberal consensus argues for inclusion rather than exclusion. Principles formulated without input from 20–5 per cent of the population would obviously be less stable than others that were more inclusive, while basic to liberal consensus is the imperative to govern people by principles they can accept. Of course these imperatives hold only if they are possible. If the cognitive divide is too great to be bridged, liberal consensus would recommend acceptable principles with the greatest possible extent. But again, the need for inclusion must be recognized. Religious fundamentalists and other authority-minded citizens do not forfeit their rights to be governed by principles they can accept, as long as they are willing to live co-operatively with their fellows. Thus we must look for principles that are able to appeal across society.

A possible alternative to such principles is to change religious fundamentalists' mindset. Requirements of common citizenship justify some measure of common education, so perhaps we can place our faith in that. I have repeatedly noted that increased education reduces anti-democratic attitudes. This has been seen in regard to intolerance, and is also a regular theme in discussions of prejudice. One reason for the association between religious fundamentalism and prejudice is that fundamentalists are generally less well educated than other citizens. Accordingly, we can hypothesize that, with increased education throughout society, differences between fundamentalists and other citizens can be narrowed, and a stronger conception of rights more widely accepted. In Chapter 3 I discussed the study of Nunn, Crockett, and Williams (1978), which concluded that in the years since Stouffer's original research the tolerance levels of Americans had increased significantly, with increased education. We have seen that Sullivan's alternative conceptualization of tolerance gives us reasons to question the Nunn group's optimism. But through increased education, the pattern that the latter posit could well become the case. Accordingly, we should distinguish between a consensus on rights that is realizable at the present time, but which would be pulled in the direction of weak rights, and a potential consensus on strong rights, but which is dependent on increased education throughout society.

However, it is not easy to say exactly how effective increased education could be. The underlying attitudes that give rise to intolerance and prejudice are deeply instilled, developed over many years. Presumably, protracted education would be required to alter them. Questions along these lines were investigated by Altemeyer. He assessed the RWA scores of seventy-six university students who had been surveyed both at the beginning and at the end of their college years (in 1982 and 1986, respectively). The sample was comprised of liberal arts majors, nursing majors, and administrative studies majors. He recorded an average drop of 11 per cent across the three groups; the scores of liberal arts majors fell especially precipitously, about 20 per cent (Altemeyer 1988: 92–3). It is important to note that scores of students who had been in the top quartile on the RWA scale ('highs') in 1982 declined on average more than twice as much as those of non-highs. This is readily explained by the fact that freshman highs had presumably lived in narrower, more confined environments before entering the university. Altemeyer surmises that falling levels of right-wing authoritarianism could be attributed to increased contact with different sorts of people, as well as formal academic instruction (pp. 93–5). The results of this study indicate that prejudice can be mitigated through increased education, though not eliminated entirely. However, Altemeyer surveyed ninety other alumni, both at the beginning of their college years and twelve years later (in 1974 and 1986, respectively). This survey showed that, in the eight years after graduation, RWA scores returned to their original levels. Altemeyer noted that the scores of respondents who had children were significantly higher than those who had remained childless (pp. 97–8). Although it is discouraging to note that the drop in authoritarianism that can be attributed to college experience was temporary, reason for some encouragement is that anti-democratic sentiments do not appear to be inexorably implanted, but can vary in response to changing circumstances.

As has been noted, questions concerning the kind of education that can be employed in a liberal society raise thorny problems. Although some level of education, which will inculcate respect for rights, is undoubtedly necessary, boundary lines are subject to dispute. Progress towards more substantive rights must be gradual, with a given increase in general respect for rights justifying education that can raise the level higher, in a somewhat dialectical fashion. However, anti-democratic sentiments rooted in religion would be particularly difficult to change. Not only are religious beliefs oftentimes especially deeply rooted, and so especially difficult to alter, but as I have noted, in a liberal society attempts to tamper with religion through education can be highly questionable.

In this connection, it bears mention that the kind of education practised in many fundamentalist schools is not likely to further the prospects of democratic consensus. On the basis of his analysis of sixteen 'major textbooks' published for fundamentalist schools, Albert Menendez concludes:

these textbooks and by extension the schools using them present only very one-sided views of history, geography, literature, and science. Furthermore, students are not encouraged to examine issues or to seek for answers to complex questions themselves. They are actively discouraged from doing so. The selection of material and the interpretations given foreclose any independent analysis and seem intent on creating a generation of adults with a mindset that can only be harmful to democratic freedoms and to interfaith harmony. (Menendez 1993: 3)[27]

Particular points illustrate this orientation. For instance a senior high school biology text attempts to relate all areas of scientific observation to God's teaching: 'If the conclusions contradict the Word of God, the conclusions are wrong no matter how many scientific facts appear to back them' (William Pinkston Jr., quoted by Menendez 1993: 118). Teachings on creationism and evolution favour the former and are hostile to the latter (Menendez 1993, ch. 5). In regard to human sexuality, homosexuality is reviled: 'God calls homosexuality a sin, and those who engage in this act are reprobates' (Pinkston, quoted by Menendez 1993: 124).

Among rights central to liberal theory, pride of place is given to freedom to practise the religion of one's choice, which includes the right to inculcate one's religion in one's children.[28] It is possible that education material of the sort Menendez describes is extreme. But more nuanced though basically similar material would likely have similar effects. Even if we believe that education presents the greatest hope for increased political tolerance and so general agreement on democratic rights into the future, we must recognize the extent to which pluralism in education, permitted in a pluralistic culture, is likely to reinforce rather than weaken intellectual and moral differences.

Means other than education have the potential to erode differences between groups. Stereotypes about minority groups flourish in ignorance. It is widely accepted that an effective way to puncture these is to encourage members of different groups to become acquainted. But contact must be of the proper sort, between social equals. Encounters between members of a prejudiced majority and members of a minority group who are their social inferiors is not likely to reduce prejudice. Prejudice will, however, be reduced 'by equal status contact between majority and minority groups in the pursuit of common goals' (Allport 1954: 281; see ch. 16).

The paradox here, of course, is that prejudice is likely to keep groups apart, thereby making the requisite constructive associations more difficult to develop. This is likely to be especially problematic for religious

[27] Menendez claims that his conclusions are consistent with finding of earlier studies; for references, see Menendez (1993: 5).
[28] For issues in regard to fundamentalism and education, see Provenzo (1990), Macedo (1995, 1997), Galston (1995), and Gutmann (1995).

fundamentalists who insist on strict separation between believers and non-believers, shunning contact with others unlike themselves. As we have noted, separatist tendencies are often invoked as one of the distinguishing characteristics of fundamentalism. Thus in some areas in which increased contact is most desired, it is unlikely to come about spontaneously.

In conclusion, then, from the point of view of liberal consensus the anti-democratic sentiments we have reviewed pose a problem that must be addressed. If differences between adherents of different religions and other world-views rule out agreement on strong rights principles—and on modes of reasoning necessary to establish them—we must seek out other principles that can bridge the gap.

5

Support for Democratic Procedures

IN spite of lack of consensus on rights and liberties, liberal citizens generally agree on another important value: support for democratic procedures. Once again, I will concentrate, though not exclusively, on the views of Americans. A central claim of this work is that the principles to which American citizens can be seen to subscribe are mainly procedural rather than substantive, centring on support for their political process. The distinction between substantive and procedural principles is generally described as between the results of decision procedures, i.e. what is decided, and the means through which decisions are made. To take a simple example, we can distinguish between a specific principle of distributive justice according to which some tax burden is assigned and different aspects of the process through which this decision is made—ranging from how the reasons for and against different proposals are handled, to specific people who occupy the offices that have power to make the decision, to how they were selected, or the overall apportionment of governmental powers according to which they function. As we will see below, problems are encountered in drawing precise lines between process and substance. In particular, maintenance of suitably democratic procedures has important substantive implications concerning the distribution of rights and liberties and other values throughout society. But on a basic level, the distinction is clear, and we can assume it at the outset of this discussion.

Discussion in this chapter is in four sections. In Section 1 I explore evidence concerning political trust, which indicates that American citizens do not support their political system. To counter this claim, political trust is distinguished from other forms of political support, especially what I will call 'regime' or 'system' support. In Section 2 I explore evidence that Americans do support their political process, including many people who lack other democratic values. In Section 3 I attempt more precise delineation of the principles to which Americans subscribe. Some implications are then drawn in Section 4.

1. POLITICAL TRUST AND SYSTEM SUPPORT

It may seem counter-intuitive to claim that Americans strongly support their political system, because of what appears to be powerful evidence to the contrary. For instance, John Hibbing and Elizabeth Theiss-Morse call their recent book *Congress as Public Enemy* (Hibbing and Theiss-Morse 1995). In their opening paragraph they note the 'astonishingly low regard' in which the American public holds its political system and institutions in the 1990s (p. 1). In a country in which candidates for federal office regularly run against 'Washington,' where 'Washington' is a term of opprobrium, this sentiment is common knowledge, and it is hardly peculiar to the 1990s. Viewing Congress as a public enemy has been a staple of American politics and culture since the last century at least. Such a view is classically expressed in Mark Twain's remark that Congress is the only indigenous American criminal class.

The popular view that Americans do not respect their government receives impressive empirical support in the large-scale decline of trust recorded in national opinion surveys. The most important survey used to measure political trust is a series of National Election Studies (NES) questions, administered regularly by the University of Michigan Institute for Social Research. Since 1958 the following four questions have been asked:

1. How much of the time do you think you can trust the government in Washington to do what is right—just about always, most of the time, or only some of the time?
2. Do you think that people in the government waste a lot of money we pay in taxes, waste some of it, or don't waste very much of it?
3. Do you feel that almost all of the people running the government are smart people who usually know what they are doing, or do you think that quite a few of them don't seem to know what they are doing?
4. Do you think that quite a few of the people running the government are a little crooked, not very many are, or do you think that hardly any of them are crooked at all?

In 1964 an additional question was added:

5. Would you say the government is pretty much run by a few big interests looking out for themselves or that it is run for the benefit of all the people?

Repeated administration of questions is highly useful in allowing us to chart changes in attitudes over time. The results have been striking, as seen in Table 5.1.[1] On the five questions, lack of trust in government rose

[1] For NES data, see Ch. 4 n. 26. Not all questions are used to construct this table, and there are slight variations in questions used in different years. But they do not affect the point at issue.

steadily through the 1960s and 1970s, maintaining extremely high levels through 1980. Distrust receded significantly during the Reagan years, but has since risen, attaining something approaching consensus levels. In other words, the most important survey of Americans' trust in their government reveals that roughly ⅔–¾ do not trust it. However, the implications of these findings depend on how they should be interpreted.

Table 5.1. *Trust in government index, 1958–1996* (%)

	Year									
	1958	1960	1962	1964	1966	1968	1970	1972	1974	1976
Average score	49	—	—	52	61	45	39	38	29	30

Year	1978	1980	1982	1984	1986	1988	1990	1992	1994	1996
Average score	29	27	31	38	47	34	29	29	26	32

Source: *National Election Studies*, table 5A.5; table generated 12 May 1998.

The difficulties in interpreting the data are seen in an exchange between Arthur Miller and Jack Citrin, which appeared in the 1974 *American Political Science Review* (Miller 1974*a*, *b*; Citrin 1974). Miller presented a grim analysis of the implications of the decline of trust between 1964 and 1970. He noted 'a strong trend of increasing cynicism for the general population', as seen in an average decline in responses to the five questions of some 17 per cent during this period (1974*a*: 952). He viewed the existence of significant levels of trust as necessary for the survival of democracy: 'A democratic political system cannot survive for long without the support of a majority of its citizens. When such support wanes, underlying discontent is the necessary result, and the potential for revolutionary alteration of the political and social system is enhanced' (p. 951).

Because the surveys show that the American people possess 'pervasive and enduring distrust of government' (p. 951), Miller entertained serious doubts about the long-term prospects of American democracy. He attributed change in public attitudes to a series of problems America encountered in the late 1960s, including the Vietnam War, civil rights changes, and a range of social problems, including campus disruptions, problems of inflation and unemployment, and pollution. Because of the polarization of public attitudes about many of these, he believed that the prospects for generally acceptable solutions were not good, while President Nixon's problems with Watergate made significant improvements in the situation unlikely.

With the benefit of almost thirty years' hindsight, we can see that Miller's analysis was fortunately overblown. Response rates concerning trust did not continue the trend of the late 1960s; decline through the

1970s was generally arrested in the 1980s although scores recorded in the 1990s have declined once again. It is possible that, had trust levels continued their consistent decline, the dire consequences Miller foresaw would have come about. But this was less likely than he apparently imagined, because of his lack of clarity about what the survey questions actually measured.

In his response to Miller, Citrin argues that Miller's analysis of the sources of political trust is overly simple. According to Citrin, Miller envisions a sort of exchange. The government provides people with policies or decisions of which they approve, and they repay the government with trust. Conversely, the response to policies of which people do not approve is distrust (Citrin 1974: 973). This model is overly simple because it fails to distinguish between different objects of trust, especially between the political regime in some larger sense and 'incumbent political leaders'. As Citrin says: 'Allegiance to the political system . . . does not preclude criticism of specific policies, authorities, or institutions; many people readily combine intense patriotic sentiments with cynicism about politicians' (p. 974). Indeed, suspicion of political officials is deeply rooted in the liberal political tradition, as seen in basic constitutional features such as the separation of powers and checks and balances. As Madison wrote in *The Federalist*, 51:

If men were angels, no government would be necessary. If angels were to govern men, neither external nor internal controls on government would be necessary. In framing a government which is to be administered by men over men, the great difficulty lies in this: you must first enable the government to control the governed; and in the next place oblige it to control itself. (Hamilton *et al.*, n.d.: 337)

But of course, Madison's suspicion of and attempt to check individual office-holders did not carry over into rejecting the political system as a whole, in support of which *The Federalist* was written.

Once we distinguish allegiance to the regime or political system on the one hand, and to specific officials on the other, we must decide which of these the trust questions measure. The wording of the questions suggests the latter. Question 1 refers to 'the government in Washington', question 2 to 'the people in government', 3 and 4 refer to 'the people running the government', while 5 refers to 'the government'. Clearly, if respondents answered according to the literal meaning of the questions, their replies would provide evidence about their views of incumbent politicians. At one point in his original article Miller seems to recognize this (1974*a*: 952).

Making a distinction between the political system and specific people running it would greatly complicate Miller's hypothesized direct relationship between government policies and people's attitude towards government. While it is likely that people's trust or confidence in political figures is directly affected by what the latter are perceived to deliver, effects on far-reaching attitudes about the overall system are less clear. An immediate source of uncertainty is the exact object of the latter attitudes. Is it the political system, the community, the country, or perhaps some other entity? Then again, exactly how do respondents conceive of these? There are enormous difficulties in deciding which of these possible entities—if any—are tapped by the NES trust questions, or whether they can be reached by other specific questions. In his response to Citrin (Miller 1974*b*), Miller provides evidence that the NES questions do tap into deeper underlying sentiments—although how deeply remains unclear. But the details here need not concern us. It is apparent that in spite of problems we encounter in identifying exactly what attitudes specific NES questions measure, we must sort out different dimensions of trust in government.

Central distinctions between possible objects of political allegiance are worked out by David Easton. Easton presents a variety of concepts which are not always easy to sort out or to map onto one another. We can begin with a threefold distinction: support for the authorities, the regime, and the political community (1965*b*: 158). Easton describes the political community as 'a group of persons bound together by a political division of labor', not 'the form or structure of political processes but rather . . . the group of members who are drawn together by the fact that they participate in a common structure and set of processes' (p. 177). In other words, support for the community is distinctive in being directed towards the other people who constitute the political system to which one belongs.

For our purposes, the other two objects are more important. Support for 'authorities' is straightforward. This is in reference to office-holders, 'occupants of the authority roles' (1965*b*: 212). Support for the regime, in contrast, is in regard to the structure of offices themselves, as opposed to the people who occupy them. These include 'the constitutional order', the rules and procedures according to which decisions are made (pp. 190–1), and also a set of norms that play a vital role in supporting these structures. Easton describes a regime's norms as 'its operating rules and rules of the game.' (pp. 200–1).

In addition to distinguishing between objects of support, Easton presents a celebrated distinction between different kinds of attitudes. 'Specific support' is characterized by a relatively short-term orientation. It is given in exchange for satisfaction of demands, and withdrawn for lack of same. Easton describes it as 'a *quid pro quo* for the fulfillment of demands' (1965*b*: 268). In earlier works he had called it 'contingent support' (p. 268 n. 2). In a 1975 article he clarifies the nature of specific support, calling attention to factors outside a direct exchange relationship. In particular, specific support includes an assessment of the overall performance of political authorities, beyond direct satisfaction or dissatisfaction with specific outputs (1975: 442–3).

'Diffuse support' is distinguished from specific support in being more long-term and substantial. The basic idea is that members of adequately functioning political systems are willing to accept political decisions they view as unfavourable, because of deeper, underlying attachment to their systems. Easton describes diffuse support as 'a reservoir of favorable attitudes or good will that helps members to accept or tolerate outputs to which they are opposed or the effect of which they see as damaging to their wants' (1965*b*: 273).[2]

Easton's presentation of two classifications—one based on objects at which attitudes are directed, and the other on the attitudes themselves—raises obvious problems in regard to how the two classifications are related. Systems of considerable complexity are possible, although as classifications become more detailed and elaborate, the attitudes in question become increasingly difficult to assess through survey questions.[3] For our purposes, much of this discussion can be set aside. Unlike empirical scholars, who study support mainly in reference to the stability or instability of political regimes, we are interested in it as a normative phenomenon, serving to justify regimes morally (rather than empirically). In accordance with my discussion of liberal principles in Chapter 1, adequate liberal principles must be accepted by most citizens, in spite of the wide range of issues about which they disagree. The principles on which I will focus centre on support for the political system in some overall sense, as opposed to the occupants of its offices. In regard to Easton's classifications, my concern is with the

[2] For refinement of Easton's views, see Easton (1975). For sophisticated recent discussion of the relationship between specific and diffuse support, see Caldeira and Gibson (1992) and Gibson and Caldeira (1992). In Easton (1965*a*) Easton overstates the independence of specific and diffuse support, for which he has been criticized (e.g. Hibbing and Theiss-Morse 1995: 12–13; Craig 1993: 8–9). Easton says of diffuse support that 'regardless of what happens', people will continue to be bound to their regime by ties of loyalty: 'This is a type of support that continues independently of the specific rewards which the member may feel he obtains from belonging to the system' (1965*a*: 124–5). Criticism of the overstatement in these particular statements is uncharitable, however, in view of numerous, more nuanced statements elsewhere in Easton's works. But one criticism that should be noted is his including empirical claims in definitions of different types of support. The precise relationship between specific and diffuse support should be addressed through empirical research rather than conceptually.

[3] Easton (1965*b*) argues that is it not part of his task 'to consider problems involved in the measurement of support as an empirical phenomenon' (p. 161). For attempts to merge the two classifications, see Easton (1975) and Westle (1989); also Craig *et al.* (1990).

objects of support, rather than characteristics of the relevant attitudes. It should be noted that support for the political system overlaps closely with what Easton calls diffuse support, but we need not explore the complexities of this relationship. I will avoid language of 'specific' and 'diffuse' support, referring instead to the attitude that interests us as 'regime' support or 'system' support, although its close relationship to diffuse support should be kept in mind. In addition, I will refer to support for office-holders as incumbent support.

For our purposes, a basic distinction between support for a given political system and for its office-holders is necessary. I do not dispute the popular view that Americans widely disapprove of their political system, frequently expressing views that could be characterized as loathing. But, as we will see, popular contempt is generally directed at the group of people who serve in government—and how they appear to behave—rather than the political system itself, to which most people are bound by strong ties of loyalty and affection.

2. SUPPORT FOR THE POLITICAL SYSTEM

As noted in the previous section, the principles on which American citizens can generally agree centre on support for the political system. The relevant principles are of two closely related kinds, centring on support for the institutional features of existing governments and for general, abstract norms of democracy. Although these two objects of support are clearly distinct, the contours of each are somewhat ill defined, and so they can overlap, especially if the American political system is described as encompassing democratic norms, as in Easton's account of political systems (above, p. 120). More significant than such theoretical imprecisions are practical difficulties with the available empirical data. In this section I will examine the results of a series of surveys which cumulatively provide strong evidence for widespread system support, although we will also see problems with the evidence. Evidence concerning support for democracy as a value is discussed in the following section.

The surveys I will examine are markedly crude in comparison to what we have seen in previous chapters. Although theorists disagree about important aspects of religion, they are able to employ developed scales which have been refined through repeated administration and in the reliability of which there is general confidence. Work on political tolerance is less polished; the reliability of scales has only recently begun to receive detailed attention (Finkel *et al.*, forthcoming: 44), while, as we have seen, there is disagreement about what tolerance is, and so how it should be measured. But a great advantage of tolerance research is the repeated administration of similar questions over almost half a century, which has afforded opportunities for sustained discussion of crucial issues. In the surveys on political support, in contrast, specific objects of inquiry vary considerably from study to study. On the whole, survey questions have not only not been tested for reliability, but there is relatively little discussion of normative aspects, especially why they focus on particular targets rather than others.[4] Moreover, many important questions have remained unaddressed. For the most part, survey questions do not carefully distinguish between support for regimes and for specific office-holders. A number of surveys have recorded strong support for abstract democratic norms. But the literature examined in previous chapters shows that such results can be misleading, because the norms many people actually hold contain tacit qualifications. The lack of studies applying norms of system support to particular circumstances is therefore a significant gap. Even if there is widespread system support on some general level, it is hard to know exactly what this means, in the absence of additional surveys that pit support for these norms against other values. To make matters worse, it is not clear how developed and sophisticated people's views are in regard to such matters. It is not unlikely that, even with more sophisticated survey instruments, results would be indecisive, because many people do not have coherent, formulated views about the different political principles to which they could subscribe.

This list of problems could be extended. But without minimizing such difficulties, we should note once again that surveys are the best evidence we have concerning people's political principles. The only alternatives to relying on this evidence are impressionistic assessments and 'armchair sociology'. As we will see, the overall direction in which the evidence points is clear, although it is difficult to formulate resulting principles with precision.

We can begin with Hibbing and Theiss-Morse's *Congress as Public Enemy* (Hibbing and Theiss-Morse 1995). Hibbing and Theiss-Morse organized a nationwide telephone survey of 1,443 respondents of voting age, conducted in 1992, which was supplemented by a series of focus groups. Their theoretically sophisticated survey provides perhaps the best evidence available concerning support for the United States political system.

Hibbing and Theiss-Morse criticize Easton for discussing the political system as an abstraction, because the political system of any given

---

[4] For valuable discussion of measurement issues in studies on a wide range of democratic values, see Finkel *et al.* (forthcoming).

country is composed of actual institutions and how they function. For example, in *A Framework for Political Analysis* (1965a), Easton writes: 'The critical questions for us do not relate to . . . the particular form of the internal structures or processes of the system' (p. 115; quoted by Hibbing and Theiss-Morse 1995: 15–16). Hibbing and Theiss-Morse argue that the 'vital objects of support in modern, developed political systems' are political institutions, which also bridge the gap between regime and authorities. They are 'where the regime meets the authorities', where individual political office-holders develop policies in accordance with the rules of their institutions (p. 16). Hibbing and Theiss-Morse therefore asked their respondents about their feelings about particular institutions. Their approach has the added advantage of providing evidence about exactly how support varies across different institutions (pp. 16–17).

Hibbing and Theiss-Morse framed their question in order to have respondents clearly distinguish between attitudes towards institutions and towards their occupants. Their language is as follows:

Now, I've asked you to rate some people in government, but sometimes when we talk about the parts of the government in Washington, like the Supreme Court, the presidency, and the Congress, we don't mean the people currently serving in office. These institutions have their own buildings, historical traditions, and purposes laid out in the Constitution. I'd like to know how warm or cold you feel toward these institutions, not the people currently in office. (p. 44)

Their survey yielded two figures for each institution, one in regard to the institution itself and one for occupants of offices. In each case, the gap between the two figures was significant. Support for the Supreme Court as an institution was 94 per cent; for the members of the Supreme Court, this was 73 per cent. Support for the presidency was 96 per cent; for the incumbent president (George Bush), support was 46 per cent. Support for Congress was a bit lower, at 88 per cent, while support for the members of Congress was an overwhelming 64 per cent lower, at 24 per cent (pp. 44–5). These levels of support for office-holders are consistent with the trust scores discussed in the previous section. Clearly distinguishing between institutions and office-holders allowed Hibbing and Theiss-Morse to establish what we can identify as a general consensus on system support, in spite of the absence of strong incumbent support. In response to other questions, 91 per cent of respondents approved (35 per cent approved strongly; 56 per cent approved) of 'the basic constitutional structure of the U.S. government', while only 8 per cent disapproved. Only nine respondents (0.06 per cent) strongly disapproved (p. 59).[5]

---

[5] Other studies of support for the Supreme Court provide figures similar to, though somewhat lower than Hibbing and Theiss-Morse's; see Tyler and Mitchell (1994:

Similar results were obtained in Hunter and Bowman's (1996) survey, which consisted of 2,047 face-to-face interviews. As we will see, this survey contained a wide range of questions in regard to social and political issues, with respondents conveniently classified according to religion, race, and other demographic variables. The responses Hunter and Bowman recorded provide important insights into the nature of system support.

Hunter and Bowman did not consistently craft their questions to have respondents distinguish between support for the political system and for office-holders. It seems likely that their slightly lower system support scores can be explained by respondents' failure clearly to make this distinction, with low levels of incumbent support serving as a drag on system support.[6] Hunter and Bowman's respondents reported low levels of confidence in office-holders. They were asked a series of questions closely related to the NES trust items. For instance, to the question 'How much confidence do you have that the people who run our government tell the truth to the public?' 3 per cent of respondents had a lot of confidence, 36 per cent some confidence, 39 per cent a little confidence, and 25 per cent no confidence (Hunter and Bowman 1996, vol. ii, table 8). When asked about their level of agreement with the statement that 'most elected officials don't care what people like you think', 69 per cent either completely agreed or mostly agreed (table 16A). Eighty-one per cent either completely or mostly agreed that 'government is run by a few big interests looking out for themselves' (table 16E). Seventy-eight per cent either completely or mostly agreed that 'our leaders are more concerned with managing their images than with solving our nation's problems' (table 16C).

Support for the political system was considerably higher. Favourable responses rose dramatically when people were asked to contrast the political system and the people running government. Asked about their level of agreement with the statement that 'our system of government is good, but the people running it are incompetent', 16 per cent completely agreed, and

803–4) (discussed below, in Ch. 8); for references and brief discussion of earlier surveys, see Tyler and Mitchell (1994: 753–6). However, employing questions that focus on 'support for the maintenance of the institution' rather than broader and less definite aspects of support for the Supreme Court, Caldeira and Gibson report somewhat lower figures over their five questions (Caldeira and Gibson 1992: 638). On their five questions, the average level of positive support among whites was 69.24%, while the percentage uncertain was 16.78%, and 14% were unsupportive (pp. 640–1). (For whites, minimum N was 794.) Given the somewhat theoretical nature of the questions Caldeira and Gibson employed, I believe that 'uncertain' responses should not be taken to indicate lack of support. For support levels among black respondents, and the wording of three of the questions used, see below, pp. 134–5.

[6] This appears to show up in the results recorded on table 12A; see below. In addition, compare the levels of confidence in different institutions of the federal government that they recorded; see Tables 14C, 14D, and 14A.

50 per cent mostly agreed (in comparison, 30 per cent mostly disagreed and 4 per cent completely disagreed) (table 16B). We should note that among those disagreeing here were, presumably, respondents who do not believe that the people running government are incompetent. Favourable responses to questions directly about the political system were high. To the question 'To what extent do you feel you should support our system of government?' 80 per cent responded positively, and another 11 per cent neutrally; only 2 per cent responded 'none at all' (table 12D).[7] To 'To what extent are you proud to live under our political system?' 76 per cent responded positively, and 12 per cent were neutral; 3 per cent responded 'none at all' (table 12B). To 'To what extent do you feel our system of government is the best possible system?' 69 per cent responded positively, and another 14 per cent were neutral; 4 per cent responded 'none at all' (table 12C). Responses were somewhat lower for 'To what extent do you have respect for the political institutions in America?': 56 per cent responded positively, and 20 per cent were neutral (table 12A). Once again, results on this question should probably be attributed in part to respondents not clearly differentiating institutions and their occupants. Ninety-six per cent of respondents selected as closest to their views either the statement that 'The US is the greatest country in the world, better than all other countries' or 'The US is a great country, but so are certain other countries' (55 per cent and 41 per cent, respectively). Only 4 per cent chose 'There are some other countries that are better than the US' (table 13).

The evidence of these national surveys can be supplemented with a brief look at a smaller survey conducted by E. N. Muller and colleagues, in conjunction with their examination of diffuse political support. Muller's analysis of diffuse support is among the most sophisticated in the literature. He developed a behavioural measure of the concept, arguing for empirical connections between respondents' levels of diffuse support and their behaviour in regard to the political system. Attempting to work out a measure of diffuse support that would clearly focus on the political system, rather than on office-holders, Muller and his colleagues developed a 'political support-alienation' (PSA) scale. They believe this 'focuses unambiguously on the political system' (Muller *et al.* 1982: 262), and has repeatedly been demonstrated to be a strong predictor of anti-system

[7] It is not clear how neutral responses should be handled, in light of the desire for consensus postulated by liberal theory. In reporting on surveys, I will indicate neutral responses but believe that in these particular cases they should be counted with positives as opposed to negatives. Presumably, the fact that people do not object to features of the government indicates that they could be brought to agree. I should note, however, that this position would dilute the commitments of liberal theory to entail that people be governed by principles that they accept or are indifferent to, as opposed to only principles they actively support.

political behaviour (p. 258; also Muller and Jukam 1977; Muller 1979). Believing that previous surveys had been weakened by 'extremely broad, crude response categories' (Muller *et al.* 1982: 242), Muller and his colleagues tested the items in the PSA scale for reliability (pp. 248–53). In the survey I will examine, PSA questions were administered in 1978 to a general population of 778 New York City adults and to 240 students and faculty members at Columbia and New York Universities. Muller and his colleagues also had the scale administered to small samples of 201 residents of San José, Costa Rica, in 1978, and 169 residents of Guadalajara, Mexico, in 1979. The questions that comprise the PSA scale are as follow:

(A) To what extent do you have respect for the political institutions in [COUNTRY]?
(B) To what extent do you think that the courts in [COUNTRY] guarantee a fair trial?
(C) To what extent do you feel that the basic rights of citizens are well protected by our political system?
(D) To what extent are you proud to live under our political system?
(E) To what extent do you feel our system of government is the best possible system?
(F) To what extent do you feel you should support our system of government?
(G) To what extent do you feel you and your friends are well represented in our political system?
(H) To what extent do you feel that your own political values differ from those of our political system? (p. 249)

Levels of diffuse support, as measured by the PSA scale, were high (all figures from p. 261). In the New York City general survey, 63.6 per cent of non-whites and 72.2 per cent of whites surveyed showed high support scores: 88.4 per cent of non-whites demonstrated positive levels of support; the figures for whites was 91.9 per cent. (The university sample, which was not divided accorded to race, demonstrated somewhat more alienation; 76.05 per cent showed positive support.) In Costa Rica the figures were even higher: 92.4 per cent of respondents showed positive levels of support.[8]

A final source of evidence for general attitudes towards the political system is people's feelings of obligation to obey the law. These were examined in Tom Tyler's survey of 1,575 residents of Chicago, conducted in 1984

[8] For additional surveys, which support the main claims made in this section, see Craig *et al.* (1990) and Almond and Verba (1965: 64–5); also 196–7, 13–15. We should recognize the possibility that strong responses on system support questions could in part result from subjects telling interviewers what they believe they want to hear. Kuklinski *et al.* (1997) argue that phenomena along these lines in part account for apparently declining racism among white Southerners. Cf. discussion of the work of Batson and different colleagues and Herek, above, pp. 93–4, 97 n. 15.

(discussed below, in Chapter 8). Previous studies had established that respondents generally hold strong feelings of obligation (see Tyler 1990: 31). Responses of Tyler's subjects (N = 1,575) supported these studies. Asked about the statement 'People should obey the law even if it goes against what they think is right', 82 per cent agreed. With 'I always try to follow the law even if I think that it is wrong', 82 per cent agreed. Eighty-four per cent agreed with 'If a person is doing something and a police officer tells them to stop, they should stop even if they feel that what they are doing is legal'. Seventy-nine per cent agreed with 'Disobeying the law is seldom justified' (Tyler 1990: 45). Responses to these questions are at or near the consensus level.[9]

In Chapter 3 we saw reasons to be sceptical about the meaning of responses to abstract questions concerning political values. The fact that respondents say that obeying the law is the right thing to do, or generally the right thing to do, could well leave room for a range of other considerations that could conflict with this moral requirement and on occasion override it. As with other abstract statements we have seen, we cannot rule out the possibility of tacit qualifications. In this case, however, there is some evidence that feelings of general obligation held in regard to specific cases. Tyler asked his respondents about the rightness or wrongness of various actions in violation of the law. In almost all cases, there was strong consensus that lawbreaking was wrong. Ninety-six per cent of respondents said it is wrong to make enough noise to disturb neighbours (very wrong, 61 per cent). Ninety-six per cent responded it is wrong to litter (very wrong, 63 per cent). One hundred per cent responded that drunk driving is wrong (95 per cent very wrong). Eighty-four per cent said that speeding is wrong (very wrong, 39 per cent). Ninety-nine per cent said shoplifting is wrong (very wrong, 92 per cent). Eighty-six per cent said parking illegally is wrong (very wrong, 37 per cent) (Tyler 1990: 44).[10]

Although feelings of political obligation should not be conflated with support for a given political system, these attitudes are obviously closely

---

[9] Responses on similar questions in a second wave of interviews (N = 804) were similar; see Tyler (1990: 46). Two additional questions, with response rates of 74% and 69%, are included at (1990: 45). In the latter of these, 69% of respondents agreed with: 'It is difficult to break the law and keep one's self respect' (p. 45). I view this question as unclear, because it raises the troublesome issue of self-respect.

[10] The value of these responses, however, is severely lessened by the fact that in his questions Tyler does not distinguish the extent to which these acts are wrong because of their consequences (*mala in se*) and because they violate the law (*mala prohibita*). For discussion of this distinction and its ramifications for questions of political obligation, see Klosko (1992: 15 ff.). For figures for levels of 'peer disapproval' in regard to these acts, see Tyler (1990: 44).

related. And so the obligation surveys provide additional substantiation of my claims concerning political support.

The levels of system support recorded in all these surveys may strike us as surprising in view of the strong anti-democratic sentiments observed in the previous two chapters. But the evidence clearly shows that large majorities of Americans support the political system, even though they would deny various rights to minority groups. In the last chapter I noted strong associations between religion—especially religion with a closed cognitive style—and anti-democratic sentiments. Thus it is important to note that evangelical Protestants are especially strong supporters of the political system. Orthodox Catholics, who are close to evangelicals in many theological respects, evince levels of system support that are similar, though slightly lower.[11]

These points are supported by Hunter and Bowman's survey. Their findings about evangelicals are generally consistent with what we saw in the last chapter. Evangelicals' responses to a variety of questions were closer than any other group to what we would expect of Altemeyer's 'right-wing authoritarians'. For instance, evangelicals were found to be unusually pessimistic about the situation of the nation. They responded more negatively than any other group in regard to whether the United States is declining or improving in regard to all of the following areas: education and schools (table 4B); family life (table 4C); the American work ethic (table 4D). They were found to be more worried than any other group about the condition of the nation as a whole (table 45); American families (table 46A); the national government (table 46B); the American economy (table 46C; here they were tied with orthodox Catholics); schools in America (table 46D); the nation's churches (table 46E); the country's 'moral and ethical condition' (table 46F), 'our elected officials in Washington' (table 46H), 'national political debates and discussions' (table 46I). On other questions, on which they were not the most worried group, the gap between evangelicals and other, more worried, groups was slight. On most of these questions orthodox Catholics were the second most pessimistic group.

Evangelicals' relatively gloomy outlook about the country was accompanied by advocacy of forms of discipline that was, again, consistently stronger than that of any other group. They scored highest (tied with orthodox Catholics) on how much they thought 'tougher laws and penalties to deter crime' would improve the country (table 47A), and responded far more strongly than any other group about how much they thought the

[11] For how evangelicals and orthodox Catholics are identified, see above, Ch. 4, Sect. 4.

country would be improved if 'more parents used spanking to discipline their children' (table 47c; also tables 93s and 96j). Evangelicals were highest in thinking that harsher sentences were very important in solving the country's crime problem (table 48d)—although they were not highest in favouring more prisons (table 48c) or more police (table 48b) to solve it. They were lowest in supporting more treatment and education to deal with crime (table 48b) and in support of legalizing drugs (table 48e). Eighty-eight per cent of evangelicals completely agreed or mostly agreed with the statement that 'Those who violate God's rules will be punished' (table 74h; 49 per cent and 39 per cent, respectively). The next highest score on this question was by orthodox Catholics, 77 per cent (table 74h: 29 per cent and 48 per cent, respectively).

Of the groups surveyed, evangelicals were least tolerant of homosexuals. On an entire list of questions, their attitudes towards homosexual people were the least favourable of any respondents, frequently by significant margins (with attitudes of orthodox Catholics generally second least favourable). These included granting homosexuals rights to marry (table 42b; also table 96d), to adopt children (table 42c), and to serve openly in the armed forces (table 42d), and requiring landlords to rent to them (table 42e). Evangelicals had the lowest rate of agreeing with the claim that a person is born with a given sexual orientation and can do little to change it (table 42a), and agreed more strongly than any other group with the statement that 'AIDS is God's way of punishing homosexuals' (table 42g). They responded most strongly that 'mere acceptance of homosexuality' is very bad for society (table 6e). By a wide margin, evangelicals agreed most that it is very wrong when adults of the same sex engage in sexual relations (table 93c). They expressed greater agreement than any other group with the view that homosexual behaviour, even between consenting adults, should be against the law (table 42f).

Hunter and Bowman's survey provides little information about attitudes towards other groups. But it is significant that evangelicals responded more strongly than any other group that marriage between blacks and whites is wrong (table 93d).

Evangelicals also possessed notably negative feelings towards the national government. Over 80 per cent either completely agreed or mostly agreed with all of the statements discussed above: that leaders in the United States are more concerned with managing their image than with solving the nation's problems (table 16c); that people in government waste a lot of tax money (table 16d); that government 'is run by a few big interests looking out for themselves' (table 16e); that the country 'is run by a close network of special interests, public officials, and the media' (table 16g); that 'most politicians are more interested in winning elections than doing what is right' (table 16L). On each of these questions, the scores for evangelicals were higher than for any other group. For instance, over 70 per cent of evangelicals completely agreed or mostly agreed that 'the federal government controls too much of our daily lives' (table 16H) and that 'most elected officials don't care what people like you think' (table 16A).

Responses to these questions paint a clear picture of evangelicals as having strongly negative attitudes towards the federal government. Their feelings are along the lines of what one would expect from the discussion of trust scores in Section 1, though consistently less favourable. Coupling these attitudes with evangelicals' tendency towards intolerance makes it striking that their attitudes in regard to system support not only are consistent with the polls discussed earlier in this section, but are the most favourable of the groups surveyed. On all four of the system support questions in table 12 (in regard to having respect for the US system of government, being proud of the US system of government, believing the US system of government is the best possible, and believing one should support our system of government; see above, pp. 125–6), evangelicals had higher percentages of respondents responding 'a great deal' than any other group. On no question was their level of overall positive scores lower than that of any group. Eighty-five per cent of evangelicals responded in the three highest categories on the question of the extent to which they feel they should support the American system of government; in comparison, in the next highest group, orthodox Catholics, 80 per cent were in these categories (table 12D). Higher percentages responded that the United States is the greatest country in the world or a great country, though there are other great countries (68 per cent, 31 per cent respectively) than any other group (table 13; see above, p. 126). Higher percentages of evangelicals reported positive feelings about the term 'patriotic' than any other group (table 44G).

Hunter and Bowman do not provide direct evidence on why evangelicals are so strongly supportive of the political system, in spite of all the negative attitudes charted here. But it seems likely that this is bound up with their overall cognitive style. As we saw in the last chapter, evangelicals are 'authority-minded'. It is likely that an attitude of deference similar to what they bring to their religious views and other areas of life carries over into their relationship with the national government. In spite of their disillusionment with how the existing government functions, they are solidly deferential to the overall system.[12]

---

[12] Instructive in this regard is the symposium 'The End of Democracy? The Judicial Usurpation of Politics' (Bork *et al.* 1996). The contributors were generally highly disappointed with recent governmental policies and decisions of the Supreme Court, which several believed were in conflict with God's law. However, although the

If this explanation is correct, then it has important implications in regard to increasing evangelicals' commitment to other democratic norms. If evangelical Protestants and other 'authority-minded' groups are deferential to the political system, then they are likely to pay especially respectful attention to moral requirements mandated by the system. Formally mandating stronger forms of tolerance and other democratic values could well legitimize them and afford them substantially greater allegiance. To quote Altemeyer (though on RWAs rather than evangelicals): 'Anti-discrimination laws can be quite beneficial. Ordinary authoritarians appear more likely to obey laws they dislike than others are. (It comes from being an authoritarian)' (Altemeyer 1996: 304). Something along these lines appears to have happened in the formerly segregated South as a result of the civil rights revolution. Within a generation support for values of racial tolerance and against racial prejudice and discrimination increased markedly.[13] It is not unlikely that similar attitudinal shifts in regard to other democratic values could be brought about by concerted political action.

In any case, whether or not this particular explanation of the attitudes of evangelicals is accepted, important points have been established. Support for the political system in the United States is extremely strong, in spite of the lower levels of support for other democratic values we have seen. One reason for this apparent disparity in attitudes is that system support levels are extremely high for specific religious groups that are likely to have especially low levels of commitment to other democratic values.

In addition to the views of evangelicals, we should briefly review evidence concerning attitudes of system support and incumbent support among different racial groups. In their survey Hunter and Bowman present valuable evidence concerning the attitudes of African Americans, Hispanics, and whites on the broad range of questions discussed in this section. This evidence is most conveniently presented in the form of a brief table (Table 5.2).

The results of the survey are inconclusive. System support scores are somewhat lower for African Americans, but not markedly so. On respect for political institutions, African Americans score 9 per cent higher than whites; on the question whether the United States is the best possible

contributors' arguments show how religious beliefs can lead people to question the legitimacy of the political system, in spite of their distrust contributors did not call for action against the system. At most, there were calls for civil disobedience, which, in accepting penalties, recognizes the system's legitimacy. Other proposals, to work through the courts and Congress and to amend the Constitution, also signify recognition of the legitimacy of the existing regime's processes.

[13] But note the recent study of Kuklinski *et al.* (1997); see above, n. 8.

Table 5.2. *Political support among African American, Hispanic, and white respondents*

Question	African American	Hispanic	White
System support (% positive)			
(12A) Respect for US political institutions	63	59	54
(12B) Proud to live under US political system	73	71	76
(12C) US system of government is best possible	63	62	70
(12D) Should support US system of government	78	71	81
(13) USA is the greatest country in the world or one of best	95	94	96
(44) Positive feelings about the term 'patriotic'	73	85	88
Incumbent support (% negative)			
(16A) Most elected officials don't care what people like you think	76	61	69
(16B) US system of government is good but people running it incompetent	74	63	65
(16C) US leaders are more concerned with their image than with the nation's problems	80	76	78
(16D) People in government waste a lot of tax money	89	87	92
(16E) Government is run by a few big interests	86	77	80
(16G) Government is run by a close network of interests, officials, and media	83	77	81
(16H) Government controls too much of our daily lives	75	51	62
(16I) People like you don't have a say in what government does	67	64	59
(16L) Politicians are more interested in winning elections than in doing what is right	81	81	79

Numbering refers to table numbers in Hunter and Bowman (1996: ii). Questions are presented in abbreviated form. Figures are limited to positive responses; they do not include neutral responses. The margin of error in the survey is ±2.

Source: Hunter and Bowman (1996: ii).

system of government, they score 7 per cent lower. On positive feelings about the term 'patriotic', they are 15 per cent lower than whites. Responses for Hispanics are generally lower than those of both whites and African Americans on these questions, though on feelings about the term 'patriotic', their responses are 12 per cent higher than African Americans, though 3 per cent behind whites.

On incumbent support responses, African Americans are consistently more distrustful than whites, by an average of some 5.1 per cent. The only question on which their score is lower (less negative) than whites is whether the government wastes tax money. Hispanics are consistently less negative towards incumbents than are either African Americans or whites. On the nine questions, their average negative response is 8.2 per cent lower than that of African Americans and 3.1 per cent lower than that of whites. There are two exceptions. On the question whether politicians are more interested in winning elections than in doing the right thing, their score is the same as African Americans' and 2 per cent higher than that of whites. On the question whether people like you have much say about what government does, their score is less negative than that of African Americans (by 3 per cent) but 5 per cent more negative than that of whites.

Hunter and Bowman's findings should be supplemented with results from James Gibson and Gregory Caldeira's sophisticated study of blacks' attitudes towards the United States Supreme Court.[14] In their survey of at least 435 blacks (and at least 794 whites) conducted in 1987, Gibson and Caldeira's main interest lay in determining and explaining levels of diffuse support among blacks. They measured these attitudes with questions designed to examine 'institutional commitment', which they describe as 'willingness to defend the basic structure of the institution against fundamental change' (Gibson and Caldeira 1992: 1121). Five statements were employed, for which respondents were asked to express support or lack of support. Two examples: 'The power of the Supreme Court to declare acts of Congress unconstitutional should be eliminated'; 'If the Supreme Court continually makes decisions that the people disagree with, it might be better to do away with the Court altogether' (p. 1129).

On the questions, responses of blacks were supportive but consistently less so than whites. Across the five statements, the percentage of blacks supportive was 54.44, in contrast to 26.9 per cent uncertain and 18.88 per cent unsupportive. The statement recording the lowest level of support was: 'The right of the Supreme Court to decide certain types of controversial issues should be limited by the Congress' (p. 1129). On this, 28.7 per cent of blacks were unsupportive, in contrast to 39.5 per cent sup-

---

[14] For their findings in regard to whites, see above, n. 5.

portive (28.3 per cent of whites were unsupportive, in contrast to 49.0 per cent supportive). Across the five questions, blacks were 14.8 per cent lower than whites on support, and 4.88 per cent higher on lack of support.

As one can imagine on the basis of the third question quoted above, given the somewhat theoretical nature of Gibson and Caldeira's questions I am not inclined to construe 'uncertain' responses as lack of support, though they must of course be kept separate from expressions of support. The fact that the views of blacks are lower than those of whites is a significant concern for proponents of liberal consensus or other democratic theories. But levels of support among blacks still place them roughly within the bounds of liberal consensus. We should also note that, as Hunter and Bowman's figures show, they maintain this level of system support in spite of generally lower levels of incumbent support.[15]

To conclude discussion in this section, one possible problem should be addressed. It could be argued that positive responses on the political system, like general support for abstract democratic norms, contains tacit qualifications. Thus we must address the possibility that the consensus examined here is no more meaningful than general consensus on democratic norms.

In the absence of more detailed survey evidence, it is not possible to say exactly what consensus on system support amounts to. However, it is important to note that this is definite in a way that democratic norms are not. Rather than responding to general questions about support for democracy, or support for such things as constitutional government or checks and balances (see the following section), respondents were asked about specific political entities, most notably the separate institutions of the American political system, in the Hibbing and Theiss-Morse surveys, while the questions in Muller's PSA scale also referred to specific institutions. The Hunter and Bowman questions repeatedly made reference to 'our system of government' or 'our political system', while scores here were comparable, though slightly lower, than those to the question comparing the United States to other countries.

It is likely that this consensus on support for the American political system is qualified in various ways. Many respondents no doubt have significant reservations about aspects of the American system of government. But support for this political system does not lend itself to the kind of clear qualifications that we saw on general democratic principles. Responses on

---

[15] For the relationship between specific and diffuse support among blacks, see Gibson and Caldeira (1992). In the Conclusion, I will briefly discuss means to broaden liberal consensus to include people who do not express support. For recent discussion of black–white differences on political trust (incumbent support), with additional references, see Emig *et al.* (1996).

questions concerning political obligation indicate willingness to accept decisions of the political process, even when these go against people's own views. In the following section I will look into abstract norms that are bound up with system support and their possible qualifications. But support for the political system appears to be relatively unqualified.

Although the evidence does not allow us to speak with assurance on reasons for general support for the American political system, it bears mention that this is consistent with commonly held beliefs. As a nation, the United States lacks unifying factors present in other countries, e.g. ethnic or religious homogeneity, or common cultural identity. Rather, disparate elements in the American melting-pot are often said to be united by adherence to a common political system and its founding tradition, as epitomized in the Constitution, Bill of Rights, and Declaration of Independence. If this is true, it would help to explain general support throughout the American population.

3. SUPPORT FOR DEMOCRATIC PRINCIPLES

Support for American democracy has implications for attitudes about democracy as a political value. Certain norms of democracy—'its operating rules and rules of the game'—are included by Easton in his concept of regime support (1965*b*: 200–1), and we will look into what this entails. Some relevant evidence has been seen in the tolerance literature, though this of course has the problems we have discussed. It is unfortunate that, in spite of the great importance of the attitudes in question, relatively little research has been conducted. There is a paradox here. Consensus levels of support for democratic norms appear to have discouraged further inquiry. The absence of measurable differences in people's commitment to these values made it unlikely that they would have predictive value, and so researchers turned to other concerns.[16] In recent years a number of surveys have been conducted on support for democratic norms in newly democratic states, especially the former Soviet Union and former East Germany (for discussion of these surveys, see Finkel *et al.*, forthcoming). The curious result is that there is better evidence on popular attitudes about democratic norms in these countries than in the United States and other developed democracies. But again, this is probably because of the general view that in the latter countries support for democratic norms is at the consensus level.

[16] I am grateful to Steven Finkel for this point.

In the absence of strong evidence about attitudes towards democratic norms in the United States, I will turn to other sources. Extensive evidence is available concerning attitudes of West Europeans, especially the biannual Eurobarometer surveys of the populations of the member states of the European Union. It must of course be borne in mind that these surveys do not examine Americans, and so the data must be used with care. However, in certain cases, especially when there is strong agreement across a large number of different countries and the belief in question is intuitively plausible, it is reasonable to assume that it would be accepted by similar levels of Americans. The hypothesis that Americans and West Europeans share at least certain democratic beliefs is supported by their similar responses on the tolerance surveys discussed in Chapter 3. Evidence concerning Europeans is of course not direct evidence about the attitudes of Americans and should not be treated as such. But in the absence of direct evidence, employing it, with suitable qualifications, seems defensible.

Eurobarometer surveys have indicated extremely high levels of support for 'democracy' as a value. Respondents in thirteen countries were asked about their attitudes towards the idea of democracy, apart from existing political systems, and about democracy as a form of government. The two questions were as follows (Fuchs *et al.* 1995: 349). First question: 'Let us consider the idea of democracy, without thinking of existing democracies. In principle, are you for or against the idea of democracy?' Second question: 'Which of the following opinions about different forms of government is closet to your own? (1) In any case, democracy is the best form of government, whatever the circumstances may be. (2) In certain cases a dictatorship can be positive. (3) For someone like me it doesn't make any difference whether we have a democracy or a dictatorship.' Responses to the first question demonstrate overwhelming support for democracy as an ideal, over 90 per cent in all countries, over 95 per cent in nine of the thirteen countries surveyed. Scores ranged from 98.7 per cent in Greece and 98.5 per cent in Portugal to lows of 92.9 per cent in both Italy and Belgium. With justification, one researcher characterizes these response rates as 'astonishingly high' (Thomassen 1995: 383).

Support for democracy as a form of government (i.e. choosing answer 1 to the second question) was less high, ranging from 92.8 per cent in Denmark and 92.2 per cent in Greece, to 64.9 per cent and 65.3 per cent in Ireland and Northern Ireland, respectively. Putting these exceptions aside, the lowest recorded levels of support were 74 per cent for Italy and 76.4 per cent for Belgium. Ten of the thirteen countries had response rates above the 75 per cent level generally used to indicate consensus. Analysing these data, Dieter Fuchs and his colleagues note that because support for democracy as a form of government is more closely related to satisfaction with the existing government, the gap between the two response rates is not surprising (Fuchs *et al.* 1995: 348).[17]

The nature of the responses to these two questions suggests that Americans would share similar levels of support for democracy, both as idea and as form of government. It seems likely that support for democracy as idea would surpass the 90 per cent level seen in all the European countries, and, in all probability, the 95 per cent level seen in nine of the thirteen countries. The question concerning satisfaction with democracy as a form of government would appear to tap into attitudes similar to those addressed by the system support surveys discussed in the previous section, especially the survey of Hibbing and Theiss-Morse (1995). Thus it is likely that support for democracy in this respect would be at a level similar to what we saw in regard to the separate institutions about which Hibbing and Theiss-Morse asked.

If this evidence allows us to postulate general support for democracy among Americans, then what people mean by 'democracy' becomes an important question. Once again, the absence of clear survey evidence makes it difficult to respond with precision. Obviously, democracy is 'a multidimensional concept' (Thomassen 1995: 384). It seems clear that democratic systems encompass related but distinguishable principles of at least two kinds: support for majority rule and support for minority rights. By majority rule I mean a collection of familiar norms, such as that decisions are to be made through free and fair voting processes, different people's preferences are to be weighed equally, and so the preferences that have the most support are chosen. There are of course different ways in which votes can be weighed or counted, no one of which is obviously best from a normative perspective. Rather, the requirement here is that procedures be 'tolerably fair', treating people reasonably equally.[18] In addition, an important component of democratic procedures is that all members of the community should accept outcomes reached. If they wish to alter what is decided, they must work within the system to do so. Other elements of majority rule could be noted. While in the absence of clear evidence it may be difficult to formulate these with precision, we can postulate features of

[17] For average levels of support for democracy in people's own countries during the period 1976–91, see Fuchs *et al.* (1995: 341). These figures were significantly lower. Four countries were above the 70% level, eight between 50% and 69%, and two below 50% (Northern Ireland at 35% and Italy at 24%.) Presumably, these responses reflected far more of what we have identified as incumbent support, which brought them down.

[18] For discussion of normative issues in this regard, with further references, see Klosko (1992, ch. 3).

possible procedures that are clearly excluded. For instance, practices such as weighing certain votes more than others, allowing some people to vote more than once, placing significant barriers to certain people's ability to vote, or using threats or intimidation to influence votes, are clearly excluded from the realm of acceptable procedures. Along similar lines, elections must actually be contested; opposition parties must not be prevented from competing on relatively even terms. If the opposition does win, the governing parties must not refuse to relinquish power. This list could be extended. In regard to actual political processes, what is commonly meant by 'free and fair elections' is a combination of reasonably fair procedures and the absence of obviously objectionable features. Departures from acceptable norms and practices are easily recognized and would disqualify a given process from being acceptable. Although we lack survey evidence concerning general exclusion of such practices, it seems safe to surmise that these views are widely shared.[19]

In addition to principles of majority rule, acceptable democratic procedures include a modicum of minority rights. Fair elections require free exchange of information, and so freedom of speech and the press, rights to stage political rallies and demonstrations, and other, similar rights, regardless of people's political views. This means that criticism of and opposition to government policies must be allowed. Effective opposition is a crucial feature of democratic processes. People must not be barred from receiving adequate information about political questions, from voting, etc. We can extend this idea. In order to be able to participate meaningfully in democratic processes, people must have at least a minimal level of education, including instruction about the political system and how it works. They must also have the leisure time necessary properly to inform themselves about political matters. Because of the close relationship between these aspects of a democratic system and rights to speak or publish as one pleases, to be free from certain forms of government interference, and so on, the dividing-line between majority rule and minority rights is difficult to draw. The two notions are not only conceptually linked but imply one another. Once again, the list of rights necessarily implied by a democratic system is difficult to draw. Though, as we will see, survey evidence is of some help, it is likely that different people conceive of the rights in question differently and would disagree about the levels of different rights that are necessary. But, as noted in Chapter 1, in spite of problems in determining the exact shape or level of different rights with precision, there is little doubt that they must be respected in some form. Absence of free

---

[19] I should note that the argument here does not rule out extending procedures in various ways to increase citizens' opportunities for democratic deliberation; for possible examples, see Gutmann and Thompson (1996).

speech, a free press, or rights for groups to associate and hold political rallies would clearly disqualify a given process from being acceptable. The political systems we are likely to recognize as legitimate democracies guarantee acceptable levels of all of these.

Once again, in order to gain insight into the nature of democratic systems, we can employ survey evidence concerning West Europeans. Important evidence on the main features of democratic political systems is provided by surveys conducted by the Allensbach Institute in West Germany in 1978, 1986, and 1990, and in East Germany in 1990 (Fuchs *et al.* 1995). The data were analysed by Fuchs, Guidorossi, and Svensson. These surveys support a conception of democracy along the lines I have sketched. Respondents were given a list of characteristics generally viewed as central features of democracies and asked which ones they believed a country must have in order to qualify as a democracy. I provide an abbreviated table (Table 5.3).[20]

Table 5.3. *Features of democracies* (%)

Feature	West Germany, 1978, 1986, 1990 (average)	East Germany 1990
Freedom of expression/of press	88	92
Equality before the law	86	88
Choice between several parties	83	85
Periodic free and secret elections	79	84
Freedom to travel	79	76
Freedom of religion	77	83
Every vote counts equally at elections	77	76

Source: Fuchs *et al.* (1995).

Fuchs and his colleagues describe the results as 'remarkable': 'Almost by common consent, the citizens of both West and East Germany consider several basic rights and some aspects of the competitive party system as the constitutive characteristics of a democracy' (1995: 331–2). In addition, as Fuchs and his colleagues note, the features identified correspond 'almost exactly to the basic institutions of a polyarchy' identified by Robert Dahl as the necessary features of a democratic system (1995: 332; Dahl 1971). The extent of agreement between citizens of West and East Germany is especially striking, because the latter was just emerging from more than forty years of communist domination. On five of the seven

[20] The figures here revise Fuchs *et al.* (1995: 331) slightly, correcting what appears to be a transcription error in the last entry, on the basis of averaging the three data points in Noelle-Neumann and Köcher (1993: 558). The wording of the question is available in Fuchs *et al.* (1995: 331) and Noelle-Neumann and Köcher (1993: 558).

features identified (all but freedom to travel and votes counting equally), agreement among East Germans was higher than among West Germans.[21]

Thus there appears to be strong agreement among Germans as to what constitutes democracy. Though we do not have comparable data for Americans, there are reasons to believe that they would respond similarly. This contention is supported by both the high levels of agreement in Germany and the commonsensical nature of the features identified.

However, even if we grant that this level of support for democratic norms can be postulated for Americans, we confront an obvious problem. Support for abstract principles could mask important tacit qualifications. Unfortunately, lacking the voluminous studies discussed in Chapter 3, we must be far more tentative here. The main surveys I will examine have been discussed in Chapter 3, those conducted by Prothro and Grigg (1960) and McClosky (1964).[22] As we have seen, these surveys were concerned mainly with tolerance for the rights of minority groups. But they also provide evidence concerning attitudes towards other democratic principles.

As noted in Chapter 3, Prothro and Grigg asked their respondents, residents of Tallahassee, Florida, and Ann Arbor, Michigan, to agree or disagree with a series of statements expressing democratic norms in abstract terms. The statements, which were intended to cover essential features of democracy, are as follows (Prothro and Grigg 1960: 282):

1. Democracy is the best form of government.
2. Public officials should be chosen by majority vote.
3. Every citizen should have an equal chance to influence government policy.
4. The minority should be free to criticize majority decisions.
5. People in the minority should be free to try to win majority support for their opinions.

As noted in Chapter 3, Prothro and Grigg discovered consensus on all these principles. Levels of agreement ranged from 94.7 to 98 per cent (p. 284). This supports extending the results of the Eurobarometer surveys to the United States. But, as we saw above, when respondents were asked about specific applications of these general statements, consensus evaporated (1960: 286). Prothro and Grigg asked respondents about five statements that were intended as 'specific embodiments' of statements 2 and 3, above, to which they refer as the 'principle of majority rule'. These

[21] For similar features identified in a mass survey in the Netherlands, in the early 1970s, when respondents were asked what they thought of when they heard the word 'democracy', see Thomassen (1995: 384–6).

[22] Also see McClosky and Zaller (1984: 317–19) on clear and contested norms. It should be noted that Sullivan and his colleagues also tested some of the statements used in the two surveys discussed here (Sullivan *et al.* 1982: 202–7).

statements are as follows (with the percentage providing democratic responses in brackets) (Prothro and Grigg 1960: 282–5):

1. In a city referendum, only people who are well informed about the problem being voted on should be allowed to vote. [49 per cent]
2. In a city referendum deciding on tax-supported undertakings, only tax-payers should be allowed to vote. [21 per cent]
3. If a Negro were legally elected mayor of this city, the white people should not allow him to take office. [80.6 per cent]
4. If a Communist were legally elected mayor of this city, the people should not allow him to take office. [46.3 per cent]
5. A professional organization like the AMA (the American Medical Association) has a right to try to increase the influence of doctors by getting them to vote as a bloc in elections. [45 per cent]

Thus we see qualifications of general principles here as well. It seems to me that the relationships statements 2 and 5 bear to the principle of majority rule might not have been apparent to many respondents, and I will set them aside. But the other three statements clearly concern democratic principles. Some 20 per cent of respondents were willing to abridge central democratic norms to avoid a black mayor, and over half to avoid a communist mayor. These responses suggest psychological processes similar to those discussed in Chapter 3.

Related results are found in McClosky's survey. This survey, also discussed in Chapter 3, included separate national and élite samples, and was conducted in 1957–8. A series of scales were employed in order to inquire into a range of democratic norms and attitudes. Especially interesting for our purposes are a set of statements used to examine people's attitudes to what McClosky identifies as 'rules of the game'. Selected items are as follows. For each statement, positive responses are undemocratic. I put the levels of agreement (i.e. of non-democratic responses) of national and élite samples respectively, in brackets after each statement (McClosky 1964: 365):

[1] There are times when it almost seems better for the people to take the law into their own hands rather than wait for the machinery of government to act. [26.9 per cent, 13.3 per cent]
[2] The majority has the right to abolish minorities if it wants to. [28.4 per cent, 6.8 per cent]
[3] I don't mind a politician's methods if he manages to get the right things done. [42.4 per cent, 25.6 per cent]
[4] Almost any unfairness or brutality may have to be justified when some great purpose is being carried out. [32.8 per cent, 13.3 per cent]
[5] Politicians have to cut a few corners if they are going to get anywhere. [43.2 per cent, 29.4 per cent]

[6] It is all right to get around the law if you don't actually break it. [30.2 per cent, 21.2 per cent]

In no case, as we can see, was the national sample's level of non-democratic responses below 25 per cent, and so on none of these 'rules of the game' was the 75 per cent agreement level that McClosky views as consensus achieved. But on most questions here—and most others in McClosky's table—the élite sample maintained democratic consensus.

In this survey the applications of democratic principles are less straightforward than in the tolerance studies—and in some of Prothro and Grigg's questions—and so the discrepancies with general principles less glaring. But clearly, the general norms here concern 'rules of the game', which significant minorities were willing to abridge for the sake of getting things done, most notably the 'great purpose' mentioned in statement 4. Questions of detail aside, these two surveys suggest that the democratic norms many citizens uphold contain tacit qualifications. Without firm evidence, however, we cannot say much more about exactly what these look like. Because of widespread differences in beliefs and attitudes throughout the American population, it is unlikely that there is a single set of democratic principles that is the focus of strong consensus. However, general support for the political system appears to provide a way round this difficulty. Democratic procedures can be used to adjudicate disputes about democratic principles. Because different citizens support the political system, they should support its determinations in this regard—as in regard to other liberal norms. This is a central principle of liberal consensus, discussed throughout the remainder of this chapter.

Support for the political system also has important implications in regard to the rights liberal citizens should support. As I have noted, for democratic decision-making to function properly, a range of rights must be protected. These include freedom of speech, free press, free association, etc. Even if liberal citizens accept weak rights principles in these areas, support for norms of democracy should entail something stronger; support for democracy can strengthen the rights principles to which people are committed and which can be justified to them. Logical connections here are sufficiently clear to establish adherence to stronger rights, even if such principles conflict with other principles people accept.[23]

Consider the case of Jones, who supports the American political system, some form of democracy, and general rights principles, but is opposed to allowing Nazis or atheists to demonstrate or publicize their views. Thus

[23] It is conceivable that subjects could reject their support for democracy in order to render their beliefs consistent. Given high levels of support, I view this alternative as generally unlikely. This issue is discussed briefly below, in the Conclusion.

the rights principles to which she adheres should be identified as weak. In a case like this, we can assume that her support of rights is qualified by other values, presumably legal moralism. She believes that various forms of destructive or hate speech (as she views them) would undermine the community's traditions or solidarity and so should not be allowed. Perhaps she would argue that such expression does not warrant protection, as the United States Supreme Court has argued that obscene material, 'which is utterly without redeeming social value', is not protected by the First Amendment (*Memoirs* v. *Massachusetts*, 383 U.S. 413 (1966)). Jones's position is not consistent with the presumption in favour of liberty presented by many liberal theorists, e.g. Feinberg's conception of liberalism (see above, Chapter 3, Section 3). But central to political liberalism is recognition of the fact that justificatory arguments for strong rights principles rest on assumptions that are not likely to be generally adhered to in pluralistic societies. Jones would no doubt recognize the value of developing certain human faculties, as discussed by Mill, or a conception of autonomy such as that discussed by Nozick (1974: 48–51). But she could well place relatively little weight on these concerns and more on other, conflicting values. Jones's desire to stamp out behaviour that is potentially disruptive of social order does not necessarily rest on a distinctive comprehensive moral view, while general considerations along these lines are not obviously indefensible. Thus it is not clear immediately that stronger rights principles that require allowing the groups in question to demonstrate could be justified to her.

But if Jones is committed to democratic political systems, it is not clear that she can continue to support restrictive rights. Access to a full range of opinions is central to democratic processes. In support of this point, I quote Alexander Meikeljohn:

> When men govern themselves, it is they—and no one else—who must pass judgment upon unwisdom and unfairness and danger. And that means that unwise ideas must have a hearing as well as wise ones, unfair as well as fair, dangerous as well as safe, un-American as well as American. Just so far as, at any point, the citizens who are to decide an issue are denied acquaintance with information or opinion or doubt or disbelief or criticisms which is related to that issue, just so far the result must be ill-considered, ill-balanced planning for the general good. (Meikeljohn 1948: 26)

Exactly which rights are necessary for effective democracy is a controversial question. We saw in Chapter 3 that democratic systems commonly place some restriction on democratic rights. But even if we grant this, the requirements of democracy provide an additional argument to strengthen the rights commitments of liberal citizens. In the case of Jones, even though she believes that free speech of atheists and Nazis is detrimental to the community and so should be restricted, her recognition that allowing these groups to speak is necessary for full democratic deliberation could lead her to curb her intolerant impulses. Obviously, in a diverse society people will respond to these considerations differently, and it is not clear that they would be profoundly persuasive to citizens with highly qualified conceptions of democracy. But taking these considerations into account, we should still recognize that this is an additional argument that could be effective in many cases. It should be noted, however, that this line of argument holds only for rights that can be shown to be integrally bound up with the workings of democratic systems (see Meikeljohn 1948: 93–102). For instance, it is not likely to be able to justify rights to publish sexually explicit or otherwise obscene materials to people who view this kind of activity as profoundly offensive or destructive of community values.

For both moral and practical reasons, disagreement about the nature of preferred democratic principles, including the scope of democratic rights such processes entail, can best be resolved democratically. On moral grounds, democratic means of settling disputes are obviously defensible, provided the mechanisms in question are tolerably fair (see Klosko 1992, ch. 3). If consensus cannot be reached through other means (see below, Chapter 7), democratic agreement can be assumed to be the most desirable alternative, especially because democratic decision-making is generally accepted and so able to be justified to almost all members of the population. On practical grounds, democratic processes, which afford rights to participate to all citizens, are likely to generate more support than other kinds of political decision-making mechanism.[24] The fact that they are widely supported in all the industrial democracies is itself a strong consideration in their favour.

The principle that democratic procedures should set the contours of democratic principles can be extended to democratic procedures as well. Although the political system and its institutions are generally supported, existing structures are not ineluctably given. Disagreements about their form too should be settled democratically. In this sense, democratic procedures are 'reflexive'; they must be invoked to determine their own shape.[25] We can call this principle the 'procedural norm of democracy'. Although people may not be aware of subscribing to it, it can be justified to them as implied by their support of the democratic political system. This is also in keeping with the practice of democratic systems, and so should be acceptable to many people.

---

[24] For discussion of one possible psychological source of support for democratic procedures, see below, Ch. 8.

[25] The term 'reflexive' is taken from Solum (1993).

Roughly formulated, this principle holds that the precise contents of a given right or other democratic principle in country X must be determined by appropriate procedures in X's political system. Among matters the political system must determine are how the right in question should interact with other democratic principles, and so the qualifications it contains.

On the basis of our discussion of democratic systems, it is possible to present a series of norms that should be included in liberal consensus. Once again, these principles can be formulated only roughly; their details must be filled in through democratic procedures. There are four main principles:

1. Support for the value of democracy as morally desirable, although this may be qualified by concern for other values.

2. Support for fair democratic political procedures.

3. Support for an important range of rights as necessary for the proper working of democratic political systems. We can refer to these as democratic rights, recognizing the likelihood of considerable overlap between them and the rights discussed in Chapter 3.

4. Support for the rule that in a pluralistic society the precise contours of the three principles noted here and other important rules and norms must be determined through the workings of democratic procedures. Once again, we can refer to this as the procedural norm of democracy.

4. PROCEDURAL LIBERALISM

The principles put forth in the last section are bound up with Americans' support for their political system and the democratic norms it embodies. The central role democratic procedures must play in delineating the principles of liberal consensus identifies this theory as highly 'procedural', as opposed to 'substantive'. There are of course significant substantive components of the principles I have outlined, especially rights principles— whether weak or strong—which are almost universally accepted, and supplemented by support for democratic rights. Democratic procedures must also work within the contours of other commitments of liberal theory discussed in Chapter 1. The dividing-line between procedural and substantive principles is inherently difficult to draw (on which, more below), while commitment to democratic procedures is itself an important substantive principle. But the point remains that the scope of the substantive principles I have identified must be determined by democratic procedures (i.e. the substance of principle 4).

Because of their dependence on the operation of political procedures, the principles I have identified are vulnerable to what could be viewed as abuse. If the majority of citizens are strongly opposed to a given minority group, then the latter could well have its rights curtailed. Although such actions could contravene basic commitments of liberal theory, the possibility still remains that hostile majorities could impose disadvantages on minorities that fall short of flagrant disregard of the latter's rights that would be necessary to disqualify such actions immediately. Clear examples we have come across are widespread desires to curtail various forms of expression in order to protect other values. I view possibilities such as this as a severe problem with liberal consensus. But it should be borne in mind that, in spite of their shortcomings, democratic procedures are able to serve the central function of political liberalism. Their importance can be seen if we look briefly at a discussion of liberal disagreements in Larmore's *Patterns of Moral Complexity* (Larmore 1987).

Like other theorists, Larmore notes that political liberalism is necessitated by pervasive disagreements in liberal societies. In the portion of his book that interests us, he discusses connections between liberal disagreements and 'a universal norm of rational dialogue' (p. 53). He argues that disagreements in liberal societies should be addressed through rational dialogue. When people disagree about specific issues, 'those who wish to continue the conversation should retreat to *neutral ground*, with the hope either of resolving the dispute or bypassing it' (p. 53).

The question that interests us here is the nature of this neutral ground. The studies I have examined, especially those concerning psychology of religion in the previous chapter, lead one to doubt the existence of substantive neutral moral grounds of the kind Larmore suggests. It seems unlikely that there is a set of premises waiting to be discovered that would (*a*) be acceptable to proponents of widely different comprehensive moral, religious, and philosophical views, and also (*b*) be sufficiently robust to allow disputants to proceed from them to generally accepted conclusions of disputed moral issues. Larmore does not explain what the necessary neutral principles are, while as we will see in Chapter 7, the most notable attempt to provide them, those derivable from 'intuitive ideas' latent in the public culture of liberal societies, discussed by Rawls in *Political Liberalism*, is unconvincing. Accordingly, one great advantage of the principles discussed in this chapter is that they constitute an adequate neutral ground in Larmore's sense. By adverting to them, disputants could resolve their disagreements through means that would be mutually acceptable. Although the principles can be viewed as lacking in terms of normative content, they do have the considerable advantages of (*a*) being likely to be widely accepted in liberal society, and (*b*) being able to fulfil the main function that the principles of political liberalism are supposed to fulfil.

To conclude this chapter, I will discuss the distinction between 'procedural' and 'substantive' liberalism, and defend this against a recent argument that seeks to collapse the two. Though the dividing-line between procedure and substance is not hard and fast, there is a clear difference.

The importance of procedural fairness (or procedural justice, terms I will use interchangeably) in liberal political theory has long been recognized. Locke of course argues that the primary purpose of government is to provide a neutral means of settling disputes. People are partial to their own interests, and so, if left to their own devices, would fall into conflict (Locke 1988, Second Treatise, chs. 2–3). More recently, prominent liberal theorists have identified the liberal public good with the practice of fair procedures rather than pursuit of specific outcomes (e.g. Benn and Peters 1959; Hampshire 1989, ch. 4; Dahl 1989).

Procedural justice, as opposed to substantive justice, centres on the moral acceptability of means for making decisions. In the words of Michael Bayles: 'Procedure concerns the process or steps taken in arriving at a decision; substance concerns the content of the decision' (Bayles 1990: 3). The universe of possible decisions is large, with corresponding diversity as to what constitutes procedural justice in different contexts (see below, Chapter 8). What all relevant procedures share is means to select from possible alternatives, whether this is the winner of a court case, the guilt or innocence of an accused party, choice of principles to allocate some good, or which of possible social policies to implement. In certain cases, a procedure itself will yield a clear outcome, for example, the winner of a lottery or the verdict in a trial. In other cases, procedures select officials who will make policy decisions, through election, appointment, or other means.

The importance of distinguishing procedural justice and substantive justice is disputed by Joshua Cohen, who argues that the operation of democratic procedures is so closely circumscribed by substantive restraints that the distinction effectively disappears. In his words, 'the distinction between procedure and substance is not a fundamental distinction in political justification' (Cohen 1994: 593; also 1996). The reason for this: 'democracy is, in its *preconditions*, *implications*, and *rationale*, a substantive as well as a procedural ideal' (1994: 600). Cohen disputes the claim that procedural agreement is easier to attain than agreement on substantive matters. As we have seen, in order for a fair democratic procedure to exist, citizens must be guaranteed a litany of rights, not only to free participation, but to unrestricted information and debate, and to adequate education (pp. 602–3). Similarly, democratic procedures cannot produce *any* decision; they must yield results consistent with citizens' basic rights (pp. 604–5). Because of the substantive prerequisites of democratic procedures, Cohen believes that the prospects for a more general overlapping consensus are on a par with the prospects for constitutional consensus on basic democratic or constitutional norms (p. 600).

Although Cohen casts valuable light on the relationship between concerns of procedural and substantive justice, I do not believe he narrows the gap as much as he would like. There are two issues here that should be distinguished. First, on a general level, though agreement on procedures clearly does carry substantive commitments, the extent of these remains to be determined. Fair democratic procedures must operate within the confines of important moral constraints and require the existence of a range of rights throughout the community. It is possible that Cohen would be able to demonstrate that, in particular areas, the implications of widely shared background assumptions could lead to agreement without resort to procedures. For example, it is clear that democratic procedures cannot yield policies that blatantly discriminate against religious minorities (see Cohen 1994: 604–5). But beyond this point, agreement is more difficult to achieve. Exactly what constitutes discrimination is a subject about which both citizens and moral philosophers disagree. Does it mean that organized prayer in public schools is disallowed? What about a moment of silence? Should religious groups be allowed to practice polygamy—or to use otherwise outlawed drugs in their rituals? It seems likely that, as a matter of practical necessity, these and countless other questions must be resolved by acceptable procedures. Secondly, the substantive commitments procedures carry could well differ with different procedures in different areas. But exactly what these are in each area must be worked out before we can ascertain the extent to which procedures are still necessary, and so how important the distinction between substance and procedures remains. In other words, procedure and substance cannot simply be said to coalesce. We require detailed examination of specific procedures and their substantive backdrops. In the absence of detailed analysis, the claim of coalescence will remain unconvincing. Until such analysis is put forth, procedures will remain central to feasible democratic theory.

6

Distributive Justice

I n certain ways opinions concerning distributive justice are similar to those we have seen about democratic rights. I will explore attitudes in regard to three main areas: preferred principles of distribution; assessments of how well society conforms to these; and attitudes towards possible governmental policies to bring society closer to preferred norms. As we will see, there is general agreement throughout society on a certain principle of distribution. But, as we have seen in previous chapters, people differ a good deal on applications to particular circumstances. It is commonly said that in American society there is less agreement on economic values than on basic features of democracy. For instance, McClosky and Zaller observe, in regard to the former, 'though mainly occurring within relatively limited boundaries, [economic debate in the United States] ranges from support for laissez-faire to support for welfare capitalism or even a mixed economy with marked socialist features' (McClosky and Zaller 1984: 294). Although in the two decades since McClosky and Zaller's survey socialist proposals have probably become less common, economic debate could still be viewed as more wide-ranging than political debate. As McClosky and Zaller note, aside from 'a handful of political extremists', few opinion leaders openly oppose values such as freedom or equality or advocate authoritarian rule (p. 294).

Claims such as these, however, are misleading. McClosky and Zaller's comparison conflates different levels of analysis. The economic disagreements they note could be described as occurring on the level of policy. But if we ascend to the level of more abstract principles, we discover consensus in the economic realm as well. In this sense, opinions on questions of distribution are like those we have seen concerning rights and democracy. However, as in these other cases, we will see that opinions become more variegated as they become more concrete.

1. PRINCIPLES OF DISTRIBUTIVE JUSTICE

Since the time of Aristotle it has been well known that there are different principles according to which goods or values can be distributed 'fairly'. Briefly, Aristotle distinguishes between 'arithmetic' and 'geometric' justice. In accordance with the former principle, people who are equal in some respect are treated equally; according to the latter, people who are unequal are treated unequally (*Politics* 3.8, 5.1). To make the distinction clear, we should distinguish four things: (*a*) the good being distributed, (*b*) the people to whom it is distributed, (*c*) the principle according to which it is distributed, and (*d*) the characteristic of the people in virtue of which the principle is applied to them. In regard to (*d*), Aristotle writes: 'We make bad mistakes if we neglect this "for whom" when we are deciding what is just' (*Politics* 1280ª13–14: Aristotle 1981: 195). What Aristotle means by 'for whom' is the characteristic of people that is relevant to the distribution in question. To take a simple example, in the American political system all citizens have the right to vote. Obviously, the good in this case is the right to vote, which is distributed to all American citizens alike. The principle of distribution is what Aristotle calls 'arithmetic' in that all subjects receive similar quantities of the good in question. In this example, the 'for whom' is American citizens. People receive the right to vote under the description of 'American citizens'—a respect in which all are equal—rather than, say, simply the description 'people', which is not the basis for distribution. Thus explicating 'for whom' is necessary to flesh out the distributive principle.

'Geometric' distribution is most clearly applicable in competitive situations. In a race, the prize goes to the winner. Or in a chemistry class, students are graded according to their performance on exams and laboratory exercises. In the race, what is distributed is the prize. The people involved are the contestants. The principle is 'geometric', treating people unequally in regard to a respect in which they are unequal, as all contestants do not receive similar prizes. The 'for whom' in this case, the respect in which people are unequal, is their performance in the race. We should note that in a situation of this kind, people are treated fairly in regard to distribution of the prize only if the conditions under which they compete are substantially equal. Thus we could say that a 'geometric' norm of distribution requires that 'arithmetic' norms be implemented in regard to opportunities to compete. Granted this proviso, the examples of the right to vote and the racing prize illustrate that, although different principles of distribution are involved, both distributions are intuitively fair. In both cases, the people involved can be viewed as having been treated 'equally'.

Studies have shown that Americans generally subscribe to principles of 'geometric' distribution in regard to economic goods. For purposes of linguistic ease, I will refer to these as principles of 'merit' and to 'arithmetic' principles as principles of 'equal distribution'. For Americans, deeply wedded to values of capitalism as well as democracy, distribution of economic goods through the free market is generally viewed as fair. The distributive principle in question upholds allocation of goods according to the qualities valued by the economic market-place, which in this regard constitute 'merit'. What Samuel Kluegel and Eliot Smith (1986) refer to as 'the dominant ideology' concerning economic inequality in the United States is a set of linked claims, which are as follows. First, there is abundant opportunity for economic advancement if one works hard. It therefore follows that people are personally responsible for their own economic fate; where one ends up depends on one's skills, talents, and hard work. Accordingly, since how well individuals do depends on their own qualities—talent and effort—although the resulting distribution of economic rewards is unequal in terms of quantities of goods people receive, it is on the whole 'equitable and fair' (Kluegel and Smith 1986: 5). I will examine the components of the 'dominant ideology' in detail to see how widely they are subscribed to, and some of their important implications.

Researchers note that Americans do not have single principles of distribution that they apply to all areas of life. According to Jennifer Hochschild, Americans apply norms of equality to the political realm and areas beyond the political, to home, school, and community. Norms of equal distribution in these areas are epitomized by the right to vote, possessed by all citizens, or equal access to educational opportunities. In economic matters, however, it is generally believed that distribution should be according to merit (Hochschild 1981: 107, 48). The United States not only follows different norms in different spheres, but does so in exaggerated forms. The country is among the most open and participatory of modern democracies in regard to politics but among the least egalitarian in economic distribution (Verba and Orren 1985: 9; McClosky and Zaller 1984: 82). If, as repeated polls indicate, belief that all people are fundamentally equal is 'axiomatic' for most Americans (McClosky and Zaller 1984: 65), then many people could be expected to find it difficult to accept such economic outcomes. Reconciliation of these views is through general acceptance of a norm of equal opportunity. For most Americans, the demand for equal treatment in economic matters requires only that everyone receive an equal chance to compete. As with the race discussed above, people can be treated fairly according to a principle of merit, as long as the principle is applied under circumstances that are equal.

There is abundant survey evidence to support this analysis of Americans' views. But before looking at this, we should note that survey questions in this area do not always distinguish clearly between moral beliefs concerning principles of distribution and more or less empirical concerns about how the economy functions. These subjects are inherently intertwined. One's view about preferred principles is naturally strongly affected by one's opinion about how these work in practice—while, to complicate matters, one's view of how the economy is functioning is likely to be strongly influenced by one's preferred principles. In particular, support for norms of distribution according to merit is closely bound up with faith in conditions under which people can compete on reasonably fair terms. In examining beliefs about principles of distributive justice, we will oftentimes see that differences are sharper in regard to such ostensibly empirical matters than about the principles themselves, though, as we will also see, many of these are not 'empirical' concerns in the usual sense. In attempting to identify liberal citizens' views of distributive justice, it is necessary to step back from specific survey responses and where they can be placed on a normative–empirical continuum, to attempt to see how responses fit together in organized views. Looking at responses to a range of questions that span the normative–empirical divide should allow us to compile fairly clear accounts of people's opinions on distributive justice.

Combining responses from a number of polls, we can see that in the United States distribution of economic goods through the free market is accepted at levels around the consensus threshold of 75 per cent. Seventy-seven per cent of McClosky and Zaller's general sample and 89 per cent of their sample of 'influentials' agreed with the statement: 'On the whole, our economic system is just and wise'. Somewhat lower, 63 per cent of the general sample and 66 per cent of influentials agreed that the private enterprise system 'is generally a fair and efficient system', while 7 per cent and 6 per cent respectively responded that it 'mostly leads to depression and widespread poverty' (p. 133). Seventy per cent of the general public and 91 per cent of élites agreed with the statement: 'We can do everything needed to get prosperity without changing the private enterprise system very much'.[1] Sixty-one per cent of the public and 85 per cent of influentials disagreed with the idea that 'sweeping changes in our economic system' would be needed to solve social problems (McClosky and Zaller 1984: 157).[2] Levels of support for the value of private property were similar, and

[1] These last figures are from a 1958 survey; for the general public, N = 1,484; for influentials, N = 3,020 (see McClosky and Zaller 1984: 14).

[2] Sniderman and his associates recorded similar levels of support for the free enterprise system in the United States and Canada. They were 'struck by the similarity of views in the two countries'. For instance, to the question 'The profit system . . .

so few respondents favoured communism or socialism (p. 140). But this should not be construed as endorsement of an unfettered free market. Federal regulation of specific industries was strongly supported. For example, 80 per cent of respondents favoured regulating the drug industry, 73 per cent the oil industry, 73 per cent food, 71 per cent utilities; the average across thirteen industries was 67 per cent (p. 146). Seventy-five per cent of the general sample and 70 per cent of élites disagreed that 'Most things would run pretty well by themselves if the government just didn't interfere' (p. 147).

Different survey questions allow us to identify various reasons why a private enterprise system is strongly supported. These include belief that competition gets individuals to work hard and perform better (see McClosky and Zaller 1984: 155; Sniderman *et al.* 1996: 100; but cf. Sniderman *et al.* 1996: 102). Forty-eight per cent of McClosky and Zaller's general survey and 39 per cent of élites responded that with the abolition of private industry 'very few people would do their best'. Twenty-one per cent and 23 per cent, respectively, responded that 'most people would work hard anyway' (McClosky and Zaller 1984: 133). Of Kluegel and Smith's sample of 2,212 American adults surveyed in 1980, only 2 per cent strongly agreed and 23 per cent agreed that 'government ownership and control of basic industries would benefit societ'. Fifty-three per cent disagreed; 22 per cent strongly disagreed (p. 165).

Another factor supporting belief in free enterprise is its congruence with central American values. On the basis of his interviews with thirty-five Connecticut state senators in 1988, Grant Reeher posits general consensus on American ideology, centring on 'traditional liberal tenets of individualism, and concomitantly, economic opportunity' (Reeher 1996: 241–2). According to this common view, the free enterprise system is simply part of the American spirit. Eighty per cent of McClosky and Zaller's general survey and 83 per cent of influentials responded 'for the most part, yes' to the question 'In your opinion, is the free enterprise system necessary for free government to survive?' 'Probably not' was chosen by 6 per cent of the general survey and 12 per cent of influentials. Eighty-two per cent of the general sample and 87 per cent of influentials agreed with the statement 'Our freedom depends on the free enterprise system' (1984: 133). Thus the free enterprise system is deeply imbued with values of freedom, individualism, and opportunity that many people associate with the American ethos (esp. Hartz 1955; see below, Section 4).

(1) often brings out the worst in human nature; (2) usually teaches people the value of hard work and personal achievement', 54% of Americans and 61% of Canadians chose (2); 16% of Americans and 17% of Canadians chose (1) (Sniderman *et al.* 1996: 88–9).

Although these considerations are doubtless significant, survey evidence indicates the great importance of an additional factor: general belief that a free enterprise system is fair. Americans overwhelmingly support the value of equal opportunity. In a 1957 sample of 103 adults in Indianapolis, Frank Westie reports that 98 per cent of respondents agreed with the statement 'Everyone in America should have equal opportunities to get ahead'; 98 per cent agreed that 'Children should have equal educational opportunities'; 97 per cent agreed that 'Each person should be judged according to his own worth' (Westie 1965: 531). In their survey of 2,762 American leaders of different types, conducted in 1976 and 1977, Sidney Verba and Gary Orren recorded similar results. In response to the question how best to deal with inequality, 98 per cent of business leaders selected 'equality of opportunity' rather than 'equality of result'; 98 per cent of Republicans chose similarly. Although scores varied among other groups of leaders, they did not vary by much. The lowest were recorded by feminists and Democrats, 84 per cent of whom selected equality of opportunity. The highest response for equality of result was Democrats, with 8 per cent, followed by feminists, blacks, and youth, with 7 per cent (Verba and Orren 1985: 72).

In view of what we have seen in previous chapters, we must ask what responses on such abstract questions really amount to.[3] But response levels on less abstract questions were similarly high. Ninety-eight per cent of Verba and Orren's business leaders and 99 per cent of their Republicans responded that, in a fair economic system, earnings are based on ability. There was more range here among groups, with 67 per cent of black leaders and 71 per cent of feminists responding that earnings should be based on ability. While 0 per cent of Republicans and 1 per cent of business leaders responded that all earnings should be 'about the same', 17 per cent of blacks, 15 per cent of feminists, 14 per cent of youth leaders, and 12 per cent of Democrats chose this option (Verba and Orren 1985: 72). But even with this variance, responses of all groups of leaders were well above consensus levels. Once again, I will return to the implications of disagreements in response to questions such as these—and at higher levels—below.

Belief that earnings should be based on ability receives impressive support in McClosky and Zaller's surveys (see 1984: 84). The same is true in Canada. Seventy-one per cent of Sniderman's Canadian sample

---

[3] On particular applications, Westie (1965) recorded departures from answers to the general questions; when discrepancies were pointed out to people, they tended to change particular responses to conform with general. This departs from the pattern noted in Ch. 3, although, because the questions dealt with race, it is possible that subjects may not have responded according to their actual feelings; for this tendency, see Kuklinski *et al.* (1997).

responded that 'people with more ability should earn higher salaries', while 12 per cent responded that 'all people should earn about the same' (Sniderman *et al.* 1996: 92).

Norms of merit distribution are supported by general belief in the availability of opportunities. Kluegel and Smith's survey provides valuable information along these lines. Subjects perceived strong opportunities for both themselves and Americans in general. In response to the question 'How good a chance do you think a person has to get ahead today, if the person works hard?' 63 per cent responded 'a very good chance' or 'a good chance', while another 26 per cent responded 'some chance'; 9 per cent responded 'little chance', and only 2 per cent, 'no chance'. Seventy per cent responded that most Americans have a 'fair opportunity to make the most of themselves in life'; 30 per cent replied that 'something usually holds them back'. Subjects were asked: 'Some people say that there's not much opportunity in American today—that the average man doesn't have much chance to really get ahead. Others say there's plenty of opportunity, and anyone who works hard can go as far as he wants. How do you feel?' In 1966, 78 per cent responded that there was plenty of opportunity, although, it is worth noting, this was down from 88 per cent who gave this response in 1952 (Kluegel and Smith 1986: 44).[4]

Subjects were generally optimistic about their own chances for advancement. They were asked: 'Compared to the average person in America, do you think the chance of getting ahead for . . . you yourself is?' Thirty-eight per cent responded much better than average (5 per cent) or better than average, 54 per cent average, and 9 per cent worse than average, or much worse (2 per cent). Subjects were asked: 'Do you think you have had a fair opportunity to make the most of yourself in life or has anything ever held you back?' In 1980, 72 per cent responded that they had had fair opportunities. In 1972, 73 per cent gave this response (p. 47). In response to: 'Thinking about your future work career, do you expect that over the next 5–10 years you will . . .' 83 per cent expected to advance rapidly or steadily; 4 per cent expected to lose some ground (p. 47). In regard to the last question, responses concerning subjects' experiences correlated with their expectations. Of those who had advanced rapidly, 82 per cent expected rapid or steady advancement in the future, and 1 per cent to lose ground. In comparison, of those who had lost ground (N = 39), 64 per cent expected rapid or steady advancement, and 8 per cent to lose ground (p. 47). But, as one can see, overall levels of optimism were quite high.

---

[4] The 1952 figure is from a National Election Studies survey (N = 1,730); the 1966 is from another study (Huber and Form 1973) (N = 342) (Kluegel and Smith 1986: 44).

Kluegel and Smith report strong correlations between people's own experiences and their views of general opportunity levels. Of respondents who identified their own chances (contemporary and future) as much better than average, 93 per cent viewed the level of general opportunity as very good or good, and 0 per cent said there was little or no general opportunity. In contrast, 59 per cent of those who viewed their own opportunity as average perceived general levels as very good or good, and 12 per cent saw little or no general opportunity. Of those who saw their own opportunities as worse than average, 41 per cent perceived general levels as very good or good, and 28 per cent saw little or no general opportunity (p. 55). Of respondents who believed they had had a fair chance to get ahead, 67 per cent viewed general opportunity as very good or good, and 8 per cent as little or none. Of those who believed they had been held back, 53 per cent saw general levels as good or very good, and 18 per cent responded 'little or none' (p. 55).

Clearly, this set of results indicates the importance of personal experience in shaping general beliefs about opportunity. Large majorities of Americans believe in their own opportunities to advance and view the system as providing similar opportunities to others. As Kluegel and Smith note, general belief in opportunity is reinforced by examination of the factors identified as having held people back. Only a minority saw themselves as having been restricted by systemic or structural factors: race, sex, the job market. These people had the strongest views about lack of overall opportunity. For instance, of those who believed they were held back by job market factors ($N = 47$), 57 per cent saw little or no or some general opportunity. Of those held back by race ($N = 32$), 50 per cent saw little or no general opportunity and another 25 per cent only some. In contrast, of those who were held back by lack of education ($N = 7$), 34 per cent saw little or no or some general opportunity, and 67 per cent very good or good opportunity. Of those held back by motivation, 32 per cent saw little or no or only some opportunity, and 68 per cent very good or good opportunities (p. 55). Thus strong majorities believed that they had been treated fairly, or, if held back, that this was because of personal factors. On the basis of their survey, Kluegel and Smith argue that underlying the 'dominant ideology' is a profusion of positive personal experience, which makes for general optimism (p. 72).[5] General support for norms of merit distribution is greatly facilitated by general belief in widespread opportunities. Because people have opportunities to compete, they deserve what they get.

[5] It is not clear how well this sentiment has survived difficult economic times for many Americans in the early 1990s. But it is unlikely that these basic attitudes are widely questioned, especially in view of the prosperous mid- and late 1990s.

In spite of faith in general and personal opportunity, there were significant differences in perceived prospects of and by different groups. This is clear in contrasts between blacks and women on the one hand and the views of white men on the other, as recorded by Kluegel and Smith. On a scale of 1 to 5 (lowest to highest), mean scores for whites and blacks in regard to prevalence of opportunity in American society were 3.8 and 3.51 respectively. For men, the mean was 3.87 and for women 3.65 (with differences). Whites viewed their personal opportunity as 3.36; blacks viewed their own as 3.13. Men place their personal opportunity at 3.42, as compared to 3.24 for women (Kluegel and Smith 1986: 63). Multiple regression indicates a statistically significant effect of being white on belief in general opportunity, Beta = 0.10. Also significant was the effect from being male, Beta = 0.09; the effect of increased education was highest of all, Beta = 0.11. That for increased income was 0.09 (all significant at the 0.05 level) (p. 65). The highest effects on belief in personal opportunity were increased education (Beta = 0.21) and increased income (Beta = 0.15). The effect of being white was Beta = 0.07. For being male, the effect on belief in personal opportunity was Beta = 0.08 (all significant at 0.05 level). (p. 65). In spite of the strong effect of increased education on belief in both general and personal opportunity, it is interesting to note that belief in lack of opportunity for particular groups was seen to increase with increased education. Among white men who had eleven or fewer years of school, 23 per cent viewed opportunities for blacks as less than average; for white college graduates, the figure was 36 per cent. Thirty-one per cent of blacks with eleven or fewer years of school believed opportunities for blacks to be less than average. For black college graduates, this figure increased to 58 per cent. Twenty-eight per cent of women with eleven or fewer years believed opportunities for women to be less than average; for women college graduates, this increased to 53 per cent (p. 70).

Findings such as these could be multiplied, but several points are clear. First, there are significant differences between perceptions of white males and women and blacks about the general levels of opportunity in society and opportunities open to different groups.[6] The fact that belief in the existence of these differences increases with education is easily explained. Substantial differences do exist in the distribution of economic goods and education in contemporary society, which presumably influence more

---

[6] Rytina, Form, and Pease present similar findings concerning effects of race and income on the belief that there is abundant opportunity in America. For instance, although 78% of all respondents (N = 354) agreed about the presence of opportunity, 90% of poor whites agreed, but 56% of poor blacks, and 58% of middle income blacks; 80% of middle income whites agreed, and 93% of upper income whites (Rytina *et al.* 1970: 707–8).

informed people's perceptions. For instance, although unemployment levels for men and women were quite close, in 1994 average annual earnings for a man were $41,118, as compared to $27,162 for a woman (US Department of Commerce 1996, table 728).[7] In 1995 similar percentages of men and women had completed high school (81.7 per cent and 81.6 per cent, respectively), but 26 per cent of men had completed college, as compared to 20.2 per cent of women—which is nevertheless a significant percentage gain for women since 1960 (9.7 per cent of men and 5.8 per cent of women had completed college) (table 242).

Blacks continue to lag behind whites in important respects. In 1995, 13.2 per cent had completed college, as compared to 24.0 per cent of whites; 73.8 per cent had completed high school, as compared to 83.0 per cent of whites (table 241). In 1994, 11.7 per cent of whites were below the poverty level, as compared to 30.6 per cent of blacks (table 730). In 1995, 7.7 per cent of blacks were unemployed, as compared to 4.3 per cent of whites (table 649); 35.7 per cent of blacks between 16 and 19 years old and 17.7 per cent between 20 and 24 years were unemployed, as compared to 14.5 per cent and 7.7 per cent of whites (table 644). In 1993 median income of blacks was $21,542, as compared to $39,300 for whites (table 721).

In spite of these differences, a second point is that, as Kluegel and Smith argue, although real, differences in outlook represented by women and blacks should not be exaggerated. As we have seen, although blacks viewed their own prospects as lower than average (a mean of 2.85, on a scale of 1 to 5), they placed general opportunity at 3.51. Perceptions of women were similar. They assessed general opportunity at 3.65 and their own at 2.73. Whites, in comparison, viewed general opportunity at 3.8 (Kluegel and Smith 1986: 63). We have seen that majorities of college-educated blacks and women believed their own group lacked opportunities (58 per cent and 53 per cent, respectively). As Kluegel and Smith observe, although sex and race differences 'are the strongest bases for potential group differences in beliefs about opportunity', it is notable that both blacks and women had generally positive views of general opportunity in society. Because less educated blacks and women saw less inequality in their own regard, neither group generally believed its prospects were limited (p. 72).

[7] Unemployment: table 628. The survey drawn on in Kluegel and Smith (1986) was conducted in 1980, while the figures presented here are from the 1996 *Statistical Abstract of the United States*. But although specific relationships have changed in magnitude to differing extents, the broader points still hold. For example, women's median income in 1980 was $11,591, while men's was $19,173 (table 725).

2. BELIEF SYSTEMS

As with the moral principles examined in previous chapters, support for principles of merit distribution is qualified in its applications to particular circumstances. But this assumes an unusual form; differences show up more on the empirical level than the normative. Although there is general agreement on norms of merit distribution, people disagree a good deal about the conditions under which people compete. We have seen that most members of society believe there is general opportunity. Some groups assess the general level differently, but these disparities are relatively slight and do not seriously undermine the dominant ideology. More significant differences show up in regard to the distribution of opportunities, i.e. the economic system's fairness. Disagreements here are most apparent in differing explanations for income inequalities. Although there is general belief in widespread opportunities, substantial portions of the population believe that some groups have more opportunities than others, while, as we will see, these differences can be traced back to important underlying factors.

We can begin with Verba and Orren's survey of assorted leaders. If we assume that leaders are generally better educated and more sophisticated than the public at large (see Verba and Orren 1985: 90), then Verba and Orren's study provides in heightened form a view of how different groups think. Different leaders had strikingly different views about economic inequalities. For instance, 93 per cent of business leaders viewed the free enterprise system as fair to workers, and only 3 per cent as unfair to workers; 88 per cent of Republican leaders viewed it as fair and 6 per cent unfair; in contrast, 47 per cent of Democrats viewed it as fair and 31 per cent unfair. More dramatic contrasts were recorded in regard to black and feminist leaders: 31 per cent of blacks viewed the system as fair and 44 per cent unfair; the figures for feminists were 23 per cent and 50 per cent respectively (p. 74). These findings were supported by a 1966–7 survey of 354 adults in Muskegon, Michigan. Joan Rytina, William Form, and John Pease report substantial differences between views of the fairness of the economic system between respondents of different races and income levels (Rytina *et al.* 1970).[8]

---

[8] On the basis of a national survey of 522 adults, Wayne Alves and Peter Rossi report a systematic variation between respondents' views on the relative importance that should be accorded to consideration of merit and need in economic distributions, with high status respondents placing greater emphasis on merit (Alves and Rossi 1978).

McClosky and Zaller's survey shows that differences such as these are related to broader differences in subjects' intellectual outlooks. McClosky and Zaller correlated respondents' opinions about the fairness of the system with a scale of democratic values. Respondents high on democratic values were seen to be markedly more critical of the system than respondents low on democratic values.[9] For instance, in response to whether the free enterprise system 'survives by keeping the poor down' or 'gives everyone a fair chance', 70 per cent of the general public sample low on democratic values responded that it gives everyone a fair chance, and 6 per cent that it keeps the poor down. Forty-five per cent of those high on democratic values responded that it gives everyone a fair chance and 15 per cent that it keeps the poor down. Eighty-three per cent of opinion leaders low on democratic values ($N = 48$) responded that the system is fair, and 0 per cent that it keeps the poor down. Thirty-six per cent of opinion leaders high on democratic values ($N = 626$) responded that it gives everyone a fair chance and 9 per cent that it keeps the poor down. Fifty-six per cent of high democratic value opinion leaders declined to choose, as opposed to 17 per cent of low democratic value opinion leaders (McClosky and Zaller 1984: 174–5). Subjects were asked whether 'working people in this country' 'usually earn about what they deserve' or 'do not get a fair share of what they produce'. Of opinion leaders low in democratic values ($N = 375$), 79 per cent responded that working people get what they deserve and only 2 per cent that they are not treated fairly. Thirty-seven per cent of high democratic opinion leaders responded that they are treated fairly and 24 per cent unfairly (p. 180).

McClosky and Zaller's study sheds valuable light on how different elements of belief systems fit together. In a classic article Philip Converse defines a 'belief system' as 'a configuration of ideas and attitudes in which the elements are bound together by some form of constraint or functional interdependence' (Converse 1964: 207). Converse describes 'constraint' as 'the success we would have in predicting, given initial knowledge that an individual holds a specified attitude, that he holds certain further ideas and attitudes' (p. 207). Converse argues that the relationship between components of a world-view can be more psychological than logical. Even if different ideas do not entail one another logically, they can be bound together psychologically. If idea *A* constrains *B*, change in the former 'would *psychologically* require, from the point of view of the actor, some compensating change(s) in the status of' the latter (p. 208). Converse suggests that important factors linking ideas are the interests of different

[9] For their scale construction, see McClosky and Zaller (1984, ch. 1, apps. I, II). 'Democratic values' centre on support for democratic rights, as discussed above in Ch. 3.

segments of the population: 'the configuration of interests and information that characterize particular niches in the social structure' (p. 211). In
addition, connections between particular sets of ideas can be traced back
to the latter's origins as integrated packages:

First, the shaping of belief systems of any range into apparently logical wholes
that are credible to large numbers of people is an act of creative synthesis characteristic of only a minuscule proportion of any population. Second, to the extent
that multiple idea-elements of a belief system are socially diffused from such creative sources, they tend to be diffused in 'packages,' which consumers come to see
as 'natural' wholes, for they are presented in such terms. (p. 211)

Accordingly, one reason the views of different opinion leaders and 'ideological élites' are frequently sharper than those of the general public is that
the élites are more familiar with the theoretical constructions out of which
general belief systems arose.[10] Examination of the psychological factors
involved in belief systems would raise issues of enormous complexity and
take us beyond the scope of this work. Accordingly, I will examine different elements of respondents' views and infer that they are connected when
this is indicated by the evidence, without attempting to explain the precise
nature of underlying forces at work.

McClosky and Zaller's study shows clear inverse relationships between
respondents' support for democratic and capitalist values. We have seen
that respondents who were measured as higher on support for democratic
values were more critical of aspects of the economic system than others
less high. More broadly, McClosky and Zaller report that respondents
higher on a scale constructed to measure one attitude were consistently
found to be lower on a scale for the other. Among members of the general
sample low in democratic values, 20 per cent were low in capitalist values
and 47 per cent high. The reverse was true of those high in democratic values: 21 per cent were high in capitalist values and 53 per cent low. Among
McClosky and Zaller's opinion leaders, of those low in democratic values
(N = 51), 8 per cent were low in capitalist values and 84 per cent high. Of
opinion leaders high in democratic values (N = 641), 22 per cent were high
in capitalist values, and 53 per cent low (McClosky and Zaller 1984: 163).

Evidence shows that variations between responses of subjects high and
low on democratic values stem from differences on wider philosophical
views—although the evidence does not allow us to characterize the wider
differences in detail or to say exactly how far-reaching they are. McClosky
and Zaller constructed scales to measure three aspects of respondents'
'ideological orientation', their attitudes towards social change, 'social

[10] An important recent study of the role of intellectual élites in the creation of mass
opinion is Zaller (1992).

benevolence', and 'faith in human nature'.[11] All three of these correlated strongly with levels of support for democratic values. For instance, of the general sample, 18 per cent of those scoring low on social change scored high on democratic values. In contrast, 53 per cent of those high on social change scored high on democratic values. Forty-two per cent of the sample of opinion leaders low on social change were high on democratic values, as compared to 87 per cent of those high on social change. More striking, 17 per cent of the sample of ideological activists low on social change were high on democratic values, while 93 per cent of those high on social change were high on democratic values. Patterns were similar for social benevolence and faith in human nature (p. 200). In all these cases, correlations were consistent, strong, and statistically significant. Especially notable are powerful relationships between these three ideological measures and support for democratic values among opinion leaders and ideological activists, members of the population who were, presumably, more consciously attuned to the components of their belief systems.

In addition to testing the three ideological measures against support for democratic values, McClosky and Zaller examined their relationships with capitalist values. As we have seen, respondents' scores on democratic and capitalist values tended to be inversely related; respondents higher on one scale tended to be lower on the other. These differences were maintained in regard to the three ideological measures. For instance, of activists low in support for social change, 84 per cent were high in capitalist values, in comparison to 10 per cent for those high in support for social change. Of activists low in social benevolence, 76 per cent were high in capitalist values, as opposed to 15 per cent of activists high in social benevolence. Of activists low in faith in human nature, 87 per cent were high in capitalist values. Only 5 per cent of activists high in faith in human nature were also high in capitalist values (McClosky and Zaller 1984: 223).

Respondents' ideologies, based on self-identification, correlated strongly and consistently with democratic and capitalist values and with McClosky and Zaller's three ideological measures. Contrasting views of democratic values among self-identified liberals and conservatives were examined above, in Chapter 3. Similar contrasts were found in regard to capitalist values. For instance, respondents were asked whether the free enterprise system 'gives everyone a fair chance' or 'survives by keeping the poor down'. In the general sample, 75 per cent of strong conservatives said it gives people a fair chance and 8 per cent that it keeps the poor down. Of strong liberals, 12 per cent responded that it was fair and 6 per cent that it keeps the poor down. In the sample of influentials, once again, the divide

---

[11] For details, see McClosky and Zaller (1984: 198–9).

was sharper: 80 per cent of strong conservatives said the system is fair, and 0 per cent that it keeps the poor down; 9 per cent of strong liberals said the system is fair and 27 per cent that it keeps the poor down (p. 226).

On each of the eight questions McClosky and Zaller used to measure support for capitalist values the *average* percentage of strong conservative opinion leaders giving the pro-capitalist response was 93.87 per cent. When asked about the effects of giving 'everybody the same income regardless of the type of work they do', 100 per cent agreed that this 'would destroy the desire to work hard and do a better job' (p. 225). One hundred per cent agreed that communism, adopted in the United States, 'would make things worse for most Americans' (p. 226). The low percentage, 80 per cent, was recorded on whether the free enterprise system is fair or keeps the poor down (p. 226). Over the eight questions, the average percentage of strong liberal opinion leaders giving the pro-capitalist response was 38.75 per cent. That is an *average* difference of some 55 per cent. The question with the highest level of support among strong liberal opinion leaders (56 per cent) concerned whether, under a fair economic system, 'people with more ability would earn higher salaries', or everyone would earn about the same (p. 227). In contrast, only 9 per cent agreed that the free enterprise system 'gives everyone a fair chance' (p. 226).

As we saw with correlations between ideology and democratic values in Chapter 3, different philosophies (or philosophical views) are evident in these responses. The consistent and overwhelming agreement of strong conservatives indicates the presence of highly articulated views. Liberals were less in agreement, and so one can assume that they had less fully articulated views. But consistent differences between their views and those of conservatives indicate at the very least that they did not subscribe to the conservative view.[12]

McClosky and Zaller's ideological measures show sharp overall differences between conservatives and liberals. For instance, of activists self-identified as strong liberals, 1 per cent were low in support of social change and 91 per cent high; 88 per cent of strong conservatives were low in social change and 4 per cent scored high. Seventy-two per cent of strong liberals were high in social benevolence and 6 per cent low. Almost precisely the reverse, 7 per cent of strong conservatives were high in benevolence and 73 per cent low. Seventy-two per cent of strong liberals were high in faith in human nature and 0 per cent low; 2 per cent of strong conservatives were high in faith in human nature and 64 per cent low. As we saw in Chapter 3, similar relationships held in regard to attitudes towards democratic

---

[12] In the many tables in McClosky and Zaller (1984, ch. 7) one sees similar patterns, with scores consistently correlating with ideological gradations from strong conservative to strong liberal.

values: 98 per cent of strong liberals were high and 0 per cent low; 14 per cent of strong conservatives were high on support for democratic values, and 59 per cent low (p. 202).

McClosky and Zaller's findings are supported by those of other researchers.[13] The study of political attitudes in Canada conducted by Sniderman and his associates, which included a separate sample of élites, confirms the relationship between political ideology and capitalist values. In Chapter 3 I noted sharp differences between attitudes towards democratic values of Canadian democratic socialist and conservative élites (clearest among members of the New Democratic Party and Progressive Conservatives, respectively). Similar patterns were seen in regard to questions concerning distributive justice. Sniderman and his colleagues report that 16 per cent of a United States general sample and 17 per cent of a Canadian general sample responded that the profit system 'often brings out the worst in human nature', while 54 per cent and 61 per cent respectively responded that it 'usually teaches the value of hard work and personal achievement'. Four per cent of Progressive Conservative partisan élites (N = 71) responded that it brings out the worst, and 87 per cent that it teaches the value of hard work. In contrast, 73 per cent of New Democratic Party élites (N = 74) responded that it brings out the worst, and 5 per cent that it teaches the value of hard work (Sniderman *et al.* 1996: 89). The Sniderman group asked whether: 'The poor are poor because . . . (1) they don't try hard enough to get ahead; (2) the wealthy and powerful keep them poor.' Of the general samples, 24 per cent of Americans and 16 per cent of Canadians responded that they don't try hard enough, and 21 per cent and 24 per cent respectively that they are kept poor by the wealthy and powerful; 55 per cent and 60 per cent declined to answer. Among Progressive Conservative élites (N = 69), 13 per cent responded that the poor don't try hard enough, 6 per cent that they are kept down, and 81 per cent declined to answer. Among New Democratic Party élites (N = 78), 0 per cent responded that they don't try hard enough, 32 per cent declined to answer, and 68 per cent responded that the poor are kept down (p. 90). Asked to agree or disagree that 'One of the big problems in this country is that we don't give everyone an equal chance', 53 per cent of the US general sample agreed and 34 per cent disagreed; 57 per cent of the Canadian general sample agreed, and 43 per cent disagreed. Twenty-one per cent of Progressive Conservative élites (N = 127) agreed and 79 per cent disagreed; in contrast, 89 per cent of New Democratic Party élites (N = 110) agreed and 11 per cent disagreed (p. 85).

[13] See Verba and Orren (1985, esp. ch. 5) and Kluegel and Smith (1986: 259–72).

These responses are not surprising. The fact that Conservative élites are consistently more pro-capitalist than the general public and Democratic Socialist élites consistently more anti-capitalist stands to reason. There is little doubt that attitudes towards the free market strongly influenced these élites in their choice of party. But again, sharp and consistent differences between strong liberals (in the United States sense) and strong conservatives point to strikingly different intellectual orientations.

If we compare the results reported in this section with those in the last, we confront a now familiar paradox. In the last section I noted general agreement on a principle of merit distribution and strong—though less strong—belief in the general availability of opportunities. In this section I have reported considerable disagreement among political and ideological élites about the fairness of the system and other matters. Immediate implications are that the general agreement in Section 1 masks important differences, and that these differences are present, in intensified form, in the views of more articulate élites. Once again, these differences are manifested especially clearly in disagreements over ostensibly factual questions about how the economic system performs. However, it is clear that these disagreements are not empirical in a straightforward sense. People assess the fairness of opportunities through the lenses of their overall philosophical orientations. As we saw with perceptions of threat, in Chapter 3 perceptions of the economic system's fairness are of a piece with subjects' overall philosophical orientations. Because these central social 'facts' are interpreted quite differently by subjects with different philosophical orientations, there is unlikely to be agreement on them until subjects come to agree philosophically.

The main ideological dividing-lines of questions of the system's fairness are familiar. The evidence supports a continuum between opposed views of self-conscious, articulate élites, with the views of the less self-conscious general public falling at varying points between. The two opposed views can be identified as 'liberal' and 'conservative'.[14] McClosky's surveys concerning the three 'ideological measures' demonstrate that more than specific political and economic differences separate the views. We are of course most interested in political and economic opinions, though without forgetting that these are embedded in wider philosophical orientations. For our purposes, the two views are most clearly distinguished by support for democratic and capitalist values. As McClosky and Zaller's surveys show, these two attitudes bear an inverse relationship; respondents higher on one scale tend to be lower on the other.[15]

---

[14] Fleshed-out versions of these views are found in Reeher's 'narratives of justice', based on interviews with Connecticut state senators (Reeher 1996).

[15] McClosky and Zaller also present a third, basically alienated, 'anti-regime' belief pattern; see (1984, ch. 8).

The liberal view is the more supportive of individual rights. The conservative view has more faith in the fair workings of the free market. Roughly and simply, the liberal view is characterized by basic optimism about human nature and social change. The liberal supports individual autonomy, allowing people to choose for themselves, and tolerance for non-conformity. Her desire to protect minorities and people who flout majority opinion is of a piece with her desire to protect individuals from unbridled market forces.

The conservative view is more optimistic in one sense, in that it strongly values the existing system, which is perceived as providing equal opportunities and dispensing rewards according to merit. Perhaps support of the existing order can be construed in a negative sense, in that the conservative is basically fearful of human nature and is concerned that change will make things worse. As we saw in Chapters 3 and 4, heightened senses of fear and threat are generally linked with low regard for democratic values. The conservative's willingness to suppress unpopular minorities and individual expression is consistent with his lack of faith in human nature and lack of benevolence towards other people. These attitudes would appear to be closely related to opposition to interference with the market, which, again, is viewed as a just dispenser of rewards. As we will see in the next section, when people are badly treated by the market, the conservative generally believes this is their own fault. Having less faith in market processes, liberals are more willing to tamper with it and attribute inequalities to its defects.

3. PUBLIC POLICIES

Disagreements over the working of the economy have direct implications in regard to public policy. For our purposes, it is important to trace connections between basic policy orientations and the underlying philosophical orientations discussed in the previous section.

Respondents' explanations of economic inequalities, including those that make social welfare programmes necessary, were generally in keeping with the dominant ideology. Most of Kluegel and Smith's respondents attributed economic inequalities to personal factors. For instance, in regard to the factors responsible for possession of wealth, 95 per cent of their respondents viewed 'personal drive, willingness to take risks' as either very important (64 per cent) or somewhat important (31 per cent). 'Hard work and initiative' were viewed as either very or somewhat important by similar percentages, 60 per cent and 32 per cent, respectively.

'Great ability or talent' was identified as very important or somewhat important by 88 per cent. Personal factors that are not ordinarily associated with merit were also viewed as important: 'political influence or "pull" ', 88 per cent very or somewhat important; money inherited from families, 93 per cent very or somewhat important (Kluegel and Smith 1986: 77).

Explanations for poverty were similar in emphasizing personal characteristics. Some of these were as follows: 'lack of thrift and proper money-management skills', 64 per cent very important and 30 per cent important; 'lack of effort by the poor themselves', 53 per cent and 39 per cent, respectively; 'lack of ability and talent', 53 per cent and 35 per cent, respectively. However, structural factors were also thought to play a role, if not quite as significant. 'Failure of society to provide good schools for many Americans' was viewed as very important by 46 per cent of respondents and important by 29 per cent. 'Low wages in some businesses and industries' were viewed as very important by 40 per cent and important by 47 per cent. The figures for 'being taken advantage of by rich people' were 20 per cent and 35 per cent, respectively. For 'prejudice and discrimination against blacks', the figures were 31 per cent and 44 per cent, respectively (Kluegel and Smith 1986: 79).[16] Kluegel and Smith conclude that, on average, 'individual factors are considered much more important than structural factors in accounting for poverty'. Four of the top five explanatory factors were individual rather than structural (the exception being society's failure to provide adequate schools) (p. 78). Explanations of wealth were similar, although differences between personal and structural factors were not as large (p. 78).

In spite of this measure of agreement, there were, once gain, significant variations among the views of different groups. Rytina, Form, and Pease report correlations between income and race and opinions concerning causes of wealth and poverty. Respondents were given open-ended questions about causes of poverty and wealth. In regard to causes of wealth, 17 per cent of poor blacks and 34 per cent of poor whites responded in terms of personal characteristics; 72 per cent of rich whites indicated personal characteristics. On why people are poor, 17 per cent of poor blacks and 30 per cent of poor whites responded in regard to personal characteristics; 62 per cent of rich whites indicated personal characteristics. On why people were on relief the last six years, 28 per cent of poor blacks and 46 per cent of poor whites cited personal characteristics, in comparison to 78 per cent of rich whites. Three per cent of poor blacks and 13 per cent of poor whites agreed with a statement to the effect that the poor don't work as hard as

[16] These are their 1980 figures; the figures for 1969 data are generally similar (p. 79).

rich people do; 39 per cent of rich whites agreed with the statement. Zero per cent of poor blacks and 19 per cent of poor whites agreed that the poor don't want to get ahead as much as everyone else does, in comparison to 46 per cent of rich whites (Rytina *et al.* 1970: 712–14).

Verba and Orren's survey of various kinds of leader supports these findings. The leaders were asked about causes of poverty in America. Fifty-seven per cent of business leaders said this was the fault of the poor, and 9 per cent that it was the fault of the system. Fifty-five per cent of Republican leaders said the poor were at fault and 13 per cent, the system. In contrast, 5 per cent of Democrat leaders viewed the poor as responsible and 68 per cent, the system. Five per cent of black leaders identified the poor and 86 per cent, the system. Nine per cent of feminist leaders identified the poor and 76 per cent the system (Verba and Orren 1985: 74).

Different accounts of the causes of economic inequalities are closely bound up with views on public policies. Thus it is not surprising that Democrats, blacks, and feminists tend to be more supportive of welfare programmes than the general public, and Republicans and business leaders less supportive.[17] Kluegel and Smith note strong relationships between belief in personal responsibility for poverty and lack of support for welfare programmes, and belief in structural or systemic causes of poverty and support for welfare (Kluegel and Smith 1986: 162). The conflicting interpretations of economic inequalities these surveys reveal are readily identifiable as conservative and liberal. We can postulate a continuum between personal and systemic explanations of economic inequality, with polar positions presumably occupied by articulate ideological élites. But while polar positions are perhaps clear, the large majority of people who fall between the poles combine both kinds of factors in their explanations. This is seen in regard to attitudes towards causes of poverty and closely related views on the need for social welfare programmes.

We have seen that Kluegel and Smith's respondents cite both personal and structural causes of poverty, though they view the former as more important. General Social Survey (GSS) data support the finding that Americans generally hold the poor responsible for their own condition.[18] In 1988–91 GSS surveys 91.4 per cent of respondents viewed 'lack of effort

---

[17] See Verba and Orren (1985, chs. 4, 6) and Kluegel and Smith (1986: 159). It should be noted that Kluegel and Smith report a negative effect of being female on support for welfare (Beta = -0.04), though this was not significant at the 0.05 or 0.1 levels. In comparison, the effect of race (non-white) was positive: Beta = 0.19, significant at the 0.05 level (p. 159).

[18] The GSS is administered by the National Opinion Research Center. Results are available on the internet at the following address: http://www.icpsr.umich.edu/gss/subject/s-index.htm (retrieved winter, 1998).

by the poor themselves' as either very important or somewhat important in 'explaining why there are poor people in this country' (internet data, codebook variable: whypoor4); 74.4 per cent viewed 'loose morals and drunkenness' as very important or somewhat important (whypoor2). But respondents also identified structural factors: 78.5 per cent responded that 'failure of industry to provide enough jobs' was either very or somewhat important (whypoor3); 75.8 per cent responded that 'failure of society to provide good schools for many Americans' was very or somewhat important (whypoor1). (But then again, in 1983–7 GSS surveys 71.4 per cent of respondents answered 'yes' when asked if everyone in this county has 'an opportunity to obtain an education corresponding to their abilities and talents' (codebook variable: educop). I assume that 'everyone' here was generally construed as 'most people'.)

These responses are consistent with general belief in opportunities *for most people*, that most people have opportunities to develop their talents and get ahead, although the extent to which their chances are equal is interpreted differently by proponents of different ideologies. The poor's inability to keep up can be explained according to different combinations of personal and structural factors. We have seen that strong conservatives believe this is basically the poor's own fault, while strong liberals absolve the poor themselves and blame the system. The majority of Americans, falling between these poles, believe that both kinds of factor are responsible.

Widespread ambivalence about causes of poverty carries over into their view of welfare programmes. In keeping with the dominant ideology, which emphasizes opportunity and individual responsibility, Kluegel and Smith's respondents had highly negative views of welfare. Forty-five per cent strongly agreed and 36 per cent agreed that the United States spends too much money on welfare programmes; 37 per cent strongly agreed and 40 per cent agreed that 'most people getting welfare are *not* honest about their needs'; 19 per cent strongly disagreed and 50 per cent disagreed that 'most people on welfare who can work try to find jobs so they can support themselves' (Kluegel and Smith 1986: 153). Given general sentiment that most people on welfare are 'lazy and dishonest' (p. 152), it is not surprising that respondents were more supportive of guaranteeing jobs to people who want to work (61 per cent) than to providing them with welfare payments. Kluegel and Smith report that the average level of support over their four welfare questions was about 30 per cent (p. 152). These responses can be characterized as *principled* objections, because welfare runs against America's dominant ideology of self-reliance and individual responsibility. But people also recognize that welfare is necessary under certain conditions and so should be available to those who truly need it. According to 1983–7 GSS surveys, 83.9 per cent of respondents either agreed strongly or agreed that welfare is helpful in 'difficult situations' (codebook variable: welfare2); 88.9 per cent either strongly agreed or agreed that it helps prevent hunger and starvation (welfare5). McClosky and Zaller report that, in different surveys conducted between 1937 and 1975, 89 per cent of Americans supported 'government old-age pensions for needy people'. Seventy-nine per cent supported government provision of free medical care 'for those unable to pay'. Sixty-nine per cent responded that the government should 'provide for all people who have no other means of subsistence'. Sixty-eight per cent agreed that 'the federal government has a deep responsibility for seeing that the poor are taken care of, that no one goes hungry, and that every person achieves a mini- mum standard of living' (McClosky and Zaller 1984: 272). But in the GSS surveys negative effects were recognized at similar levels: 85 per cent of respondents either strongly agreed or agreed that welfare makes people work less hard (welfare1); 60.1 per cent of respondents either agreed strongly or agreed that welfare discourages young women who get preg- nant from marrying the father of the child (welfare6).[19]

Thus Americans' support of welfare can be characterized as both ambivalent and grudging. Because of the dominant ideology, they are concerned that the poor not be responsible for their condition. As David Miller observes, belief that payments go to people who don't need them underlies scepticism about the welfare system. Thus the traditional dis- tinction between the deserving and the undeserving poor lives on (Miller 1992*b*, 573–4). It is not unlikely that the combination of general antipathy to welfare and belief that it is going to people who could do without it, on the one hand, and recognition that it is necessary for certain people, on the other, is in part responsible for the deeply flawed systems that resulted. In the words of Kluegel and Smith, 'welfare programs are publicly accepted and implemented but rarely permit a decent or dignified life for most recipients' (1986: 175).

A popular reconciliation of conflicting attitudes has emerged in recent years. Given Americans' belief in self-reliance, it is not surprising that a consensus has developed that the poor should be supported, but that they should be required to work for what they receive. For several decades polls have revealed overwhelming support for work requirements. Of respon- dents in 1988–91 GSS surveys 82.2 per cent strongly favoured or favoured 'requiring that people must work in order to receive welfare' (codebook variable: workfare). McClosky and Zaller report that 89 per cent of respondents (to a Gallup poll published in 1975) responded similarly on a similar question (McClosky and Zaller 1984: 272). According to Steven

---

[19] For additional polls on attitudes towards welfare, see Teles (1996, ch. 3).

Teles, in his recent study of the federal welfare system, it is because work is central to the individualist and 'hierarchist' strains in America's culture that work requirements have become 'politically unavoidable': 'the heart of the public's concern for the welfare dependent is their lack of self-sufficiency and their continual dependence upon the government for subsistence not generated from the sweat of their own brow. The American public unmistakably demands that people on welfare should work' (Teles 1996: 170–1). Accordingly, it is not surprising that several states passed welfare reform measures during the early and mid–1990s, culminating in the federal welfare reform act of 1996.[20]

Similar combinations of attitudes are seen in the area of affirmative action. On this issue, Americans clearly oppose giving people advantages that are perceived as unearned. In a 1994 GSS survey 84.08 per cent of respondents opposed preferences 'in hiring and promoting blacks' (codebook variable: jobaff; results similar on affrmact: 82.9 per cent opposed). According to McClosky and Zaller's survey, 15 per cent responded that 'laws requiring employers to give special preference to minorities when filling jobs' are a good idea, as opposed to 53 per cent who responded that they are a bad idea. Seventy-six per cent responded that laws requiring special preferences for minorities when filling jobs are unfair to qualified non-minorities. A similar percentage responded that special preferences for women are unfair to men (McClosky and Zaller 1984: 91–3).

But efforts that did not afford what was viewed as preferential treatment were supported. Opposition to affirmative action did not amount to lack of support for the value of equality. Fifty-seven per cent of McClosky and Zaller's general sample responded that 'efforts to make everyone as equal as possible should be increased'. Fifty-three per cent supported spending tax money to provide college education for those who can't afford it (p. 91). In GSS surveys conducted between 1983 and 1987, 42 per cent of respondents supported government grants to help low income people attend college; 53 per cent supported federal loans. Fewer than 5 per cent supported no government assistance (codebook variable: aidneedy). According to Tom Smith's seven-country study (on which, more below), 75 per cent of Americans strongly agreed or agreed that 'the government should provide more chances for children from poor families to go to university'. This was higher than Australia and Hungary (71 per cent and 72 per cent), though lower than the other countries studied (of which, Italy was highest, with 89 per cent) (Smith 1989: 63).

Before concluding this review of the evidence, I should discuss an additional important source of data. In addition to collecting information in

[20] For discussion of issues involved in reforming the welfare system, including moral arguments for and against reform, see Teles (1996, afterword).

public opinion polls on the beliefs and values of liberal citizens, researchers have conducted different types of laboratory experiment to observe choice of distributive principles by small groups. Because my main concern is the principles liberal citizens would adopt, and there is abundant survey evidence on this, I will devote relatively little attention to experiments.[21]

We can focus on one interesting example, a series of experiments conducted by Norman Frohlich and Joe Oppenheimer.[22] In the experiments of greatest interest to us, Frohlich and Oppenheimer asked their subjects to choose between four principles of distributive justice: maximizing the average income; maximizing minimum income (a principle similar to Rawls's difference principle); maximizing the average level but with a floor, so no one would fall below a certain level; and maximizing the average within a determined range, so no one would fall below a certain minimum or rise above a certain maximum. Subjects were university students in two United States cities, Manitoba (which at that time had the only socialist government in North America), and Warsaw. Groups of five subjects were asked to discuss and choose principles for themselves, under conditions in which they did not know their own places in the resulting income distributions, but were given information on how distributive principles would affect income levels and distributions in society. Ninety-eight five-person group experiments were run; these were highly successful in reaching agreements. The principle of maximum average income with a floor was the overwhelming choice, in all locations. It was chosen by 77.8 per cent of groups; maximum average was chosen by 12.3 per cent; 8.64 per cent chose maximum average in a range; maximum floor alone was chosen by 1.23 per cent (Frohlich and Oppenheimer 1992: 60). Transcripts of the discussions that led to choice of principles provided insight into participants' rationales. According to Frohlich and Oppenheimer, the preferred principle was viewed as allowing a balance of competing 'claims of entitlements and needs, while preserving incentives for productivity' (p. 169). It provided 'a guarantee that no one would "starve" and would also allow those with luck, ambition, or talent (or some combination of these) to increase their earnings without limit and without unnecessary taxation' (p. 63).

Though it is not clear that choice of a given principle under the condi-

[21] The amount of attention given to laboratory material in this chapter is in contrast to discussion of procedural justice, in Ch. 8. Having relatively little general information on procedural justice, we rely far more heavily on laboratory and other kinds of studies.

[22] For reviews of additional sources of information on views of distributive justice, see Tyler *et al.* (1997) Miller (1992*b*).

tions devised by Frohlich and Oppenheimer identifies it as a principle of justice in any ultimate sense, their results support the findings discussed throughout this chapter. Given our concern with principles that liberal citizens could agree upon, the fact that they were consistently able to reach agreement is itself significant, as is of course the nature of the principle generally selected. The preferred principle, which rewards superior performance, can be identified as distribution according to merit. But, as we have seen throughout this chapter, subjects also recognized the need to circumscribe this principle with measures to protect those least able to compete. The fact that this principle was chosen consistently across all four locations studied is also significant. The values of mildly fettered individualism were preferred by Polish and Canadian students as well as Americans.

4. 'CAPITALIST DEMOCRACY'

Combinining the evidence seen throughout this chapter, we can draw important conclusions. Once again, in spite of general support for the dominant ideology in the United States, opposed conservative and liberal élites differ sharply in regard to the fairness of the system, with the former attributing inequalities to personal factors and the latter to problems with the system. For the majority of people, falling between these poles, explanations are complex, combining factors of both kinds. Because it is basically consistent with the dominant ideology, the public's overall view can be characterized as individualistic, but individualistic with exceptions. Central to this view is acceptance of norms of merit distribution and belief in high levels of general opportunity. But this overall view is ambivalent on questions of the system's fairness. Because of strong beliefs that many of the poor are responsible for their condition, there is overwhelming support for workfare programmes and opposition to affirmative action. But this view also recognizes legitimate exceptions and so an important role for social welfare programmes.

The distinctiveness of basic American views comes more clearly into focus if we compare them to those in other countries. In a seven-country comparison conducted during the mid–1980s, Tom Smith notes that the United States was tied with Australia for lowest percentage of GDP devoted to welfare spending (at 17 per cent, in the mid–1980s), and lowest in public support for welfare programmes. For instance, 21 per cent of Americans (N = 1,564) either agreed or strongly agreed that 'the government should provide a decent standard living for the unemployed'. Next lowest was Australia, with 35 per cent. In comparison, 68 per cent of Italians agreed or strongly agreed, 64 per cent of British respondents, and 63 per cent of West Germans (Smith 1989: 71). Over five items used to assess support for welfare, the average level of American support was lowest, at 38 per cent. Australia was at 42 per cent; the other five countries at 60 per cent or above (p. 62). Interestingly, of the five countries, the United States had the second lowest level of support for spending more on benefits for the poor, at 58 per cent (Australia was at 59 per cent). The country with lower support was the Netherlands, at 55 per cent, though, as Smith notes, support will depend on what each country already spends (in the mid–1980s the Netherlands was spending 27.6 per cent of GDP on welfare programmes) (pp. 62 and 75 n. 1).

Smith argues that America's comparatively low support for welfare should in part be explained by its 'ideology of opportunity' (p. 67). Along with Australian and British respondents, in analysing the factors responsible for individual success, Americans were found to place greatest reliance on personal attributes (hard work, ambition, good education, natural ability, in that order) (p. 68). Supporting belief in opportunity was Americans' optimistic assessment of their own position. According to Smith, only Australians 'even begin to approach the American figure'. Eighteen per cent of American respondents saw themselves in the top three (of ten) rungs in the social structure. No more than 10 per cent of respondents so placed themselves in any of the other countries studied (p. 67).

In light of their limited support for welfare programmes, it is not surprising that Americans are generally opposed to more far-reaching redistributive programmes. It is notorious that 'there is no socialism in the United States'. Unlike the European industrial democracies, the United States has never had a significant socialist movement (for discussion, see Hochschild 1981, ch. 1). Poll responses have been consistent with this observation for many decades. In 1937, during the Great Depression, Americans were asked if 'the federal government should follow a policy of taking money from those who have much and giving money to those who have little'; 30 per cent agreed (Hochschild 1981: 18; N not reported; but see below, p. 177). In December 1939 they were asked if 'there should be a law limiting the amount of money an individual is allowed to earn in a year'; 24 per cent said 'yes' (Hochschild 1981: 18; N = 2,048). Jumping ahead to 1969, Americans were asked if 'every family in this country should receive the same income, about $10,000 a year or so'; 13 per cent agreed (p. 18; N = 1,002). These responses are perhaps counter-intuitive, because the United States has generally had greater income inequality than the other industrial democracies (Hochschild 1981, ch. 1).

Additional studies support this account of Americans' orientation.

Only 7 per cent of McClosky and Zaller's general sample agreed that 'under a fair economic system all people would earn about the same'. Only 6 per cent agreed that it would be fairer to pay people according to their economic needs than according to how hard they work. Five per cent agreed that 'giving everybody about the same income regardless of the type of work they do would be a fairer way to distribute the country's wealth than the present system' (McClosky and Zaller 1984: 84).

Americans' failure to support significant redistribution is obviously bound up with general belief in the positive value of economic inequality. In Kluegel and Smith's survey 55 per cent of respondents agreed or strongly agreed that more equality of incomes 'would avoid conflicts between people'. Thirty-nine per cent agreed or strongly agreed that incomes should be more equal, because every family's needs are the same. Fifty-five per cent agreed or strongly agreed that incomes should not be made more equal, 'since the rich invest in the economy, creating jobs and benefits for everyone'. Eighty-two per cent agreed or strongly agreed that incomes 'cannot be made more equal since it's human nature to always want more than others'. Seventy per cent agreed or strongly agreed that incomes should not be made more equal, 'since that would keep people from dreaming of someday becoming a real success' (Kluegel and Smith 1986: 106–7). This lack of support for significant redistribution is especially interesting in light of the finding that Americans are not only aware of poverty in the United States but overstate its magnitude. While approximately 12 per cent of Americans had incomes below the poverty line in 1980, on average Kluegel and Smith's respondents perceived about 31 per cent of the population as poor (pp. 117–18).

Americans are not alone in supporting economic inequalities. Comparison with other countries reveals that this attitude is widespread. Because of their less developed social welfare systems, Smith characterizes the United States and Australia as 'capitalist democracies', rather than 'social democracies' (as are Britain, Italy, the Netherlands, West Germany). Thus it is interesting that, on a series of questions concerning the need for financial incentives, the average level of Americans' support was 66 per cent, fifth highest of the seven countries examined. Of the seven countries, the United States was fourth in belief in the need for financial incentives to get people to work hard, and in belief that they are necessary to get people to take extra responsibility. The United States was sixth in belief in the need for financial incentives to get people to acquire skills and qualifications, and to get them to study for a vocation (Smith 1989: 69).

One area in which Americans have been found to support government intervention is to reduce income inequality. Although inequality is generally not only accepted but viewed as valuable, large percentages think it should be reduced in degree. In response to a GSS question asked repeat-edly since 1972, 47.5 per cent of Americans supported the idea 'that the government in Washington ought to reduce the income differences between the rich and poor'; 20 per cent were neutral on the issue and 32.5 per cent opposed (codebook variable: eqwlth). In 1976, 47 per cent agreed that 'the government should tax the rich heavily in order to redistribute wealth' (Hochschild 1981: 18). Thirty-eight per cent of Kluegel and Smith's sample responded that, ideally, they think there should be more equality of incomes than there is now. Only 3 per cent favoured complete equality of income, while 7 per cent favoured 'less equality of income than there is now' (Kluegel and Smith 1986: 112). Aside from business leaders, all groups of leaders in Verba and Orren's study supported a smaller gap between pay at the top and bottom of the income scale. Not surprisingly, however, groups differed widely on how much the gap should be reduced. Business and, to a lesser extent, Republicans viewed the current earnings gap as equitable; feminists, and to a lesser extent, labour and intellectuals, viewed it as most unfair (Verba and Orren 1985: 159).

In spite of widespread, if not universal, support among Americans for narrowing economic inequality, there is less sentiment along these lines in the United States than in other modern democracies. Of the seven countries examined by Smith, Americans were least in agreement with the claim that income differences are too large: 56 per cent of Americans agreed. Next lowest were Australia, with 58 per cent, and the Nether-lands, at 66 per cent. In comparison, 65 per cent of British respondents agreed and 86 per cent of Italians (Smith 1989: 66). Over four Eurobarometer surveys conducted between 1976 and 1987, inhabitants of twelve European Union countries were asked whether it was impor-tant to 'try and reduce the number both of the very rich people and of the very poor people'. Over the four surveys across the twelve countries, the average responding that this was either important or very important was 80 per cent. High response rates included 96 per cent in Italy in 1976 and 93 per cent in both Greece and Poland in 1987. The low response rates were in Britain: 53 per cent in 1976 and 50 per cent in 1978 (though the figures in Britain for 1983 and 1987 were 70 per cent and 69 per cent, respectively). These were the only two recorded response rates below 60 per cent (Roller 1995: 69).

The clear thrust of comparative studies is fully in keeping with conven-tional views of the American spirit. The United States is commonly seen as a land of opportunity—of limitless opportunities for those willing to work hard. It would take us beyond the scope of this book to explore in detail reasons behind this distinctive American orientation. But briefly, by all indications, it is deeply embedded in American culture. American individualism and self-reliance are tropes. Consider the opening of a recent book on American political culture: 'Few observers of American political culture have failed to comment on the individualistic character of the American people. Most truisms are not without validity, and this one is no exception' (Ellis 1993: 3). Smith writes of the United States—and Australia, his other capitalist democracy: 'Our two capitalist democracies are both new nations, former frontier societies peopled by a diverse mix of immigrants. Although they are extensions of Western society in general and British society in particular, the USA and Australia also represent new beginnings—self-made nations that "grew up" democratic and capitalist' (Smith 1989: 60).

The surveys I have examined confirm that sentiments in the European industrial democracies are far more egalitarian than in the United States. Although the value of economic incentives, and so of economic inequality, is generally recognized—in some cases, as we have seen, at levels higher than in the United States—this is more firmly held in check by egalitarian impulses than in the United States. Though we find a similar combination of egalitarian and inegalitarian attitudes in the United States, the mix is tilted decidedly towards distribution according to merit. Once again, as Smith says, the United States is a capitalist democracy rather than a social democracy.

According to Clive Bean, who compared attitudes towards civil liberties and economic policy in six countries, attitudes in the United States and Australia are distinctive:

Australia and the United States together betray the legacy of having been 'settler societies'. The concept of what constitutes a 'fair go' in these nations appears to revolve around individual endeavour with a smaller emphasis than elsewhere on the government playing a major role and a greater endorsement of private wealth and of not imposing on the wealthy to share their riches.[23] (Bean 1991: 95)

5. IMPLICATIONS

In American society agreement on norms of merit distribution is somewhat analogous to what we have seen in regard to democratic rights. There is general consensus throughout society that what people receive should

---

[23] Bean's six countries were: Australia, West Germany, Great Britain, Austria, Italy, and the United States. Data were from the International Social Survey Programme's first role of government survey, conducted in 1985–6. For the United States, there were 987 respondents.

reflect their contributions. People who are more highly educated, have more valuable skills, and otherwise contribute more should receive more. We have also seen that most people believe the overall economic system provides considerable opportunity, both to themselves and to people in general. But this level of agreement rests on a substructure of disagreement about the extent to which the economy is fair to everybody and, closely linked, the extent to which principles of merit should be supplemented by norms of equal distribution.

Underlying disagreements are most clearly seen in areas that do not fit well with the dominant ideology. People with disparate political and economic views accept different explanations of poverty and wealth, and what should be done about the former. There is little disagreement about the need to address problems of poverty. Requirements to feed the hungry, care for the sick and elderly, and otherwise protect the defenceless are clearly accepted throughout American society. But a crucial provision is that subjects of assistance must truly need it. They must not be able to fend for themselves. Given different underlying philosophies people bring to these issues, it is not surprising that there is considerable disagreement on what constitutes true need. Although overall policy parameters on the issues have been in place for many years, at the present time in the United States the social welfare system is in flux, and it is not clear how new policies will work in practice.

In spite of general agreement on basic distributive norms in the United States, the areas of disagreement we have seen reveal a lack of philosophical consensus. Views advanced by liberal and conservative élites differ in fundamental respects. Although principles of merit distribution are generally accepted, applying them to concrete circumstances will oftentimes cause controversy. Once again, while disagreements here can be viewed as concerned with factual aspects of the economy's workings, they are permeated by philosophical differences. Like disagreements discussed in previous chapters, they are likely to yield solutions that would be generally acceptable only through democratic procedures.

But this should not be taken to mean that movement towards acceptance of greater equality is necessarily at a standstill. The dominant ideology's core principles exist within a wider context, and it is in these surrounding areas that both increased agreement and the implementation of public policy measures to promote equality appear possible.

In at least two main areas, the dominant ideology clearly implies increased equality, in both theory and practice. These concern caring for the truly needy, and providing genuine equality of opportunity throughout society. In regard to the former, there is a range of people who are obviously not able to provide for their own basic needs. The sick and the elderly, children without families, and other similar groups obviously fall into this category, and most Americans strongly support caring for them. Such convictions imply adequate provision of obvious necessities, such as food, housing, and a safe environment. Because people have indisputable needs for additional services such as health care, requirements to provide these as well to people who would not otherwise receive them can be readily justified to most Americans. Arguments along these lines require agreement on the controversial issue of identifying the people truly unable to fend for themselves. But for a significant range of people, there can be little doubt about their need for assistance.

Extending principles of basic care to additional classes of people would be more controversial. Central to recent welfare reforms have been widespread beliefs that many people receiving assistance were not truly needy. With sufficient motivation, they would be able to find work and care for themselves. In other words, their dependent position should be attributed to personal rather than structural factors. Central to disagreements in this area, then, are controversies concerning the nature of 'need' and 'desert'. These are clearly philosophical issues, about which people disagree. Because interpretations of complex social problems such as poverty depend heavily on subjects' overall philosophical views, it is unlikely that people with sharply different perspectives could be brought to agree on many aspects of these issues. For instance, people will disagree as to whether the economy provides employment opportunities for everyone who wants to work, and whether it is feasible for people to be required to work if they have small children and no adequate child care options. Different answers to these questions and others like them have clear implications for how we identify the segments of the population that should receive government assistance.

A case in point concerning different views of need and consequent social policies is seen in 1996 federal welfare reforms. As part of the social security system, supplemental security income (SSI) provides income support to families with disabled children, the parents of whom are often unable to work because of the need to care for them. By the mid-1990s the number of SSI recipients had exceeded 1 million. In keeping with their more restrictive conception of true need, Republican lawmakers argued that not all recipients were truly disabled. As part of the 1996 act, SSI eligibility requirements were tightened, resulting in more than 140,000 recipients being declared ineligible. Not surprisingly, subsequent consequences of the reforms have been widely viewed as unjustifiably harsh. At the time of writing, the revised requirements are under review (*Weekly Edition*, National Public Radio, 21 March 1998). What is clear in this instance, and other similar examples one could name, is that public policy areas are arenas in which conflicting philosophical views can be worked out, and that theoretical assumptions can be revised by resulting experience.

Because of strong philosophical disagreements between segments of the population and no other clear means of settling philosophical and policy disputes, agreement must be provided by democratic processes. However, regardless of the difficulties we face on many controversial issues, there is a core of cases that are reasonably clear-cut. For instance, for classes of people who cannot conceivably fend for themselves, policy requirements are straightforward, and can be justified to almost all Americans with relatively little difficulty.

As experience with SSI reforms indicates, large-scale social experimentation can provide information that will help to narrow disagreement about even highly controversial issues. For example, as welfare reform programmes are implemented, we will learn a great deal about whether the economy can actually provide jobs for all welfare recipients who are required to work, and, closely related, about social support services necessary to enable former recipients to work. Determinations as to who is truly needy and the extent to which poverty is caused by structural as opposed to personal factors are closely bound up with empirical claims concerning how the economy has worked, and predictions about how it will work in the future. As information concerning the latter is supplied by future performance, disagreements about the nature of the needy can be narrowed—perhaps to a large extent—although it is unlikely that all disagreement can be cleared up. It seems clear that if changes in welfare policy result in large-scale, visible misery, large numbers of people will conclude that more must be done for at least some people than denying them benefits and requiring them to find employment. It seems likely that the evidence produced by new public policies will make decisions on these questions relatively easy to justify to most Americans.

Other policies could be readily justified by showing that they are necessary for genuine equality of opportunity. We have seen that real equal opportunity is central to the dominant ideology and so necessary to support claims that economic outcomes recipients receive are what they deserve, and so are fairly acquired. Because of the clear importance of education to people's future prospects, Americans are strongly committed to providing equal educational opportunities. Thus widespread practices of funding schools through property taxes, which result in vastly greater expenditures in affluent districts than in poorer, can be easily criticized. Similarly, although, as we have seen, Americans generally oppose affirmative action measures that are perceived to provide preferences, genuine equality of opportunity requires an end to racial discrimination. If minority groups are not to be favoured, neither can they be subjected to additional hurdles. And so policies to prevent racial (and other) discrimination should be put in place and vigorously enforced. Once again, because Americans are strongly committed to equal opportunity, policies along these lines can be readily justified to them, while the specific form such policies should take can be decided upon by democratic procedures.

7

Rawls's Political Constructivism and Democratic Values

HAVING reviewed central beliefs of liberal citizens, we can pause and reflect upon what has been established. We have two main conclusions. First, we have seen that, in spite of deep-seated disagreements between proponents of different comprehensive views, there is strong consensus on central political values concerning the need for democratic procedures and individual rights, on distributive norms based on merit, and that people should have equal economic opportunities. As noted in the first chapter, beliefs along these lines are fundamental commitments of liberal theory. It is to be expected that inhabitants of contemporary liberal societies would support them.

We have also seen that this measure of consensus rests upon a substructure of underlying disagreements. In spite of respects in which they agree, people with different comprehensive views interpret central values differently. As is seen perhaps most clearly in regard to democratic rights, liberal citizens differ in how they define their scope and their force, as indicated by the circumstances under which they believe rights can be overridden by other concerns. Such disagreements reflect deep differences in overall philosophical or world-views.

Responses to survey questions indicate patterns in respondents' views. It is likely that connections between different doctrinal components throughout the population are less strong than among political and intellectual élites. But overall patterns appear similar. Our evidence does not enable us to characterize the overall views of less articulate segments of the population with precision. But indications are that, for the bulk of the population, range and diversity among belief systems are considerable. Combining these differences with near unanimity on central values leaves us with a situation that is accurately described in Rawls's account of 'overlapping consensus': agreement on a range of central principles, which people interpret differently from the perspectives of their own comprehensive views. In large part, the evidence does not provide detailed accounts of exactly how different people interpret principles. But there are strong indications that these conform to recognized liberal and conservative viewpoints, which may well fall along the continuum noted in the last chapter. In addition, the moral epistemologies explored in Chapter 4 provide some insight into how people with different comprehensive views reason on moral matters.

The generally held values I have identified are of great importance. They demonstrate that the basic commitments of liberal theory posited in Chapter 1 can be justified to almost all members of society, thereby providing support for democratic procedures, equal opportunity, and a protected area of individual rights, although as I have noted, details in regard to all these principles must be filled in. Commitment to democratic procedures is especially important, because they provide means of resolving disagreements not only about other liberal principles, but about the form and scope of democratic procedures themselves. Democratic procedures provide a means for justifying solutions to contested issues as products of procedures that are generally accepted. In the Conclusion I will briefly address the fact that the principles discussed are generally, though not universally, supported. Aside from this problem, the inhabitants of pluralistic societies have been shown to agree on a range of principles sufficient to settle their important disagreements. One can hypothesize that, in some measure, the stability and durability of contemporary liberal societies rests on this consensus.

The area of agreement we have seen admits different construals. Working within this general area, proponents of different comprehensive views could argue for particular interpretations of general principles most consistent with their own value orientations. Because of their profound nature, the disagreements separating people are unlikely to be resolved by arguments alone. In the final analysis, they must be settled politically, with solutions acceptable throughout society on this basis, as long as outcomes remain within the parameters of the abstract principles. To a good extent, political debates in contemporary democratic societies could be construed along these lines, with proponents of different political views advancing their preferred interpretations. Expression of opinions of course has some effects; minds are changed and viewpoints influenced. But with resulting distribution of opinions falling far short of consensus, resolutions must be achieved by democratic procedures. Throughout this work I have generally attempted to present accounts of general principles that are developed in the direction of greater economic equality and expanded rights. For reasons I have discussed, the need to support democratic rights and general acceptance of equality of opportunity have implications that move in this direction. But arguments in other directions are also plausible. Once again, differences between preferred interpretations of society's basic norms must be resolved politically.

In spite of the extent to which liberal consensus could be pushed towards more egalitarian goals, it could be criticized for falling short in this respect. Rawls in particular has attempted to develop a form of political liberalism with substantially greater egalitarian content. Because Rawls is the dominant figure in political liberalism, his view must be addressed, while examining his constructive procedure will support the empirical method discussed in Chapter 2 (and practised throughout this work).

1. RAWLS'S 'POLITICAL CONSTRUCTIVISM'

In *Political Liberalism* Rawls employs a distinctive method of 'political constructivism' to establish his well-known principles of justice (Rawls 1993). Rawls's principles are familiar and need not be discussed in detail here (Rawls 1971: 60–1, 302–3).[1] The first guarantees equal liberty for all members of society. The second has two parts. It guarantees, first, that positions in society are open to everyone and distributed according to fair equality of opportunity, and, secondly, that economic inequalities benefit the least advantaged members of society, Rawls's famous 'difference principle'. Rawls's method of political constructivism is complex. As in *A Theory of Justice*, the principles of justice are the outcome of a process of choice, conducted in the original position, behind a veil of ignorance. The original position is a 'device of representation', to help focus our moral ideas. Given problems caused by the pluralism of liberal societies, the principles arrived at must be acceptable to adherents of society's different comprehensive views. Accordingly, Rawls holds that argument must be from 'intuitive ideas' that he believes are deeply rooted in liberal culture, and so subscribed to by adherents of different comprehensive views. Rawls describes public culture as comprised of 'the political institutions of a constitutional regime and the public traditions of their interpretation (including those of the judiciary), as well as historic texts and documents that are common knowledge' (1993: 13–14).

The specific intuitive ideas on which Rawls focuses are a view of society as a fair system of co-operation and a conception of the person as possessing two moral powers, concerning abilities to form and revise her own conception of the good and to live on fair terms of co-operation with

---

[1] For a recent statement of the principles, see Rawls (1993: 5–6).

others. Though Rawls does not describe in detail how the intuitive ideas tie in with the choice of principles in the original position, it is clear that they are represented by central features of the original position and the deliberations of the representative individuals. Because these particular conceptions of the person and of society are built into the structure of the original position, principles of justice chosen under these conditions are thereby identified as the most suitable principles for free and equal citizens possessing the two moral powers, who seek to live on fair terms of co-operation with others.

Because the principles of justice must be acceptable to adherents of different comprehensive views, Rawls argues that justice as fairness is a 'free-standing view'. This means that it is not constructed on the basis of the existing comprehensive views found in society, as through the convergence method, but rather through the intuitive ideas. Rawls divides the process of construction into two stages. In the first, principles of justice are constructed without reference to existing comprehensive views. Rawls says of the principles of justice: 'Their content is not affected in any way by the particular comprehensive doctrines that may exist in society' (1993: 141). Once the principles of justice are chosen in the first stage, they are reviewed in regard to whether they would be acceptable to proponents of society's comprehensive views, or, as Rawls terms this, in regard to their contributions to 'stability'. If the principles are lacking in this regard, suitable adjustments may be necessary (Rawls 1993: 65–6). I will return to considerations of stability, below.

Rawls's principles have more robust normative content than those that would result from the convergence method. Thus, arguably, they could represent a superior solution to the problem of political liberalism. For the sake of argument, we can assume that they would be the outcome of the method Rawls describes.[2] But this goes only part of the way towards making his case. Basic features of the selection process itself must be justified. In *A Theory of Justice* Rawls notes that different versions of the conditions under which principles of justice are chosen will yield different sets of principles: 'We may conjecture that for each traditional conception of justice there exists an interpretation of the initial situation in which its principles are the preferred solution' (1971: 121). In order to avoid vicious circularity, Rawls must show that the features he presents rather than others should characterize the choice situation. The fact that he never makes this argument in detail is a serious shortcoming of his account of political liberalism—though this does not necessarily mean that reasons for these features do not exist. I will attempt to piece together Rawls's defence of the

---

[2] An excellent argument for this outcome is Cohen (1993).

method—or the defence he would give if pressed—from points he makes in different contexts in *Political Liberalism*, and in some of his articles leading up to it.[3]

After exploring some general difficulties with Rawls's method, I will focus on two main problems: (*a*) his concentration on selected intuitive ideas in liberal public culture; and (*b*) his account of justice as fairness as a 'freestanding' view.

2. PROBLEMS WITH RAWLS'S METHOD

In order to consider Rawls's method, we must inquire into exactly what his account of political liberalism is intended to accomplish. Assessment of means depends heavily on the end. There is, however, a problem here, in that Rawls sets two goals, which do not necessarily coincide. The 'first fundamental question about political justice in a democratic society' he presents is as follows: 'what is the most appropriate conception of justice for specifying the fair terms of social cooperation between citizens regarded as free and equal, and as fully cooperating members of society over a complete life . . .?' (1993: 3). The aim here is to identify the *best* possible principles, with the criteria clearly normative. The second question concerns what Rawls calls 'toleration understood in a general way' (p. 3). Rawls wishes to find a means of bridging the multiplicity of reasonable doctrines that arise in liberal society. This aim is practical: to identify principles on which adherents of different doctrines can agree, in order to contribute to social stability (pp. 3–4). Rawls's conception of how his principles are justified is in keeping with the practical task:

justification is addressed to others who disagree with us, and therefore it must always proceed from some consensus, that is, from premises that we and others publicly recognize as true . . . Thus the aim of justice as fairness, as a political conception is practical, and not metaphysical or epistemological. That is, it presents itself not as a conception of justice that is true, but one that can serve as a basis of informed and willing political agreement between citizens viewed as free and equal persons. (1985: 229–30; similarly 1987: 6, 1989: 250)

He writes similarly in *Political Liberalism*:

The aim of justice as fairness, then, is practical: it presents itself as a conception of justice that may be shared by citizens as a basis of a reasoned, informed, and

---

[3] The main articles on which I draw are Rawls (1980, 1985, 1987, 1989). Also important are Rawls (1982, 1988).

willing political agreement. It expresses their shared and public political reason. (1993: 9)

Though his remarks on justification emphasize the practical side of his project, Rawls places greater weight on the normative. He addresses this in the first of the two fundamental questions and in the first of the two stages of political construction. His main goal in *Political Liberalism*, establishing an overlapping consensus in society, is also inherently normative. An overlapping consensus is not any agreement, but one of a certain kind. As we will see below, Rawls believes that, because of the way it is constructed, an overlapping consensus has moral depth. In addition, it addresses a range of moral concerns, including an expanded conception of individual rights and principles of distributive justice. An overlapping consensus is also accepted by its adherents in a particular way. Rawls contrasts the overlapping consensus with a *modus vivendi*, which is conceived on the model of a truce, the outcome of political bargaining. Because a *modus vivendi* is adhered to for self-interested reasons, its terms reflect the balance of power between contending factions and so are subject to renegotiation as the balance shifts (1993: 147). Unlike a *modus vivendi*, an overlapping consensus is a moral conception, based on what we can call principled acceptance. Its adherents will not withdraw their support if the relative strength of their view increases and it eventually becomes dominant (pp. 147–8).

However, in spite of respects in which the overlapping consensus goes beyond this lesser form of agreement, the need to respond satisfactorily to practical concerns places restrictions on Rawls's political construction. Central features of his justificatory apparatus are based on the practical task. If his only goal had been pursuit of moral truth, he would have argued according to basic tenets of his comprehensive view—from the moral premises he regards as most certain. Because his method of political constructivism is intended to give rise to a view that is 'political' rather than comprehensive, it is not based on premisses endorsed by Rawls but on those that can be generally accepted throughout society. The inescapability of Rawls's practical task is seen in his requirement that construction be from intuitive ideas in the political culture and the need for a second stage in the construction process. But I believe Rawls does not consistently keep his practical goal in view. Doing so would make his political liberalism more political than he himself acknowledges.

Rawls confronts an immediate difficulty in attempting to find the most appropriate conception of justice for a pluralistic society. Because liberal societies are torn by fundamental differences, he believes that disagreements over principles of justice are likely; the 'public political culture may be of two minds at a very deep level' (1993: 9). In order to find 'a basis for public agreement', Rawls works from fundamental elements of the public culture, the intuitive ideas. We collect 'such settled convictions as the belief in religious toleration and the rejection of slavery and try to organize the basic ideas and principles implicit in these convictions into a coherent political conception of justice' (p. 8). The intuitive ideas are intended to be generally subscribed to in ways that principles of justice are not. Rawls describes them as 'public and shared ideas' (p. 90).

Rawls's procedure raises immediate problems. Because of the burdens of judgement, it seems unlikely that adherents of conflicting comprehensive views will readily agree that a specific conception of justice is best suited to free and equal people who have to live together. Among the many issues over which adherents of different views will probably disagree are the precise characteristics of free and equal people. 'Freedom' and 'equality' are 'essentially contested' concepts (Gallie 1955–6; Connolly 1983, ch. 1). On the basis of what we have seen in previous chapters, it is likely that probing beneath the surface concerning even fundamental aspects of American culture such as the rejection of slavery and history of religious toleration will uncover sharp differences in how these themes are understood, or more important, how central they are. In the absence of strong evidence to the contrary, there is little reason to believe liberal citizens will agree more readily about these aspects of their moral views than about others. Indeed, one reason Rawls advances for his method of construction is conflicting strands in liberal societies concerning how the values of freedom and equality should be reflected in the rights of citizens (Rawls 1993: 4–5).

In the second stage of construction, Rawls addresses the possibility that principles derived in the first stage will not be generally accepted. He notes the need for 'acceptable changes' in the principles to bring them into accord with society's comprehensive views (Rawls 1993: 66). However, he sets this problem aside, assuming—'on the basis of a number of plausible considerations'—that it will not arise (p. 66). If we are less sanguine about this problem, we can see that Rawls glosses over serious difficulties, especially the need to take appropriate steps in the first stage of construction to make sure the resultant principles will fit with society's views. Because of his emphasis on the pluralism of liberal societies and the burdens of judgement, the burden of proof is clearly on Rawls to show that justice as fairness would fit. He notes that his claims can be 'verified only by actually elaborating a political conception of justice and exhibiting the way in which it will be supported' (Rawls 1987: 6–7; similarly, 1993: 15). But Rawls never attempts to meet this challenge. One commentator characterizes his view as 'wildly optimistic' (Jones 1995: 526–7). *Political Liberalism*—and the articles leading up to it—are strikingly lacking in detailed examination of the comprehensive views of actual liberal societies.

I do not contend that a fit between Rawls's principles and liberal culture is impossible. But Rawls's particular method of construction, pursuing as it does the best possible principles that can be drawn from selected intuitive ideas, is defensible only if his principles will fit. Because of the strong possibility that they will not, a more advisable procedure would focus on the need to generate principles that would, and then to work up from these ones that different members of society would view as normatively preferable. In other words, if the goal is to find serviceable principles, the order of the two stages of construction should be reversed. In effect, the method of convergence reverses this order.

Because of the need to find principles that will be accepted by people with different comprehensive views, a preferred method would aim first at generating a set of principles that are as uncontroversial as possible. The method of convergence begins with an attempt to find areas of agreement between existing comprehensive views. Once we have determined the range of principles that can be justified to liberal citizens, we can move on to argue for preferred conceptions of individual rights, democratic procedures, and distributive justice, although, as we have noted, proponents of different comprehensive views will argue for different conceptions of these values.

The convergence method attempts to avoid controversy as far as possible. Notion X is by definition uncontroversial—or as uncontroversial as possible—if it is adhered to by the different groups in liberal society, even if members of each group interpret it differently from their own perspectives. In different works Rawls puts forth methodological rules concerning the need to avoid controversy. In 'The Idea of an Overlapping Consensus' he writes: 'The question is: what is the least that must be asserted; and if it must be asserted, what is its least controversial form?' (Rawls 1987: 8). Along similar lines: 'the aspects of our view that we assert should not go beyond what is necessary for the political aim of consensus' (p. 14; similarly 1985: 229–30). Although we find nothing as strong as the first of these quotations in *Political Liberalism*, Rawls restates the second: 'we do not put forward more of our comprehensive view than we think needed or useful for the political aim of consensus' (1993: 153). Given the need to avoid controversy, it is not clear that Rawls should move away from generally accepted moral beliefs to the intuitive ideas.

One reason for Rawls's move to intuitive ideas is his apparent belief that public culture is fractured. He claims that 'public culture may be of two minds at a very deep level' (1993: 9). Once again, it is not clear exactly what he means, and he presents little or no evidence in support of his view. In light of the material discussed in the preceding chapters, the burden would be upon Rawls to show that liberal citizens *do not* agree in these areas.

To some extent, Rawls himself acknowledges general agreement on democratic values. Having been made aware of this by an article written by Kurt Baier (Baier 1989), Rawls addresses this possibility in *Political Liberalism*.[4] Although Baier believes that consensus on Rawls's principles of justice does not exist in contemporary American society, he contends that a different consensus does, a 'constitutional consensus'. Baier describes this as general agreement on 'procedures for making and inter-preting law and, where that agreement is insufficiently deep to end dis-agreement, on the selection of persons whose adjudication is accepted as authoritative'. As Baier notes, the constitutional consensus performs important functions akin to those Rawls assigns to the overlapping con-sensus, promoting stability in society and fostering essential civic virtues of 'tolerance, respect and reciprocity'. He also claims that agreement on institutions and procedures is supported by agreement on a general prin-ciple of justice associated with the proper functioning of institutions.[5]

Rawls's account of constitutional consensus is similar to Baier's (Rawls 1993: 149 n. 15, 158 n. 24), and he appears to accept Baier's contention that one presently exists in the United States (p. 149). Like Baier, Rawls believes that in American society there is greater agreement on political and civil rights than on matters of economic distribution. He includes the former but not the latter in his view of constitutional consensus, which he contrasts with overlapping consensus, describing the former as consensus on 'only certain fundamental procedural political principles for the con-stitution' (p. 149).

While there is agreement on certain basic political rights and liberties—on the right to vote and freedom of political speech and association, and whatever else is required for the electoral and legislative procedures of democracy—there is dis-agreement among those holding liberal principles as to the more exact content and boundaries of these rights and liberties, as well as on what further rights and liberties are to be counted as basic and so merit legal if not constitutional protec-tion. (p. 159)

Even though Rawls notes these important limitations, he recognizes that the moral content of constitutional consensus is significant, emphasizing respect for certain rights, while willingness to put one's own preferences aside and accede to the results of decision procedures is an important

---

[4] I should acknowledged my debt to this article, which did much to shape my think-ing.

[5] Baier (1989); all references are to p. 775. For Rawls's response to Baier, see Rawls (1993: 158–68).

political virtue and one central to the liberal tradition. Rawls also notes that the practice of constitutional politics fosters 'the cooperative virtues of political life', reasonableness, a sense of fairness and willingness to compromise (p. 163).

However, in spite of its virtues, and the respects in which constitutional consensus is similar to overlapping consensus, Rawls views it as inadequate. His reasons are as we have seen. Constitutional consensus falls short in not addressing questions of economic distribution—i.e. the subject of Rawls's second principle of justice. Constitutional consensus also has a weaker conception of rights, the content of which is unacceptably subject to 'the shifting circumstances' of political bargaining (p. 161). Rawls also objects to the means through which constitutional consensus is derived. Its precepts do not stem from shared ideas of the person and the nature of society, but are 'accepted simply as principles', and so lack moral depth (p. 158). For these reasons, Rawls argues for overlapping consensus and his method of constructivism.

Once again, however, Rawls's reasoning can be criticized. Though overlapping consensus may be desirable—and constitutional consensus may not be morally ideal—Rawls's movement to this higher form of consensus (pp. 164–8) is difficult to defend, absent convincing evidence for its existence, or at least its plausibility. Perhaps Rawls could argue that forms of consensus other than the overlapping consensus are inherently flawed or otherwise unacceptable. Certainly, evidence for these claims is required if he believes it is necessary to move away from the moral consensus that he recognizes as existing in liberal society. But Rawls does not develop arguments along these lines. His criticisms of constitutional consensus and the way it is derived presuppose the superiority of his method.

It could perhaps be argued that, in putting forth the overlapping consensus, Rawls is really talking about a different level of consensus, a view of what is ideally possible, rather than what is more likely to be realized. But if this is Rawls's purpose, there are still problems with his strategy. Rawls does not make clear how concentrating on an ideal—remote—possibility is an advisable means of responding to practical problems of political instability, with which he is deeply concerned in *Political Liberalism*.[6] Rawls could perhaps argue that other possible solutions to problems of stability cannot work, that a constitutional consensus will likely suffer from the instability that he believes besets *modus vivendi*. But, as we will see below, an argument along these lines is vulnerable to objections on empirical grounds. For many years the stability of liberal societies has not been in doubt. And if it were, it is not clear that the difference between

[6] For problems of political instability, see below, Sect. 5.

overlapping consensus and constitutional consensus would make a decisive difference. Along with these questions, we should ask about an additional central feature of Rawls's strategy, why he believes we should ground an ideal consensus on actual intuitive ideas latent in the culture of liberal society. The overall method of arguing from intuitive ideas is not adequately defended in *Political Liberalism*. It is to this subject that we now turn.

3. INTUITIVE IDEAS

As noted above, Rawls believes that principles of justice should be developed from selected 'intuitive ideas' latent in the public culture of democratic societies. He describes these as 'a fund of implicitly shared ideas and principles'. The main ideas on which he focuses are 'that of society as a fair system of cooperation over time, from one generation to the next', and 'the idea of citizens (those engaged in cooperation) as free and equal persons'. His other main idea is 'a well-ordered society as a society effectively regulated by a political conception of justice' (Rawls 1993: 14).

Rawls's procedure of arguing from intuitive ideas is an alternative to the method of convergence. Rawls is clearly aware of convergence. At one point he describes two ways in which principles can be constructed, using as his example an index of primary goods. The first way is 'to look at the various comprehensive doctrines actually found in society and specify an index of such goods so as to be near to those doctrines' center of gravity, so to speak' (p. 39). This obviously corresponds to convergence. In contrast to this, justice as fairness 'elaborates a political conception as a freestanding view . . . working from the fundamental idea of society as a fair system of cooperation and its companion ideas' (p. 40). Rawls's hope is not that his principles 'are fair to comprehensive conceptions of the good associated with such doctrines, by striking a fair balance among them, but rather fair to free and equal citizens as those persons who have those conceptions' (p. 40; cf. 1985: 228, 1993: 8).

My questions, of course, concern why Rawls proceeds in this way, and whether his procedure is justified. To begin with, Rawls never explains central aspects of his procedure, including the precise nature of intuitive ideas. In different contexts he describes these as 'certain fundamental ideas seen as implicit in the public political culture of a democratic society' (1993: 13); 'public and shared ideas' (p. 90). More fully: 'the political culture of a democratic society, which has worked reasonably well over a considerable period of time, normally contains, at least implicitly, certain fundamental intuitive ideas from which it is possible to work up a political conception of justice suitable for a constitutional regime' (p. 38 n. 41).[7]

These and other formulations are so vague and abstract that it is difficult to know what Rawls means by them. But he is committed to the claim that most liberal citizens would accept a set of beliefs closely related to those he expounds in *A Theory of Justice* and subsequent works, if these were presented in a certain way. Rawls undoubtedly believes that intuitive ideas not only correspond in some sense to what people believe and could recognize, but constitute the basis for developing moral principles they would also recognize and accept, if the latter could be shown to be derived from the intuitive ideas. This is confirmed by Rawls's view of how political principles can be justified to people by proceeding from premises they 'publicly recognize as true' (1985: 229). In order for acceptance to be 'free and willing' (1987: 5 n. 8), there must be a strong correspondence between the content of the principles and subjects' other political beliefs: 'No political conception of justice could have weight with us unless it helped to put in order our considered convictions of justice at all levels of generality, from the most general to the most particular' (1993: 45).

Rawls's appeal to *intuitive* ideas distinguishes these from the political views that people consciously hold at a given time. Obviously, if there were a strong correspondence between what people consciously believed and the contents of the two principles of justice, they would easily accept them. An intuitive idea, instead, appears to be one that people are not necessarily aware of holding but to which they are committed because of their other beliefs. In 'Kantian Constructivism in Moral Theory' Rawls speaks of 'underlying notions and implicitly held principles': '[The] aim of political philosophy, when it presents itself in the public culture of a democratic society, is to articulate and make explicit those shared notions and principles thought to be already latent in common sense' (1980: 518). Confronted with proper political principles, then, people will recognize them as expressing ideas they implicitly hold. This construal is supported by the reflective equilibrium method discussed in *A Theory of Justice* and referred to in *Political Liberalism* (1971: 19–21, 46–53, 577–86; 1993: 8, 28).

But even if we accept an account of intuitive ideas along these lines, we must recognize that arguing from them is not without costs. If a central aim of political liberalism is to address each group according to ideas to which it subscribes, it is not necessarily advisable to select from people's overall moral views two—and only two—intuitive ideas from which to

---

[7] There are similar descriptions in the articles leading up to *Political Liberalism*; see e.g. Rawls (1985: 225, 1987: 4 n. 7, 6, 1988: 252, 1989: 235).

generate principles. People should be more likely to accept ideas drawn directly from views they hold, as opposed to constructed implications— some attenuated implications—drawn from only some of their intuitive ideas, which, again, they may not even be aware of holding.

Rawls would obviously respond by appealing to the pluralism of liberal societies. The fact that people do not agree on fundamental matters of justice makes it necessary to organize public culture around particular focal points: 'if we are to succeed in finding a basis for public agreement, we must find a way of organizing familiar ideas and principles into a conception of political justice that expresses those ideas and principles in a somewhat different way than before' (Rawls 1993: 9). '[S]ince no political agreement on those disputed questions [concerning matters of justice] can reasonably be expected, we turn instead to the fundamental ideas we seem to share through the public political culture' (p. 150). Once again, justice as fairness focuses on free and equal people co-operating in society.

But aside from difficulties with Rawls's claims concerning the depth of disagreement in society, he never presents evidence that people agree on the intuitive ideas. In 'Kantian Constructivism' he describes the ideas as 'conjectured to be implicit' in liberal culture (1980: 569). He notes that the intuitive ideas chosen must be the most central possible; justice as fairness must be based on 'more central fundamental ideas' than other conceptions (1993: 167–8). But he does not demonstrate that this is true of his two central ideas. He never explains exactly how a given intuitive idea is derived from aspects of public culture, or shows how, of a number of possible intuitive ideas, a particular one rather than others should be the focus of theoretical attention. Explaining how disparate elements in liberal culture can be reconciled into a single set of intuitive ideas would be highly difficult. As it seems, the method of reflective equilibrium would require moving back and forth between different possible accounts of the intuitive ideas and American culture, to try to show the centrality of certain ones and how they should be construed, before beginning to construct political principles upon them. But Rawls bypasses this stage by stipulating that American culture is embodied in a small set of examples he presents concerning religious toleration and the rejection of slavery, and then that these examples yield the intuitive ideas he identifies.

Rawls's lack of adequate explanation is especially troubling because one of the specific ideas he chooses, his conception of the person, is not particularly plausible. Once again, in order to fulfil their function, particular ideas must actually be basic features of public culture, common to its different comprehensive views.[8] Central to the conception of the person

[8] Since the practical goal is to derive principles that would fit with society's comprehensive views, it is possible that one could do this by employing intuitive ideas that

Rawls employs is a strong measure of moral autonomy. He argues that the ability to examine one's moral beliefs and revise one's conception of the good 'is not a means to but is an essential part of a determinate conception of the good'.[9] He continues: 'The distinctive place in justice as fairness of this conception is that it enables us to view our final aims and loyalties in a way that realizes to the full extent one of the moral powers in terms of which persons are characterized in this political conception of justice' (1993: 314). We can refer to the ability to revise one's conception of the good as 'moral revisability'.

Once again, it is striking that Rawls never explores liberal public culture in detail to demonstrate the centrality of this conception of the person. It is especially important that he do so, because religious conservatives do not place at the centre of their view of the person ability to revise and change one's conception of the good. As we saw in Chapter 4, central to the moral outlook of many religious conservatives is belief in 'an external, definable, and transcendent authority', to use Hunter's words. This has profound implications for their view of personal identity, which centres upon the need to pursue and live according to moral truth. Belief in such a moral standard 'defines, at least in the abstract, a consistent, unchangeable measure of value, purpose, goodness, and identity, both personal and collective'. '[O]rthodox communities order themselves, live by, and build upon the substance of shared commitment to transcendent truths and the moral traditions that uphold them' (Hunter 1990: 44, 126; see above, pp. 110–11). As we have seen, something of the order of one-fifth to a quarter of Americans subscribe to views along these lines. If Rawls wishes to convince us that his view of the person actually bridges conflicting comprehensive views, he must show that it undergirds religious comprehensive views as well as secular.[10]

Rawls is clear that the conception of the person he discusses is intended as a political conception, as opposed to a philosophical or metaphysical account. One sense in which ability to revise one's view of the good is

are less central to public culture, as long as principles that would be accepted could be generated through them. But this is an unlikely procedure, unless one could show how it would work. Rawls would have no easy time defending such a procedure as the best way to derive principles that would be likely to be widely accepted.

[9] Though Rawls relies on a strong conception of autonomy, his view should be distinguished from the 'comprehensive liberal theories' of Kant and Mill, which are explicitly based on controversial, strong notions of autonomy (Rawls 1993: 78, 199–200). Rawls's position is that his conception of autonomy is not rooted in a comprehensive view. It is found, rather, in intuitive ideas widely shared throughout society—though it appears that this contention would be difficult to sustain.

[10] Similar points about the clash between Rawls's view of the person and the religious views of many Americans are made by Galston (1989: 714, 1992: 130–1), Wenar (1995), and Exdell (1994: 447).

essential to a political conception of the person is that changes in what one values, even sudden and dramatic changes, do not affect one's 'public or institutional identity' or standing in society (Rawls 1993: 30–1). For instance, the fact that a person becomes a devout member of some religious sect rather than an atheist does not affect his rights as a citizen or his ability to hold property. We can concede that, in this sense, the ability to revise one's conception of the good probably is central to the conception of the person found in liberal political culture. However, Rawls goes well beyond moral revisability in this sense, making it central to his conception of the person and the moral powers.[11]

Because the two main intuitive ideas are modelled by the constructivist procedure pursued in *Political Liberalism*, religious conservatives could well have strong doubts about Rawls's resultant principles of justice. It is open to Rawls to dismiss this criticism. Religious conservatives may not be 'reasonable' in his sense, as, in order to be reasonable, one must recognize the burdens of judgement (Rawls 1993: 54–66). Rawls argues that he is justified in excluding unreasonable doctrines from consideration because his theory is intended to produce an overlapping consensus of reasonable doctrines (pp. 36, 63–4). For the sake of argument we can grant that the views of religious conservatives are not 'reasonable' in Rawls's sense. However, as discussed in Chapter 2, there are powerful normative and practical consideration in favour of including as many inhabitants of society as possible in a liberal consensus. At one point Rawls notes that he is optimistic in assuming that, aside from certain forms of fundamentalism, all the main historical religions are reasonable comprehensive views (p. 170). The problem, however, is the likelihood that views Rawls would classify as fundamentalism, i.e. different forms of religious conservatism, are adhered to by so high a percentage of the American population. A conception of 'reasonable' principles that immediately excludes 20–5 per cent of the population requires strong justification. Moreover, as Leif Wenar points out, Rawls's conception of the person would be rejected by adherents of many non-religious comprehensive views: e.g. followers of Bentham, Hume, and Hobbes (Wenar 1995: 50). Further reflection would probably identify additional groups.[12]

---

[11] Though there is little doubt that Rawls goes beyond autonomy in the first sense (political autonomy) to identify autonomy in the stronger sense as central to liberal culture, it is not clear that this plays an important role in his derivation of the principles of justice. See Rawls (1993: 311 n. 23); compare sect. 82 of *A Theory of Justice*, which does not rely on autonomy in the strong sense. It is not clear why Rawls presents so strong and controversial a view of the person, in spite of the injunction to avoid controversy discussed above (p. 190). For related criticisms of Rawls's view, see Wenar (1995).

[12] Members of many other religious groups would probably also object to Rawls's

In the absence of strong evidence to the contrary, then, it seems likely that Rawls's view would not be recognized by a large percentage of the American populace. Once again, if we require a broader consensus, we can argue from ideas that people already accept, instead of principles derived from controversial intuitive ideas not shared by substantial numbers of liberal citizens.

4. A 'FREE-STANDING' VIEW

Questions about Rawls's use of intuitive ideas lead directly into others concerning his two-step procedure. Because justice as fairness is a 'free-standing view', its construction is in two stages. In the first, as we have seen, principles of justice are worked up from intuitive ideas latent in the public culture. Only in the second stage is the question of 'stability' raised. What interests us here is that only at this stage do society's different comprehensive views come into play. As they are derived in the first stage, the principles' content 'is not affected in any way by the particular comprehensive doctrines that may exist in society' (Rawls 1993: 141).

Rawls does not explain exactly why comprehensive views must be excluded in the first stage but not the second. For the most part, discussion of his method centres on contrasting it with other possible methods, though not defending its superiority.[13] It seems that Rawls's main argument is that a method akin to convergence would make political liberalism 'political in the wrong way'. In two contexts in *Political Liberalism*, Rawls uses this language (1993: 39–40, 142). Although he does not elaborate on this problem in this work, he presents more of his reasoning in 'The Domain of the Political and Overlapping Consensus'. In this article Rawls expresses 'misgivings' that the view of overlapping consensus advanced in his previous articles had suggested that political philosophy is 'political in the wrong way'.[14]

conception of the person. It should be noted that members of these groups, and the ones mentioned in the text, are clearly *excluded* from Rawls's consensus, while, once again, he presents no evidence as to the percentage of the population that would be included. In contrast, the surveys discussed in Chs. 3–6 show far fewer members of society clearly excluded.

[13] See Rawls (1993, ch. 3), esp. the list of topics to be discussed (p. 89).

[14] Throughout *Political Liberalism*, Rawls draws relatively little on 'The Domain of the Political and Overlapping Consensus', in comparison, for example, to 'The Idea of an Overlapping Consensus'. But there is nothing in *Political Liberalism* to suggest that he has rejected its arguments. Barry too uses 'The Domain of the Political' to flesh out certain points in *Political Liberalism* (Barry 1995a: 891–2). The 'previous articles' mentioned are apparently Rawls (1985, 1987).

He developed the two-step method to avoid this problem (see 1989: 250–1). Rawls writes:

We must, however, be careful that a political conception is not political in the wrong way. It should aim to formulate a coherent view of the very great (moral) values applying to the political relationship and to set out a public basis of justification for free institutions in a manner accessible to free public reason. It must not be political [i] in the sense of merely specifying a workable compromise between known and existing interests, nor political [ii] in looking to the particular comprehensive doctrines known to exist in society and in then being tailored to gain their allegiance. (p. 250)

The reasons for rejecting sense (i) are evident. As Rawls says in *A Theory of Justice*, 'to each according to his threat advantage is not a principle of justice' (1971: 141). However, considerations against sense (ii), which corresponds to the method of convergence, are less apparent. Because Rawls does not present his arguments clearly, I will attempt to reconstruct them.

Rawls apparently views a consensus based on convergence as inherently precarious. As his contrast between overlapping consensus and *modus vivendi* makes clear (see above, p. 188), he is worried about principles derived from agreements based on an existing balance of power, which are subject to renegotiation as the balance shifts. Hence it is likely that Rawls fears that, if principles were chosen on the basis of existing comprehensive views, their substance would be 'affected by the existing balance of political power between comprehensive doctrines' (1993: 142). He obviously wishes to avoid such a bargaining situation, presumably because of concern about the stability of the resulting principles, which would recall the *modus vivendi*: 'social consensus founded on self or group interests, or on the outcome of political bargaining: social unity is only apparent, as its stability is contingent on circumstances remaining such as not to upset the fortunate convergence of interests' (p. 147).

If this is Rawls's main ground for preferring the two-step procedure, it is unsatisfactory for three main reasons. First, the image of different people, or proponents of different groups, engaged in political bargaining recalls Rawls's initial presentation of his social contract theorizing, in 'Justice as Fairness'. This model was found to be unsatisfactory because people who are aware of their interests have no reason not to hold out for concessions.[15] One reason Rawls introduced the veil of ignorance in *A Theory of Justice* was to get round this problem, as people who do not know their particular interests are not able to bargain in the usual sense (1971: 139–41; also 1993: 23). His fear concerning political bargaining is obviously closely bound up with *Political Liberalism*'s contrast between

[15] Rawls (1958); for discussion, see Wolff (1977, ch. 5).

the two kinds of agreement. The overlapping consensus, which is constructed on the basis of intuitive ideas rather than directly from society's comprehensive views, differs from a *modus vivendi* in not being adhered to for self-interested reasons. And so its adherents will not withdraw their support if the relative strength of their view increases and it becomes dominant (1993: 147–8). Because Rawls believes that the balance of power on which a *modus vivendi* rests can be precarious, he views the distinction between *modus vivendi* and overlapping consensus as important to social stability. If we liken the method of convergence to the kind of political bargaining that gives rise to a *modus vivendi*, then Rawls would have grounds on which to criticize this.

It is not clear, however, that the method of convergence is actually a form of political bargaining. Its governing rationale, as we have seen, is to attempt to identify principles that are held in common and so can be justified to people with different comprehensive views. The contractarian idea of bargaining is therefore out of place here. Once a core of ideas on which people can agree has been identified, proponents of different views are free to argue for their preferred construals, with democratic procedures selecting eventual principles. But identification of the area of overlap is largely an empirical endeavour, as pursued throughout the foregoing chapters, rather than an exercise in rational maximizing.[16]

Secondly, Rawls's exposition raises questions about the extent to which the two stages are in fact separate, and so whether the content of the principles is actually 'not affected in any way by the particular comprehensive doctrines that may exist in society' (1993: 141). As it stands, this claim is incorrect. Derivation of the principles in the first stage is not *ex nihilo*. Intuitive ideas rooted in the public culture of course play an essential role in their construction. Rawls does not explain why, if construction of the principles is inherently tainted by exposure to comprehensive views, intuitive ideas drawn from existing comprehensive views are admissible, but beyond this point not allowed. Excluding other, possibly relevant aspects of comprehensive views is also counter-intuitive because of the practical aims of political constructivism. Principles derived in the first stage are not intended solely to be as just as possible, but must also fit with society's comprehensive views. As we have seen, at times Rawls notes this (1993: 65,

---

[16] If there are disagreements about the nature and scope of shared principles in society, we could still employ means less drastic than Rawls's requirement that all knowledge of society's comprehensive views be expunged. Construction of principles could proceed behind a partial veil of ignorance, which blocked representative individuals' knowledge of their own comprehensive views, but not those of society. In Rawls (1993: 24 n. 27) Rawls discusses reasons for eliminating the representative individuals' knowledge of the comprehensive views of the people they represent, but does not justify eliminating general knowledge of comprehensive views.

78). He also notes that if the principles selected in the first stage would not fit properly, 'acceptable changes' must be made (pp. 65–6). Accordingly, the stages are not as separate as Rawls asserts, and so it is not clear why he excludes knowledge of everything but the two basic intuitive ideas from the first stage.

A third consideration concerns another possible reason for excluding comprehensive views. Central to Rawls's idea of 'political' liberalism is that people should be able to *endorse* the principles from their own points of view, according to their own comprehensive views. Rawls writes: 'to attain such a shared reason, the conception of justice should be, as far as possible, independent of the opposing and conflicting philosophical and religious doctrines that citizens affirm' (p. 9). Part of what Rawls means by public justification is that, in a liberal society, coercive public power should not be used in ways that citizens cannot affirm (p. 68). However, this entails that *justification* of the use of power not be rooted in a particular comprehensive view. It does not require that *construction* of the relevant principles be fully independent of conflicting comprehensive views, as long as principles constructed by working from different existing comprehensive views can be justified to each citizen in his own terms, on the basis of his own comprehensive view.

It seems then that Rawls's reasons for fearing that principles worked up from existing comprehensive views would be 'political in the wrong way' can be countered. The method of convergence should be able to generate principles that can be generally endorsed, without the problems we have seen in working from selected intuitive ideas or insisting that construction of principles be without reference to existing comprehensive views.

5. STABILITY

We have seen that Rawls appears to believe in the existence of a constitutional consensus in the United States at the present time. But he believes this is unacceptable or undesirable in various ways. In order to be persuasive, an argument along these lines must provide a convincing account of how the areas of difference between overlapping consensus and constitutional consensus are not only desirable but necessary. It must show that constitutional consensus falls short in crucial ways, so that remaining at that level is not a viable option.

Although Rawls does not directly connect up his idea of constitutional consensus and the convergence method, he believes the former can be derived from areas of overlap between existing views. Because it is also quite close to the agreements discussed in Chapters 3–6 of this work, for the sake of discussion in this section we can treat Rawls's constitutional consensus as more or less interchangeable with that uncovered by our use of the convergence method, without fear of undue distortion. Though Rawls's ideas on shortcomings of the constitutional consensus can be found in different contexts in *Political Liberalism*, they are somewhat unclear, and so, once again, I will attempt to reconstruct them. His direct discussion of the contrast between constitutional and overlapping consensus is largely unhelpful, because it is concerned to show that the latter is not 'utopian' (1993: 168, 158), rather than that it is necessary.[17]

At first sight, it would be difficult for Rawls to show that constitutional consensus is obviously unsatisfactory. He notes that overlapping consensus is not necessary 'for certain kinds of social unity and stability', and that constitutional consensus is 'sufficient for less demanding purposes and far easier to obtain' than overlapping consensus (p. 149; see also p. 230). Presumably, Rawls believes that constitutional consensus contributes to the forms of social unity and stability found in existing liberal societies, in which the requisite agreement can be found. He adds, moreover, as we saw above, that the smooth functioning of political institutions itself encourages 'the cooperative virtues of political life', reasonableness, a sense of fairness, willingness to compromise, and 'willingness to cooperate with others on political terms that everyone can publicly accept' (p. 163). If all this is true, then one must ask how constitutional consensus falls short.

Rawls holds that constitutional and overlapping consensus differ mainly in terms of breadth and depth.[18] In regard to the former, the overlapping consensus encompasses a wider range of principles, basically more secure views of substantive rights and more developed principles of economic distribution. Its superior depth is in reference to the fact that participants trace their views back to fundamental intuitive ideas rooted in the political culture. The principles that constitute a constitutional consensus are less firmly grounded.

Rawls believes that, as a result of these differences, overlapping consensus will be superior from a normative standpoint and also possess greater 'stability'. The essence of the normative criticism has been discussed

---

[17] See also Rawls (1996, pp. xlvii–viii). In addition, Rawls's main account of the differences between the two kinds of consensus (1993: 144–68) is less clear than it might be, because much of this discussion is drawn, with only slight revisions, from Rawls (1987), which was written before Baier's seminal article had brought the idea of constitutional consensus to Rawls's attention. Sect. 7, on the movement from constitutional consensus to overlapping consensus, is new, but the context into which it is inserted is not sensitive to the relationship between the two forms of consensus.

[18] He also discusses differences in specificity (pp. 164–8), though these seem less significant (see n. 19, below).

above. Even if we concede Rawls's belief that principles that provide more substantial economic protection are morally superior to those in a constitutional consensus, he has not shown that these will be accepted by the diverse inhabitants of liberal societies. In the light of our discussion of the beliefs of liberal citizens, there is good reason to doubt Rawls's claim in this regard. He clearly provides insufficient evidence that the difference principle will be the focus of agreement throughout society, or that his method is the one best suited to develop superior principles that will also be able to secure agreement.[19]

This leaves considerations of *stability*. We have seen that Rawls faults the *modus vivendi* because, owing to its lack of moral depth, its participants will withdraw their allegiance in accordance with shifts in the balance of power (above, p. 188). Rawls apparently believes that something similar holds in regard to constitutional consensus. Though he does not discuss this matter directly, he apparently believes that a constitutional consensus too is lacking in stability.

In order to assess Rawls's argument, we must discuss the nature of 'stability' and the distinctive way he employs this concept. As noted above, as the term is encountered generally in discussions in political science and sociology, 'stability' refers to attributes of a system of political institutions. For instance, according to Seymour Martin Lipset, a stable democracy is one that has enjoyed 'the uninterrupted continuation of political democracy since World War I *and* the absence over the past twenty-five years of a major political movement opposed to the democratic "rules of the game"' (Lipset 1960: 30). According to this common view, a 'stable' democracy is characterized by smoothly functioning democratic institutions. By extension, other stable governments possess similar features. For ease of reference, I will refer to stability in this sense as stability in the usual sense or political stability.

The idea of stability plays a significant role in Rawls's theory. For instance, he writes that '*all* differences' between *Political Liberalism* and *A Theory of Justice* can be traced to problems in the view of stability put forth in the latter (1993, pp. xv–xvi; my emphasis). Thus it is important to realize that Rawls discusses an unusual sense of the term, a psychological

[19] For empirical evidence that the difference principle would *not* be the focus of consensus in society, see Miller (1992*b*) and Frohlich and Oppenheimer (1992) (discussed above, pp. 173–4). Rawls believes it is unlikely that there will be a set of principles of distribution that everyone will agree upon. Rather, it is 'more realistic and more likely' that there will be a number of competing distributive principles, which will include justice as fairness (1993: 164). If this is true, then the difference between overlapping consensus and constitutional consensus in regard to principles of economic distribution is narrowed, and Rawls's grounds for rejecting the latter are also narrowed.

sense, which centres on the way in which the inhabitants of a regime hold their moral principles. Stability in this sense, to which we can refer as 'moral' stability, is an important component of Rawls's argument in *A Theory of Justice*. In *Political Liberalism* also, in keeping with his view of moral psychology (1993: 81–8), Rawls argues that people are more likely to act on their moral principles when they believe that their political system functions in accordance with them, and other citizens are also likely to behave in accordance with them (pp. 86, 163). It is because of an overlapping consensus's superior ability to generate stability in this sense that we should prefer it to constitutional consensus.

Two sides of this argument should be distinguished. The first is the relationship between moral and political stability. The second concerns other reasons why moral stability is desirable. I will discuss these, in turn.

In *Political Liberalism* Rawls is deeply concerned with questions of political stability. He believes that Western liberalism emerged from a cauldron of conflict between different groups during its formative centuries. Of special importance is the origin of religious toleration, which arose out of European religious wars in the sixteenth and seventeenth centuries. The fact of ineradicable pluralism led to 'discovery of a new social possibility: the possibility of a reasonably harmonious and stable pluralist society' (1993, p. xxv). Building on this example, Rawls argues that the task of political philosophy is set in motion by 'deep political conflicts'. It is utopian not to believe such conflicts exist. They generate the requirement that political philosophy bridge significant differences: 'We turn to political philosophy when our shared political understandings . . . break down' (p. 44). It is notable that to illustrate such conflicts Rawls uses the example of disagreements between the American North and South over slavery (p. 45). Such cases demonstrate the importance of finding means for groups to coexist in peaceful, stable societies.

But it is not enough for Rawls that groups merely coexist. As we have seen, coexistence on the basis of a *modus vivendi* is inadequate. An example of a *modus vivendi* is the relationship in the sixteenth century between Catholics and Protestants, who came to endorse the principle of toleration out of necessity rather than conviction (p. 148). In contrast to a *modus vivendi*, an overlapping consensus is morally stable because its adherents support it for reasons that go beyond convenience. Toleration is rooted in their comprehensive moral views—though supported differently by the views of different groups—and fostered by the sense of justice that develops in a well-ordered society (pp. 140–50). As we have seen, participants in an overlapping consensus are likely to adhere to it even if the balance of power shifts (pp. 147–9). Thus the search for overlapping consensus is strongly motivated by these practical concerns.

Rawls is aware that considerations of stability (as he construes this) have gone largely undiscussed by previous theorists (p. xvii). I believe this neglect is justified. One can ask whether considerations of stability are sufficient to bear the weight he places on them. It would be difficult for him to argue that stability in his sense is necessary for the smooth functioning of liberal societies—for political stability. As we have seen, his criticism of *modus vivendi* centres on the claim that it will lack political stability. But a similar argument is not convincing in regard to regimes characterized by constitutional consensus. A striking fact of post-Second World War political life is the overall stability of liberal democracies. Rawls's understanding of modern democratic societies appears to be hampered by common misconceptions, by belief in what is referred to as 'consensus theory'. As described by James Wright, this view holds that democratic political arrangements are inherently fragile; they 'naturally tend toward collapse in the absence of any countervailing mechanism' (Wright 1981: 12). Because of the weakness of liberal institutions, proponents of consensus theory believe it is important to promote democratic values throughout society, in order to counteract destabilizing tendencies. Because the representative individuals share Rawls's adherence to consensus theory, they are deeply concerned with preserving the stability of liberal societies, and so favour moral principles that support this.

The facts of political sociology over the past half-century, however, sharply contradict Rawls's assumptions. Brief reflection will reveal that, virtually without exception, the industrial democracies have been remarkably stable for more than fifty years. To quote Wright once again: 'The notion that democracies are somehow inherently unstable, that they naturally tend toward collapse, is very difficult to square with this and most other aspects of world political history since World War II' (1981: 67). He continues: 'In the modern world, democracies prove not to be inherently unstable, as much theory suggests, but rather obdurately stable under almost all circumstances' (p. 67). If this is true, then the representative individuals will not be much concerned with political stability, and considerations of moral stability will interest them even less. Their choice of moral principles will be based almost entirely on other factors.

If we assume that modern democracies are characterized by constitutional consensus—which probably plays some role in their political stability—it would be difficult for Rawls to argue that lack of stability in his sense undermines political stability. Moreover, his claim that stability in his sense contributes significantly to political stability is supported by little or no evidence and is not intuitively convincing. Rawls says that he is interested in a specific kind of political allegiance: 'the bases of allegiance [a liberal conception of justice] generates in virtue of the distinctive content of its principles' (1993: 161 n. 26). In his latest discussion Rawls refers to this as 'stability for the right reasons' (1996, p. xxxix n. 5). In comparison to other factors that political observers since ancient times have identified as sources of political stability—e.g. absence of economic, religious, racial, and ethnic differences—one wonders how great a role is played by specific aspects of the content of liberal principles. Accordingly, although, once again, overlapping consensus may be desirable, Rawls has not made a strong case that its superior contribution to political stability is sufficiently important to justify jettisoning a method of political construction that is able to generate constitutional consensus in favour of one that is otherwise lacking support but possibly able to generate overlapping consensus.[20]

It is still open to Rawls to argue that stability in his sense is inherently valuable and so for the superiority of his method because it yields principles that are better in this respect. Considerations along these lines appear to be more important to Rawls than political stability. Briefly, he claims the superiority of a regime with moral principles that encourage the co-operative virtues, thereby helping people fully to develop their moral powers—in this case, specifically, the 'reasonable'. Rawls describes this as ability 'to understand, apply, and to act from the reasonable principles of justice that specify fair terms of social cooperation' (1993: 103–4). However, he does not provide evidence for his crucial claim that the motivating force of moral principles with particular content is greater than that of other factors. Even if we concede that the factor he notes plays some role in influencing behaviour, he does not address the question of how this factor interacts with others that also influence conduct, e.g. self-interest, religion, national identification. In order for moral stability to be a central consideration in the representative individuals' deliberations, it must play a significant role in stimulating co-operative behaviour, but this Rawls has not shown.

It is likely that the prominent role Rawls accords this factor is bound up with his conception of the person, as possessing the two moral powers. It appears that his postulation of the 'reasonable' is less controversial than the aspects of his conception of the person discussed above (pp. 195–7). However, as we have seen, Rawls presents little evidence that his particular conception of the person is deeply rooted in the public culture of liberal societies. Absent convincing arguments that inhabitants of liberal societies would accept this conception of the person, Rawls would find it difficult to demonstrate that a society in which moral principles are held

---

[20] For further reasons to question Rawls's arguments concerning the role of political stability in the choice of principles of justice, see Klosko (1994).

in accordance with his notion of stability is for this reason significantly superior to one in which they are not.

In sum, even if we concede that a society with an overlapping consensus is preferable in various ways to one with only a constitutional consensus, Rawls does not make a convincing case that the latter is radically defective and so it is necessary to jettison the method of convergence and move to overlapping consensus. The point bears repeating that, even if Rawls did make this case, this still would not demonstrate that his particular method is the one best suited to develop an overlapping consensus. The possibility would remain that some other method was better suited to this task, and without the severe flaws in Rawls's political constructivism.

The arguments of this chapter should be taken to support liberal consensus indirectly. Rawls's method of political constructivism is beset with problems in its resort to intuitive ideas, the specific ideas it employs, its attempt to be 'free-standing', and the other respects I have discussed. A strong liberal might well be attracted to this method because of the nature of the principles to which it gives rise. But even if we allow that Rawls's principles would be generated by his method, he does not adequately defend his use of this method instead of others. The litany of problems I have discussed indicate that he would have no easy time doing so.

8

Procedural Justice

ALTHOUGH it is unlikely that the specific factors Rawls identifies contribute significantly to political stability, other aspects of normative principles may well do so. Social psychologists have long recognized that people's attitudes towards organizations are strongly affected by their views about how the latter distribute objects of value. As noted above, concerns of distributive and procedural justice can be distinguished. The former centre upon the justice or fairness of a given pattern of distributed outcomes. Procedural justice involves the fairness or justice of the procedures through which distributions are made. In regard to decisions in a given system, distributive and procedural justice are generally closely linked. Fair procedures lead to fair outcomes, while fair outcomes generally result from fair procedures. But the two are distinguishable in practice as well as theory. In recent years a body of research has established the importance of people's opinions about the procedural side of distribution, which have been found frequently to outweigh the distributive side in affecting support for organizations.

Social psychologists who have studied procedural justice proceeded originally from a view of human nature and decision-making taken from economics and public choice. According to this view, people are self-interested in a narrow and short-term sense. They can be expected to support organizations and political systems that give them what they want. Along the lines of specific political support, their main concern should be outcome effects. Procedural justice researchers have been critical of this model. The classic study of John Thibaut and Laurens Walker *Procedural Justice: A Psychological Analysis* (Thibaut and Walker 1975) demonstrated that outcome effects are neither the sole nor the strongest determinants of satisfaction with a political process. Thibaut and Walker's subjects preferred certain kinds of legal proceedings to others, without immediate regard to differences in outcomes. Briefly, they preferred adversarial procedures to non-adversarial, because of the opportunities to participate that the former provide. In adversarial proceedings subjects have more control over the decision-making process than in other kinds of procedures, e.g. inquisitorial, in which the presiding official has a far greater role. Thibaut and Walker argue that questions of control are central to procedural justice. Fair procedures place decision-making authority in the hands of participants themselves; in unfair procedures authority is disproportionately vested in third parties.

Essential support Thibaut and Walker provide for this claim is evidence concerning the attitudes of disputants in various settings. Whatever justice is, 'it is not likely to be done nor to be perceived done unless the determinative procedure matches reasonably well the procedural requirements imposed on disputants by their social environment' (p. 4). Thibaut and Walker performed a series of studies, using American undergraduates as subjects, and, for purposes of comparison, students in Great Britain, France, and West Germany. Throughout, adversarial procedures were consistently found to be preferred, and this conclusion held when subjects were placed behind a version of Rawls's veil of ignorance (Thibant and Walker 1975, ch. 11).

In subsequent decades researchers have built on Thibaut and Walker's study. Among topics that have been investigated are people's preferences in regard to a variety of different procedures and aspects of procedures, including, as with Thibaut and Walker, differences between preferences of inhabitants of different countries.[1] Effects of people's opinions about procedural justice have been observed in a litany of areas: legal settings; encounters with police and other public officials; in business in regard to such areas as lay-off decisions, grievance procedures, pay rises, employee assessments, and job interviews; and political and educational contexts.[2] Perceptions of procedural justice, or the lack thereof, have been found to have strong effects, independent of the outcomes of decisions, in all these areas. For our purposes, it is important to review findings in regard to how procedural justice affects subjects' commitment to organizations, especially political organizations. In addition, researchers have studied the nature of procedural justice itself. Philosophers have traditionally analysed the concept mainly in terms of formal criteria procedures should satisfy. For instance, in the most detailed study in the literature Michael Bayles bases his analysis on different procedures employed in the legal system and so focuses on formal characteristics of procedures, e.g.

---

[1] See LaTour *et al.* (1976) for the United States and Germany; Lind *et al.* (1978) for the United States, West Germany, France, and Britain; Leung and Lind (1986) and Leung (1987) for the United States and Hong Kong; Lind (1994) for the United States, Hong Kong, and Japan; Lind *et al.* (1997) for the United States, Germany, Hong Kong, and Japan.

[2] For overviews of procedural justice studies in different areas, see Lind and Tyler (1988) and Tyler *et al.* (1997: ch. 4).

consistency, adherence to precedents, and conformity to rules (Bayles 1990). However, empirical researchers have argued that, in assessing the fairness of given procedures, people are concerned with additional factors as well. In the years following Thibaut and Walker's study researchers moved well beyond their focus on issues of control. Additional factors that have been examined are discussed in Section 3.

In this chapter I will briefly discuss procedural studies in different areas, concentrating on two main themes: (*a*) procedural justice's contribution to system stability, in the following two sections; and (*b*) people's views about the nature of procedural justice, in Section 3. Although research in the latter area is somewhat preliminary, I will explore evidence suggesting that attitudes towards procedural justice are able to bridge the divides between diverse groups in contemporary pluralistic societies.

1. THE 'FAIR-PROCESS' EFFECT

A major reason why procedural justice is of interest to political theorists is its ability to lessen the impact of unpleasant decisions. This 'cushioning' effect is referred to in the literature as the 'fair-process effect' (Folger *et al.* 1979). For illustration, we can observe it in a study of employees, reactions to lay-offs conducted by Mary Konovsky and Robert Folger (Konovsky and Folger 1991).

Konovsky and Folger surveyed 353 lay-off victims in regard to how their justice perceptions affected their reactions to being laid off. The justice of employer procedures was assessed through different criteria, concerning such matters as whether employers applied standards consistently, were unbiased, and provided opportunities to correct errors. Additional criteria concerned whether employers gave convincing explanations for their actions. A global measure of procedural justice was also included, which consisted of two items: 'My employer tried hard to be fair' and 'My employer made the layoff decisions in the fairest way possible' (p. 637). In addition to the effects of procedural justice, Konovsky and Folger studied subjects' responses to tangible outcomes, including the amount of severance benefits they received. Dependent variables were subjects' desire for legal regulation of lay-offs and their willingness 'to recruit for and speak positively about' their former employers (p. 632).

Konovsky and Folger's results showed positive associations between lay-off victims' fairness perceptions and their willingness to speak well of their former employers and lack of desire for legal regulation of lay-offs. The effect of fair lay-off procedures was 'above and beyond' outcome concerns and the effects of explanations (pp. 643–4). Accordingly, this study suggests that what is perceived to be fair treatment can mitigate negative feelings generated by the severely negative experience of being laid off. The study has obvious practical implications for employers, who should not confine their efforts to increasing severance packages, but should also attend to making lay-off decisions in ways that will be perceived to be as fair as possible (p. 644).

Numerous similar studies can be cited. For instance, in a study of reactions to performance evaluations by some 300 government employees, M. Susan Taylor and her associates arranged to have one group of managers evaluate employees through procedures in which concerns of due process received added attention (Taylor *et al.* 1995). These included ensuring employees received adequate notice and a hearing in which communication was encouraged, and taking additional steps to make sure assessments were based on evidence. Taylor and her associates found that employees assessed according to these procedures evaluated the competence of their supervisors more favourably than did members of a control group, even though the evaluations they received were substantially lower than those of the control group (p. 518). Along similar lines, in a study of employee reactions to pay rise decisions, Folger and Konovsky found that distributive concerns were the predominant factor in satisfaction with rises. But procedural concerns were more important in influencing subjects' commitment to their organization and trust in their supervisors (Folger and Konovsky 1989).

The effects noted in these business settings have been observed in other areas. For instance, Tom Tyler studied defendants in traffic and misdemeanour court (Tyler 1984). He found that outcomes of cases strongly influenced subjects' opinions of the fairness of procedures but exerted no independent influence on assessments of the judge or court system. Views of the fairness of procedures more strongly affected these assessments than opinions regarding either output level or output fairness. Tyler notes the implication, that this study points to procedural justice 'as a key element in explaining support for legal authorities': 'defendants charged with minor offenses who fare poorly at trial will not denigrate the judge or the system so long as they believe the outcomes are fair ones reached by fair procedures' (Tyler 1984: 70).

In another study Tyler and Folger found that, in encounters with the police, subjects' opinions concerning the quality of services provided by the police and how good a job the police were doing were influenced more strongly by procedural factors than by whether the police officers issued citations (Tyler and Folger 1980).

Extending procedural justice research to educational settings, Tyler and Andrew Caine found that for undergraduate students asked to recall a course they had taken, opinions concerning the fairness of the teacher's grading procedure exerted a far stronger influence on their assessments of the teacher's fairness and overall quality than various outcome measures associated with the grades they had received (Tyler and Caine 1981, study 2, pp. 646–9). Though assessments of outcomes affected views of procedural fairness, when these factors were distinguished through regression analysis, procedural effects were found to be at least three times as important as outcome effects (p. 648).

Once again, findings along these lines could be multiplied, in business, legal, and other settings. I will examine studies of political settings in the following section. This body of research demonstrates strong procedural justice effects that are independent of and oftentimes more powerful than outcome effects, especially in regard to matters of organizational commitment. Researchers have noted that procedural justice effects are frequently most powerful when outcomes are negative, thereby acting to cushion the effects of negative circumstances. This finding, again, is of great importance in regard to gaining acceptance of untoward decisions. In the words of Tyler and Folger, this cushioning effect 'is critical, given that there are rarely resolutions of disputes that can provide all parties with everything they want or feel they deserve' (Tyler and Folger 1980: 282).

The evidence suggests that procedural justice effects such as those I have noted can be traced to two different psychological processes. According to a self-interest explanation, individuals care about procedural justice because they believe fair procedures will produce more advantageous outcomes over the long run. According to a 'group values' model, individuals are moved by concerns for their place in larger social groups.[3] The two explanations are not incompatible; both processes can be at work in specific cases (Vidmar 1990; Tyler 1994b; Lind et al. 1990). The 'sense-making' explanation, provided by Joel Brockner and Batia Wiesenfeld (1996), is compatible with different construals of the underlying psychological processes. According to this account, procedural justice effects result from subjects scrutinizing decisions in order to understand their significance. Because people are especially motivated to look into negative decisions, they are likely to pay closer attention to procedural aspects of these. Indications that such decisions were made fairly can be reassuring, interpreted as evidence that future decisions could be more favourable. In

---

[3] Variations of the self-interest model are presented by Thibaut and Walker (1975) and Folger (1986, 1987); the main supporter of the group values model is Tyler (see 1989, 1990). It is not necessary to discuss the strengths and weaknesses of the two approaches here. But it seems clear that more than bare self-interest is at work, as is seen in how procedural justice affects self-esteem (Koper et al. 1993).

spite of the decision in question, evidence of fair procedures can also be reassuring about subjects' status within the group.

But on the other hand, procedures that appear to be unfair can be interpreted as indicating the subject's lack of status in the group and/or the likelihood of similar unfavourable decisions in the future. The combination of an unfavourable outcome and what are perceived to be unfair procedures can interact in ways that reinforce negative feelings. Such 'frustration effects' can have especially severe consequences in delegitimizing a decision-making organization (Folger and Greenberg 1985; Greenberg 1987). Effects along these lines are supported by voluminous research, both field and laboratory studies.[4]

A sense-making analysis of procedural justice calls attention to aspects of decision-making processes beyond the formal characteristics traditionally discussed. Procedures are of course carried out by people. And so decision-making has a necessary interpersonal dimension (Tyler and Bies 1990; Bies and Moag 1986; Greenberg 1994; Greenberg and McCarty 1990). In looking for clues about a given decision, the subject can scrutinize the behaviour of the people he deals with, in addition to more formal aspects of the procedure. Accordingly, experienced managers have long recognized that treating subordinates with respect is important for maintaining morale and organizational commitment. Such treatment can also be identified with procedural justice. According to one Fortune 500 executive interviewed by Robert Bies and Debra Shapiro: 'In my twenty years as a manager, I've learned that much of what is meant by being "fair" really means treating people with respect. For example, I always explain to my people *why* I did what I did. . . . My people think it's only fair' (Bies and Shapiro 1987: 200).[5]

Having seen that procedural justice effects can cushion the impact of negative decisions and so help to legitimize institutions in different areas, we turn to how these effects bear on political institutions.

---

[4] For references, see table 1 in Brockner and Wiesenfeld (1996: 194–9); also the discussion in (1996: 192 n. 5); for the effects of unfair decisions, see Lind and Lissak (1985). For procedural justice effects being especially important in negative decisions, see e.g. Cropanzano and Folger (1991: 138): 'To date the research seems to indicate that people are not concerned with procedural fairness following a fair distribution.'

[5] The subjective side of procedural justice also lends itself to manipulation. Managers surveyed by Jerold Greenberg emphasized appearing to be fair over actually being fair (Greenberg 1988). Knowledgeable managers are also able to use Machiavellian means to provide the appearance of fairness without corresponding conduct (Greenberg 1990). Lissak and Sheppard found that managers care about factors other than fairness more than fairness (e.g. resolving the dispute, making sure it won't happen again), whereas fairness is a more important concern for non-managers (Lissak and Sheppard 1983: 53–7). For their sample of 118 police officers, fairness was the most important criterion, followed by 'getting at the facts' (pp. 59–60).

2. PROCEDURAL JUSTICE AND POLITICAL LEGITIMACY

We have seen that procedural justice effects influence people's view towards small claims courts and the police. In a series of studies Tyler and different associates argue that the legitimacy of different political institutions is procedurally based.[6] In other words, views about the fairness of an institution's procedures are essential to its support. Legitimacy in turn influences acceptance of the institution's actions. Thus Tyler puts forth a *procedure–legitimacy–acceptance* connection (Tyler and Rasinski 1991; cf. Gibson 1989c).

Tyler explored connections between the fairness of Congress's procedures and the institution's legitimacy with a sample of 502 Bay Area residents (Tyler 1994a, study 3). Legitimacy was assessed through several measures: willingness to accept and act upon the institution's decisions; feeling a moral obligation to accept the decisions; and willingness to act on behalf of authorities, for instance to vote for them. Also included in legitimacy was attitudinal support for institutions, or trust, and other related attitudes (p. 813). Respondents were asked about their views in regard to five aspects of Congressional action: favourability of outcome; neutrality of decision-makers, i.e. whether they listen to people on all sides of issues in making policy; degree of participation or voice respondents were afforded; decision-makers' trustworthiness; and their respect for the public. Responses on these questions were correlated with attitudinal support for Congress and 'feeling an obligation to obey government rules' (p. 822).

The study established strong effects of the components of procedural justice on evaluations of Congress and its legitimacy. While voice had weak effects on these attitudes, neutrality, trustworthiness, and respect had strong effects, generally outweighing those of outcome favourability (pp. 824–5). These results were also consistent across a range of demographic categories—a finding to which I will return. Accordingly, this

---

[6] For references for additional studies of procedural justice on a national level, see Tyler (1994a: 827). Although Tyler's work is clearly of great importance, his concerns as a social psychologist limit its relevance for political philosophy, including for our purposes here. Throughout his many studies Tyler is interested primarily in showing that procedural justice effects support a 'group value' or 'relational' conception of human nature, and the inadequacy of a conception based on narrow self-interest. Accordingly, he generally makes little attempt to establish absolute levels for different procedural justice effects in society, concentrating primarily on showing that these levels are higher than those associated with concerns of outcomes or self-interest.

study supports the claim that the use of fair decision-making procedures enhances the legitimacy of national institutions (p. 827).[7]

In a related study, also using Bay Area residents, Tyler examined attitudes towards the United States Supreme Court (Tyler 1993). This study is particularly valuable, because it focused on the court's decisions in regard to abortion rights, an issue about which people are sharply divided.

Respondents were asked about their views of the court's legitimacy through five questions (e.g. 'Do you favor the [court's] having the power to declare acts of Congress unconstitutional?') They were also asked about the extent of their agreement with court decisions, and their views of the morality of abortion. The dependent variable was acceptance of the role of the court in deciding whether women have abortion rights. Views on the legitimacy of the court were found to be the strongest factor measured as far as determining whether it should have the authority to decide on this issue (pp. 49–50). In order to explore connections between procedural justice and legitimacy, respondents were asked a series of questions about Supreme Court decision-making. These included their agreement with decisions and their belief that decisions are generally fair and that decisions are made in a fair way. The fairness of decisions was taken to be a measure of distributive justice; whether they were made in a fair way measured procedural justice. Results strongly supported the procedural justice basis of legitimacy. For procedural justice, Beta = 0.45; for distributive justice, Beta = 0.26; for agreement with decisions, Beta = 0.16 (all significant at the 0.001 level) (p. 50). In Tyler's words: 'evaluations of court procedures are the primary influence on legitimacy' (p. 51).

Respondents were asked further about their willingness to accept the Supreme Court's role in deciding whether abortion should be legal. Though results were less strong, procedural justice influenced both views that the court should and should not have this authority more strongly than did agreement with decisions or distributive justice.[8]

---

[7] The results of the other two studies discussed in Tyler (1994*a*), which were experimental, based on scenarios, were consistent with those of the third study, discussed here.

[8] For whether the court should have the authority, Beta = 0.18, $p < 0.001$, as compared to agreement with decisions, Beta = 0.07, n.s., and that decisions are fair, Beta = 0.05, n.s. For whether the court should not have the authority, Beta for procedural justice = 0.22, $p < 0.001$, as compared to 0.13, $p < 0.05$ for whether decisions are fair, and for agreement with decisions, Beta = –0.02, n.s. But it should be noted that while these three factors explained 52% of the variance in regard to the legitimacy of the Supreme Court, they explained much less variance in regard to the question whether the court should have the authority in question: only 6% of the variance in views of people who believed the court should have it, and 8% of those who believed it should not (p. 50). For connections between institutional legitimacy and belief that the court should have the authority in question, see also Tyler (1993: 49) and Tyler and Mitchell (1994: 762–3).

Tyler's results in these studies are similar to those achieved in an earlier inquiry, conducted with Kenneth Rasinski and Kathleen McGraw (Tyler *et al.* 1985). Tyler and his colleagues surveyed 584 college undergraduates on the absolute levels of benefits they received from the federal government, their level of benefits as compared to those received by the average citizen, the fairness of the benefits they received, and the fairness of the procedures through which government benefits are distributed. Dependent variables included endorsement of government institutions, trust in government, and outcome satisfaction. Leadership endorsement was based on ratings of six political figures: Howard Baker, Carter, Edward Kennedy, Mondale, Nixon, and Reagan. Institutional endorsement was based on ratings of the federal government, the presidency, Congress, and the Supreme Court.

Results showed that judgements of fairness outweighed outcome level for all three dependent variables concerning political evaluation (p. 706). Differentiation of fairness into distributive and procedural components showed that procedural justice was 'the key variable influencing overall views about government'. For instance, for leadership endorsement, for procedural justice, Beta = 0.29, $p < 0.001$; for outcome fairness, Beta = 0.07, n.s. (p. 708).

Tyler, Rasinski, and McGraw conducted a second study, based on interviews of 300 residents of Chicago, in 1983. Respondents were asked a variety of questions about the benefits they received from the federal government, whether they agreed with the government's economic and social policies, and whether these policies were fair to them. The were also asked about four aspects of the procedural justice of the Reagan administration's policy-making process, e.g. whether President Reagan considered the views of all sides in making decisions, and whether he was unbiased and impartial (Tyler *et al.* 1985: 710). Dependent variables included feelings about President Reagan, about his job competence, and views of him as a person. Respondents were also asked to assess governmental performance and about their trust in government.

As in the previous study, regression analysis showed that the major influence upon satisfaction with President Reagan and with government in general was perceived fairness. Once again, further analysis showed that 'Within fairness, procedural justice emerges as the key input.' On the basis of these two studies, Tyler, Rasinski, and McGraw conclude that 'citizens act as naive moral philosophers in evaluating government, judging its actions against abstract criteria of fairness'—especially criteria of procedural fairness (p. 717).

The results in these studies receive additional support from a survey of 156 college undergraduates performed by Tyler and Caine (Tyler and

Caine 1981, study 4; see above, pp. 211–12). For dependent variables, respondents were asked a series of questions about national leaders (Carter, Kennedy, McGovern, Ford, Reagan, and Nixon), and about government institutions (the federal government, Congress, and the Supreme Court). Independent variables included outcome level and outcome fairness, the latter assessed according to respondents' views on whether they received the outcomes they deserved. Procedural fairness was assessed by asking subjects about the fairness of the procedures by which 'government decisions are made' and 'government benefits are distributed' (Tyler and Caine 1991: 651). Since outcome levels were found to be related to judgements of procedural fairness, Tyler and Caine concluded that these influenced judgements of procedural fairness. But procedural effects were found to be far stronger than outcome effects in influencing evaluations of both institutions and political leaders.[9]

The last study I will discuss is the survey conducted for Tyler's book *Why People Obey the Law* (Tyler 1990, cited above). The 'Chicago study' involved telephone interviews with 1,575 residents of Chicago in 1984, 804 of whom were reinterviewed a year later. Tyler's analysis addresses basic attitudes concerning the legitimacy of legal authorities in general and citizens' compliance with the authorities' directives, the law. Tyler examined citizens' views of the police, courts, and the law. Once again, his interest lay in connections between procedural justice, legitimacy, and compliance.

As in the earlier study conducted with Folger (see above, p. 211), Tyler found that respondents who had had recent personal experience with legal authorities were strongly affected by procedural aspects of the encounters. Cushioning effects of procedures were 'quite robust'. Effects of experience on the legitimacy of the institutions were 'driven by procedural judgments and . . . unrelated to outcome' (Tyler and Folger 1980: 100). In fact, among those viewing procedures as fair, 'no relationship' between outcome level and dependent variables bearing on legitimacy was found: 'In other words, if people receive fair procedures, outcome is not relevant to their reactions. If they do not it is. As was hypothesized, fair procedures are a cushion of support against the potentially damaging effects of unfavorable outcomes' (p. 101).

[9] See also Tyler and Degoey (1995), in which procedural justice effects are assessed in regard to the Public Utilities Commission in San Francisco and conservation measures it implemented to address the California water shortage in 1991. The sample was San Francisco residents (N = 636). Tyler and Degoey conclude: 'Whether authorities make their decisions following fair decision-making procedures and deliver satisfactory decisions plays a key role in engendering a willingness to empower the authority as well. Furthermore, views about the legitimacy of an existing authority are almost solely influenced by the procedural fairness to [*sic*] that authority' (p. 493). See also Tyler and Lind (1992).

A general argument can be constructed on the basis of the findings I have reviewed. In certain respects, this goes beyond the evidence accumulated to date and so must be viewed as somewhat speculative. But the evidence indicates its likelihood, and it could well be confirmed by further studies. Basically, I believe something like Tyler's postulated connections between procedural justice, legitimacy, and compliance hold.[10] Political stability in large part stems from the citizenry's belief in the overall fairness of institutions (distributive and procedural, but primarily the latter). Factors in addition to procedural justice undoubtedly influence political legitimacy. But a powerful cumulative case can be made if we consider Tyler's Chicago study in the context of the other studies of legitimacy discussed above, and along with the other studies I have reviewed concerning fair process effects and connections between procedural justice and organizational commitment in a range of areas. These studies strongly suggest that people's allegiance to authorities depends in large part on their perceptions of procedural fairness, and that allegiance can be retained in spite of how people fare in particular decisions, if they believe the decisions were made in a fair manner. Because many decisions authorities make produce losers as well as winners, ability to retain the allegiance of losers is obviously important. Something like this seems to be at work in the American political system—and perhaps other democracies as well. The high levels of system support discussed in Chapter 5 are likely in large part procedurally based.

3. CRITERIA OF PROCEDURAL JUSTICE

Discussion of procedural justice in the previous sections is incomplete in a central respect. I have reviewed procedural justice effects in a range of situations, but have not attempted to say exactly what procedural justice is. Clearly, for our purposes, we cannot simply assume that it is what philosophers have traditionally conceived it to be: consistent application of standards across cases, rigorous adherence to precedents, etc. Rather, since our main concern is how it affects liberal citizens, we must take into account common views of procedural justice in our account of its nature.

[10] Though the legitimacy–compliance link is important in Tyler (1990), it is not directly related to our concerns and so it is not necessary to discuss it here. A series of studies have established that, in general, people's assessments of the morality of a given law strongly influence their willingness to obey it; for references, see Tyler (1990: 37). For references for studies of connections between lack of legitimacy and willingness to participate in political protests, see Tyler (1990: 33–6).

As noted above, in early empirical studies Thibaut and Walker identified procedural justice with issues of control (Thibaut and Walker 1975). They distinguished 'decision control' from 'process control'. The former concerns control over the decision itself; the latter involves control over the presentation of evidence in the decision-making process (Thibaut and Walker 1975, 1978; Houlden *et al.* 1978). But since the time of Thibaut and Walker researchers have shown that, as viewed by most people, procedural justice can encompass a variety of factors in addition to control.

The classic account of the basic elements of procedural justice is by Gerald Leventhal, who presents what he calls 'six rules of fair procedures' (Leventhal 1980: 30).[11] The six elements Leventhal identifies are as follows (pp. 40–6).

1. The 'consistency rule' requires that allocative processes 'be consistent across persons and over time'.
2. 'Bias-suppression' requires that authorities not base their decisions on self-interest or personal allegiance.
3. The requirement of 'accuracy' is that decisions should be based on the best information possible.
4. The 'correctability rule' is that opportunities should exist 'to modify and reverse decisions made at various points in the allocative process'.
5. The requirement of 'representativeness' is that input into the allocative process should conform to the needs and interests of people or groups affected by it. This requirement can be satisfied by participation and power-sharing arrangements.
6. Finally, the 'ethicality' rule requires that allocative procedures be consistent with wider ethical or moral concerns of the people involved.

This list obviously goes well beyond Thibaut and Walker's concentration on control. Only the 'representativeness' rule closely conforms to control, mainly process control, or voice. Presumably, one reason for the narrowness of Thibaut and Walker's focus is the narrowness of the allocative processes they studied. In legal models, in which opposed parties submit their dispute to a third party for judgement, it seems that concerns of decision and process control would be more salient than in other allocative situations.

Further research on procedural justice, which included a wide range of allocative settings, has called attention to other concerns, beyond those discussed by Leventhal. Leventhal makes the valuable point that the components of procedural justice can interact differently in different situations, with greater emphasis placed on some elements rather than others,

---

[11] These form the basis for many discussions of the elements of procedural justice recounted above.

depending on the setting (p. 46). Further studies have confirmed this suggestion, thereby undermining the idea of a single essence of procedural justice applicable to all allocative processes.

Insight into what people view as the elements of procedural justice is provided by surveys in which respondents were asked open-ended questions. For example, in his study of defendants in traffic and misdemeanour court (Tyler 1984; above, p. 211); Tyler asked his subjects: 'What about the way your case was handled was fair (or unfair)?' (1984: 62). Respondents most frequently mentioned the opportunity to present evidence (26 per cent), the nature of the case's outcome (12 per cent), and the judge's 'manner' (12 per cent) (p. 67). Three brief points can be made about these responses. First, they do not correspond to standard or traditional criteria of procedural justice. Presumably consistent treatment across cases was not widely mentioned, because defendants had little knowledge of how their treatment compared with those of other defendants facing similar charges. It is not unlikely that, if such information had been available, consistency would have been an important factor (see Tyler 1990: 153–4). Secondly, the fact that the case's outcome was one of the three factors indicates that ordinary respondents may not hold sophisticated views of procedural justice, and may not clearly distinguish factors that go into fair procedures from others that concern fair outcomes. In other words, they may not be clear on differences between distributive and procedural justice. Finally, as the similarities between Tyler's results here and those of Thibaut and Walker indicate, one factor that may have influenced Tyler's results was the kind of process he examined. It is not unlikely that people involved in other sorts of decision procedures would identify other aspects of their experience as fair or unfair.

A similar study was conducted by Greenberg (1986). He asked fifty-six middle managers in industrial companies to think of a particularly fair or unfair performance evaluation they had at one time received, and then to identify the factors that made it fair or unfair. Other middle managers then grouped their responses into categories, and still others rated these for importance (on a scale of 1 to 9, low to high). Five factors bearing on fair procedures were identified. The most important was 'consistent application of standards' (6.9); next was soliciting input prior to the evaluation and making use of it (6.1); third was 'two-way communication during interview'. Also mentioned were evaluator's familiarity with subject's work, and ability to challenge the evaluation (p. 341).

One can see that the factors cited in this study are rather different from those in Tyler's. This is most likely a result of different situations. Because the subjects Greenberg examined were likely to have had access to information about other cases, consistency emerged as the most important criterion. Results were thus more in accord with traditional notions of procedural justice.

The possibility that people's views of fair procedures vary across situations is supported by a study conducted by Blair Sheppard and Roy Lewicki (Sheppard and Lewicki 1987). Sheppard and Lewicki's subjects, forty-four executives, were given a list of seven different areas of managerial duties (planning, staff development, delegating, etc.) and asked to think about a specific instance of each in which a boss had treated them fairly and another in which they were treated unfairly. They were then asked to identify the 'principle' or 'rule' that the boss followed or ignored in each case that made his actions fair or unfair (p. 164). Responses included 510 managerial behaviours, which involved 747 rules. Grouping these produced a list of sixteen rules. This included all six of Leventhal's criteria, plus additional principles, e.g. the golden rule, timeliness ('take timely action and provide sufficient lead time'), and reasonableness ('use common sense when making a decision or enforcing a policy') (pp. 166–9). Three of the principles were viewed as generally applicable (consistency, reasonableness, and golden rule), while the other nine were applicable to different aspects of managers' tasks. Accordingly, this study illuminates the highly complex nature of procedural justice assessments, and how criteria vary not only across different kinds of procedure but across different domains of decision-makers' responsibilities (see also Barrett-Howard and Tyler 1986).

If we take it as established that criteria of procedural justice vary with situations, the issue then becomes identifying the criteria relevant to political legitimacy. Once again, the most extensive research in this areas has been conducted by Tyler. I will look at three studies, concerning personal experience with courts and the police, and assessments of Congress and of the United States Supreme Court.

As part of his Chicago study, Tyler inquired into the nature of procedural justice.[12] From his 1,575 respondents, he selected 651 who had had significant personal experience with the Chicago police and/or courts the previous year. To assess their views on the nature of procedural justice, he examined the relationship between their views of how fairly they had been treated and responses on a number of specific attributes of their treatment. The main factors considered were largely taken from Thibaut and Walker and Leventhal (Tyler 1988: 111–13) and were shown to explain most of the variance (69 per cent) in citizens' judgements about the fairness of their treatment (p. 121). Perhaps surprisingly, consistency was found to be

[12] I discuss mainly Tyler (1988) here. In Tyler (1990) there is detailed discussion of the same sample, and assessments of what constitutes procedural justice, but the results reported are similar.

relatively unimportant (Beta = 0.04). The most important factors were the authorities' efforts to be fair (Beta = 0.30), their honesty (Beta = 0.23), and their ethicality (Beta = 0.21). Aside from the relationship with consistency, which was not statistically significant, in all these relationships, $p <$ 0.001 (p. 122). Tyler found that the criteria had a 'positive, overlapping quality', so that 'citizens judge the fairness of process by using a variety of positively interrelated criteria' (p. 123). Not surprisingly in view of the different kinds of experiences Tyler's subjects had had, there were some differences between assessments of criteria in regard to disputes and non-dispute situations. The former emphasized opportunities for input and consistency of treatment; the latter placed greater weight on efforts of police officers or judges to be fair (p. 127). Tyler concludes as follows: 'Judgments about "how hard" the authorities tried to be fair emerged as the key overall factor in assessing procedural justice' (p. 129). He notes considerable distance between this account of the elements of fair procedures and familiar definitions in the philosophical literature. Accordingly, as Tyler notes, we must ask who 'owns' a moral concept, the philosophers who have produced sophisticated exegeses, or ordinary citizens, who are affected by decision procedures and hold divergent views (1990: 155).

In spite of the importance of Tyler's study, it seems that the gap he postulates can be narrowed considerably. Though subjects identify specific aspects of their treatment as contributing to its 'fairness' or 'justice', reflection suggests reasons to be sceptical about their responses. If we distinguish factors that make a decision fair in a substantive sense and others that do not themselves contribute to fairness but provide evidence about substantive fairness, we can see that Tyler's subjects regularly conflated these two categories. In effect, they used 'fairness' and 'justice' in loose senses.[13] In cases (such as those Tyler examined) in which subjects had direct contact with decision-makers, it appears that they were heavily influenced by aspects of the encounters. This could well be explained by the sense-making account of procedural justice discussed above. Subjects assessed the behaviour of decision-makers for evidence concerning the fairness of decisions, incorporating this into their evaluations of procedural justice. Even though they were asked what makes procedures fair, their responses overstated the importance of what we can call 'atmospherics', behavioural clues used to assess procedures.[14]

[13] For discussion of this point, I am grateful to Ernie Alleva.
[14] According to Tyler and Lind (1992), the three main factors behind procedural justice judgements are indications of standing, indications of trust in authorities, and neutrality of decision-makers. It is notable that all studies cited as supporting the first—the most heavily interpersonal of the three—involved direct contact with decision-makers (Tyler and Lind 1992: 153–5).

When we move to national political institutions, with which subjects do not have direct contact, aspects of interpersonal interaction are of course no longer of concern. In regard to these institutions also, we should distinguish (*a*) considerations that make a decision-making process fair and (*b*) factors that people focus on. But one could hypothesize that, with the element of personal contact removed, atmospherics will be less important and so judgements will be based more closely on the factors that philosophers traditionally discuss. Research findings will be seen to bear this hypothesis out. And so in regard to national political institutions, the factors Tyler focuses on in his innovative account of procedural justice largely drop from view.[15]

As we turn from encounters with the police and lawcourts to Congress and the Supreme Court, we lose the element of personal experience central to the Chicago study, and so can expect subjects to pay less attention to interpersonal aspects of procedures. The studies I will examine were conducted by Tyler (and discussed above, in Section 2). First, as noted above, Tyler surveyed 502 Bay Area adults on their attitudes towards Congress. He examined the effects of four aspects of Congressional decision-making on views about Congress's procedural fairness. These were: *voice*, whether average citizens can present their views to Congress; *neutrality*, whether Congress is generally honest in its decision making, considers the views of all interested parties, and collects the information it requires to make decisions; *trustworthiness*, whether Congress tries to be fair in making decisions; and *standing*, whether Congress is concerned with protecting the rights of the average citizen. (Tyler 1994*a*: 824). The relevant dependent variable, the fairness of Congressional decision-making, was assessed through two items: 'The way Congress makes decisions is fair' and 'The way Congress decides who will benefit from government policies is fair' (p. 823).

The results of the study support the influence of these factors on general evaluations of Congress's procedural justice. Strong relationships were found with neutrality, and trust. The relationship with standing was weaker and that with voice considerably weaker and not statistically significant. For neutrality, Beta = 0.31; for trust, Beta = 0.25, both

---

[15] It should be noted that, to the extent that people concentrate on interpersonal aspects of legal proceedings because they do not have the information needed to assess consistency, making this information available could improve their understanding. Thus it seems that relatively mild educational processes could make procedural principles centring on consistency justifiable to many liberal citizens. In Tyler's studies of the nature of procedural justice in national institutions—on which I rely in the following pages—subjective factors largely drop from his analysis, as he concentrates more on traditional features of fair procedures.

significant at the 0.001 level. For standing, Beta = 0.14, $p < 0.01$; for voice, Beta = 0.03, n.s. (p. 825).

Similar factors were found to influence fairness judgements concerning decision-making by the Supreme Court. The analysis conducted by Tyler and Gregory Mitchell was based on the same Bay Area sample (Tyler and Mitchell 1994; see above, p. 215 ff.). Four aspects of court decision-making were examined: neutrality ('honesty, lack of bias; decision on facts, not influenced by political pressures'), trustworthiness ('motivated to be fair; consider arguments; care'), control ('opportunity to present evidence; influence over decision'), and standing ('respect'). The results showed strong relationships between neutrality and trustworthiness and court fairness (Beta = 0.48 and 0.34, respectively; both statistically significant). The relationship with standing was weaker (Beta = 0.10, n.s.). There was a negative relationship with control (Beta = –0.13, n.s.) (Tyler and Mitchell 1994: 775). Once again, this study tells strongly against Thibaut and Walker's claims concerning control's centrality to procedural justice judgements.

Consistent results in these studies provides evidence that neutrality and trustworthiness are central to people's assessments of the procedural fairness of national political institutions, with other factors less important. Given connections between procedural justice and legitimacy, it seems that the neutrality and trustworthiness of institutions strongly influences people's support. There is a large element of common sense in this finding. Were citizens to discover that either Congress or the Supreme Court was not honest, was biased, was influenced by political pressures, or was not motivated to be fair (etc.), this would surely call its decisions into question. Consistent findings that institutions violated these principles would undermine their legitimacy.[16] Studies show that Americans' distaste for Congress is largely due to the perception that its decision-making is heavily influenced by political factors (Hibbing and Theiss-Morse 1995).

Examination of Tyler and Mitchell's poll results helps to flesh out these findings. Among their respondents, support for the Supreme Court was high. Eighty-six per cent of respondents said they had either a great deal of or some respect 'for the Supreme Court as an institution of the government' (Tyler and Mitchell 1994: 802). On another question, only 3 per cent of respondents strongly supported or somewhat supported getting rid of the Supreme Court (p. 803). Eighty per cent strongly or somewhat agreed that the court 'does its job well', and 75 per cent that it 'can usually be

---

[16] I should note that support for the court was not unqualified. A majority, 53%, agreed strongly or somewhat that the Constitution gives the Supreme Court too much power (Tyler 1994a: 803).

trusted to make decisions that are right for the country as a whole' (p. 803).[17]

Responses were similar on aspects of the court's decision-making. Eighty-nine per cent of subjects responded that decisions made by the court are usually or sometimes fair (as opposed to 9 per cent seldom fair, and 1 per cent never fair). Seventy-seven per cent agreed strongly or somewhat that 'the way the Supreme Court makes its decisions is fair' (p. 808). Seventy-nine per cent responded that the court's 'recent decisions' have been very or somewhat fair (14 per cent not very fair). Eighty per cent said that 'the way they've made their decisions' has been very or somewhat fair. Eighty-seven per cent responded that it is very or somewhat likely that, if a group to which they belonged went before the court, 'the Court would make its decision in a fair way' (pp. 809–10).

On specific aspects of procedural justice, responses were similar. Seventy-two per cent agreed strongly or somewhat that Supreme Court justices are 'generally honest—giving the real reasons for their decisions'. But only 61 per cent agreed strongly or somewhat that the court 'gives equal consideration to the views of all of the different groups in America'. Seventy-five per cent agreed strongly or somewhat that the court gets the information it needs to make informed decisions. However, 75 per cent agreed that Supreme Court decisions are influenced a great deal or somewhat by political pressure (p. 811). Apparently, views on these two questions concerning bias, especially the latter, are held somewhat in isolation from the other factors I have noted.

On trustworthiness, 83 per cent agreed strongly or somewhat that the court tries to be fair in making its decisions. On respect for rights, 77 per cent agreed strongly or somewhat that the court 'is concerned about protecting the average citizen's rights' (p. 812).

As noted in the previous section, support for the court has important practical implications. This leads people to accept its ability to make controversial decisions. The same is true of their support for Congress, which is also bound up with characteristics of its decision-making.

It is not clear how confident we can be in drawing general conclusions from the studies of national institutions I have examined. Tyler's main studies on attitudes towards the Supreme Court and Congress are based on a single study of Bay Area residents. Clearly, replication of his results with diverse samples will be necessary to establish his conclusions. However, even though at present these findings are not firmly established,

---

[17] Additional discussions of Supreme Court legitimacy include Murphy and Tanenhaus (1969) and Sarat (1975, 1977). For other studies of support for the United States Supreme Court, see above, Ch. 5, Sect. 2.

they are suggestive and could have important implications. To the extent that conclusions along these lines can be confirmed, they indicate that liberal citizens are generally willing to accept decisions, including ones with which they disagree, as long as they believe the decisions are made through fair procedures. As we have seen, people generally view procedures as fair if they are: 'neutral', i.e. decisions are made honestly, on the basis of the facts, with a lack of bias, and not (unduly) influenced by political considerations; and if decision-makers are trustworthy, i.e. motivated to be fair, and respectful of people's rights. To the extent that decisions made in these ways are able to generate consensus in diverse liberal societies, they are of great relevance for our concerns.[18]

Of crucial importance for our purposes is the congruence between procedural justice studies of national institutions and findings in regard to system support in the United States and other democratic countries. We have seen that support for political institutions is at consensus levels; procedural justice research helps to explain this. We can hypothesize that, in large part, people support national institutions because they believe they make decisions fairly. The high percentages of subjects viewing Supreme Court decision-making as fair would presumably be found to hold in the country as a whole in regard to other national institutions as well, contributing to support for these institutions in spite of outcome effects of particular decisions.

In regard to generating consensus in diverse societies, an additional aspect of procedural justice is significant. Researchers have consistently found that procedural justice judgements are not influenced by demographic characteristics. In the Chicago study Tyler examined relationships between respondents' views on procedural justice and their sex, age, race, education, liberalism, and income. He found that demographic characteristics do not have significant influence on views of procedural justice: 'In other words, different types of people within American culture define the meaning of procedural justice in a similar way' (Tyler 1988: 132). 'People think about procedural justice in a similar way even if characteristics of their backgrounds differ' (Tyler 1990: 157). Similar results obtained in Tyler's study of attitudes towards Congress. Views of procedural justice did not vary significantly with subjects' race, gender, education, income, age, or ideology. Thus Tyler concludes: 'the same issues are central to pro-

---

[18] Results of mediation and arbitration programmes show that some procedures are more successful than others at generating consensus; see McEwen and Maiman (1981, 1984), Adler *et al.* (1983), and Pruitt *et al.* (1993). In general, these procedures were viewed as significantly more fair by losers in cases, who consistently complied with judgements against themselves more highly than losers in other kinds of procedures.

cedural justice judgments for all groups'. He posits a 'general agreement about how fair decision making procedures should be defined' (Tyler 1994*a*: 826).

These findings have been confirmed in other studies, including one directed by E. A. Lind, Yuen Huo, and Tyler, on preferences for dispute resolution procedures among African Americans, Hispanic Americans, Asian Americans, and European Americans. This study uncovered only slight differences between the views of different groups (Lind *et al.* 1994).[19]

There is some evidence that similar factors influence procedural justice judgements across cultures. Lind inquired into preferences concerning procedures in the United States, Germany, and Hong Kong, using undergraduates in each locale as subjects (Lind 1994). Subjects were asked to recall an interpersonal dispute and to answer questions about the procedures used. Results showed '*no* significant differences among the sites in either the antecedents or the consequences of justice judgments' (p. 33). Subjects were guided in their choice of procedures by views of the fairness of the procedure's previous use, without regard to whether or not they had obtained a favourable outcome. In choosing procedures, American and Germans were influenced more than Chinese by previous outcomes, but in no case did outcome receive more weight than fairness judgements. In determining fairness judgements, in all three cases, standing and neutrality had more influence than control; in two of the three (United States and Hong Kong), trust was also more influential (pp. 34–5). Lind concludes: 'the overwhelming impression that one gets is of remarkably similar empirical relations, in spite of the fact that the data were collected in widely different sites' (p. 35).[20]

[19] See also Tyler and Degoey (1995). Fossati and Meeker (1997) discovered significant differences between men's and women's views of court system fairness, but these were due almost entirely to the males' greater direct experience with the court system. Tata and Bowes-Sperry (1996) report differences between men and women in the importance accorded to distributive and interactional justice, but 'no significant difference' between their views on procedural justice (p. 1329). It seems to me that, in view of what is seen above, in Ch. 4, studies of the relationship between religion and procedural justice judgements could be important, but I have not come across such studies.

[20] Results in Lind *et al.* (1997) are similar. This study is based on surveys of American, German, Chinese, and Japanese undergraduates. In all four cultures procedural justice judgements were largely determined by the same factors. Leung (1987) finds differences between procedural preferences of American and Chinese students, but these were basically due to differing desires about what the procedures were supposed to produce.

4. IMPLICATIONS

The implications of general agreement on criteria of procedural justice are clear. Not only can institutions gain the allegiance of citizens by demonstrating certain decision-making characteristics, but members of different groups in diverse societies are likely to respond similarly to the same procedural attributes. In a best-case scenario, consensus could be formed around the fairness of decision procedures, even in the absence of agreement on important moral principles and even if, as is inevitable, decisions are more advantageous to certain groups than to others. Because of the fair process effect, discussed above, members of disadvantaged groups are more likely to accept decisions if they view them as fairly made. Because of the apparent generality of procedural justice judgements, it may be possible for all groups to agree on acceptable procedures, in spite of their other differences.[21]

At the present time, we do not have the data firmly to establish the relevant connections for contemporary liberal democracies. But in the light of the numerous studies reviewed in this chapter, it seem likely that general views on the fairness of decision-making procedures help to legitimize national institutions and to contribute to willingness to accept decisions that are made.

As Tyler and Lind note, previous survey research has shown that, when people are asked how they would be treated in dealings with legal and political authorities, they almost always say that they would be treated fairly. This is in spite of their awareness that individuals are often treated unfairly. This discrepancy is widely reported. Tyler and Lind characterize it as 'an illusion of personal justice' (Tyler and Lind 1992: 155; for further references, see pp. 155–6). Because expectations have been found to shape perceptions of procedural justice, people who expect to be treated fairly are more likely to believe that they have been (Brockner *et al.* 1992, 1995; Tyler *et al.* 1989). The survey results reported by Tyler and Mitchell (1994) are consistent with these observations, and support connections between fairness and legitimacy. But once again, the Tyler–Mitchell study is based on a single sample and much more work is needed solidly to confirm its conclusions.

As noted in the last section, the body of research discussed in this chapter has obvious connections with the high levels of support for democratic procedures seen in Chapter 5. It is not possible to say exactly what

---

[21] However, for possible ideological uses of fair process effects to promote political and social domination, see Tyler and McGraw (1986).

percentage of this support can be attributed to perceptions of procedural fairness. But the research I have reviewed suggests that its influence is considerable. To the extent that members of different groups respond similarly to similar procedural attributes, this should contribute significantly to consensus support for national institutions, in spite of differences between inhabitants of modern pluralistic societies.

Conclusion

HAVING inquired into major beliefs of liberal citizens, I can present my conclusions. First and most important are the principles they could accept. As argued in Chapter 1, agreement on basic principles is a moral requirement in liberal societies and of practical significance for their smooth functioning. We have seen problems with the evidence from public opinion surveys. Certain results are not as clear as I would wish. In some cases, consensus is weaker than others, for example on system support for African Americans. In this case, we must count neutral responses, in order to achieve consensus levels—thus yielding consensus in regard to principles people do not oppose rather than those they support directly. But in spite of these problems, in an overall sense the evidence supports strong consensus on a set of principles.

As we saw in Chapters 5 and 6, even in modern, diverse societies there is general agreement on the value of democracy and democratic procedures in the political realm, and principles of merit distribution and equality of opportunity in the economic. In addition, in spite of the disagreements about rights seen in Chapter 3, on an abstract level they are almost universally supported. The principles that constitute the core of liberal consensus are as follows:

(*a*) support for democracy as a central political value;
(*b*) the need to support democratic political procedures;
(*c*) a range of rights for all citizens, which must be generally respected;
(*d*) respect for those rights necessary for the proper functioning of democratic processes;
(*e*) distribution according to merit, supported by real equality of opportunity, in the economic sphere.

As I have noted, these principles constitute an outline that must be filled in. In regard to all five principles, including (*b*), details must be provided by democratic procedures. In this sense, democratic procedures are 'reflexive'; they must be invoked in order to flesh out their own nature. In Chapter 5 I referred to this principle as the 'procedural norm of democracy'.

It bears repeating that, in filling out these principles, democratic procedures must work in accordance with the basic commitments of liberal theory. We have also seen that, in order to work properly, democratic procedures require general respect for an important range of rights. Among these are extensive freedom of speech and of the press, freedom of association, the right to hold political events and rallies, and other, similar rights along these lines. This is the justification for principle (*d*). Little evidence I have reviewed indicates that people directly support it. In this sense, it is different from the other four principles. But it is clearly implied by principle (*b*) and so can be claimed for that reason.[1] Like the other principles, (*d*) also must be filled in by democratic procedures, and so, like (*b*), should be viewed as reflexive.

The content of liberal consensus is a variant of what can be termed 'procedural liberalism'. Its core ideas centre more on means of resolving disputes than on detailed stipulations of what resolutions should look like, though of course there are parameters within which resolutions must fall. In modern liberal societies there is greater agreement on principles that deal with procedures than on matters of substance. General support for democracy and equality of opportunity are substantive principles on which there is general agreement, though again, only on an abstract level. Specific workings-out of these and other principles are subject to widespread disagreement and require procedural resolution.

Because of the fair-process effect discussed in the last chapter, procedural principles appear likely to contribute strongly to political stability, as long as they are generally viewed as fair. According to a best-case scenario, there would be general agreement throughout society on criteria of procedural justice. Though this claim receives a measure of support in the studies reviewed in the last chapter, more research is needed to confirm it. But if the results we have seen hold up, then people with different cultural, racial, and ideological backgrounds will assess democratic procedures according to similar criteria—neutrality, trustworthiness, respect for rights—and so agree about their basic fairness, again in spite of underlying disagreements.

Perhaps the greatest shortcomings of liberal consensus are the limited conception of rights it is able to support and the degree of economic equality it is able to foster. Because inhabitants of a diverse society have fundamentally different world-views, they do not generally subscribe to a strong conception of rights. As we have also seen, consensus on merit distribution allows for substantial 'deserved' inequality, with market distribution generally taken to constitute desert. Accordingly, in terms of content, the

---

[1] See above, pp. 143–5. Because it is in a sense subsidiary to (*b*), it could be viewed as a sub-principle or corollary of (*b*), as opposed to a principle in its own right.

principles developed by the variant of political liberalism pursued in this work fall short of what can be regarded as strong liberalism.

I will concentrate on individual rights here. Let us return to the position of Joel Feinberg, discussed in Chapter 3. According to Feinberg, to be a liberal is to place overweening value on individual liberty, although liberty must be restricted by 'liberty-limiting principles'. As we saw, Feinberg limits these to restrictions necessary to prevent harm or strong offence to other people (see above, Chapter 3, Section 3). Although Feinberg argues for a strong presumption in favour of liberty, with proposed restrictions requiring justification, in a diverse society many people will weigh conflicting values differently. As we saw above, many people support 'legal moralism'. They believe certain acts are inherently wrong or conflict with values associated with the community and so should be restricted, even though they do not cause identifiable people harm, or are done with participants' consent. In a diverse society people will disagree about the range of actions that are wrong for these reasons and how to weigh these values against restrictions on individual liberty. Although individual liberty is always an important concern and can be limited only for good reasons, it does not necessarily always outweigh values other than harm and strong offence. Demonstrating that it always has superior weight would require appeal to underlying considerations which may well not be generally accepted in a pluralistic society. I have noted that Feinberg, an adherent of strong principles, has difficulties with public gladiatorial contests. This is not the only example. Other problematic activities are harmful, even if done with participants' consent, e.g. boxing, or cause pain—needless pain—to animals, e.g. bull-fighting, cock-fighting, or fox-hunting. Especially troublesome cases concern possible restriction on certain forms of expression, which, as we saw in Chapter 3, are likely to be supported by large percentages of the community, and could be justified as required to preserve community values. Activities in question include non-patriotic expression such as flag-burning or mocking the president. Sexual expression, especially disseminating and consuming pornography, would also be included. Although strong liberals may not find appeals to community values convincing, the voluminous evidence reviewed in Chapter 3 shows that many members of society are not strong liberals.

Enormous grey areas are encountered in regard to such restrictions, which cause problems for liberal consensus. The principle of democratic rights, (*d*), will protect certain activities, but only those integrally linked to the political process. In this regard, one could ask whether burning the flag or wearing death-masks to presidential speeches fall into the category of political expression that should be protected. People are likely to disagree. Deeply troubling issues are encountered in regard to sexual practices. In a poll of 1,200 Americans conducted for the *Washington Post* in August 1998, 53 per cent of respondents said that sex between two adults of the same sex is 'unacceptable and should not be tolerated'. Another 18 per cent described it as 'unacceptable, but should be tolerated by society' (*Washington Post*, 11 September 1998, A40). Given sentiments like these, it is not surprising that homosexual sex is outlawed in many jurisdictions in the United States, while anti-sodomy laws were upheld by the United States Supreme Court in 1986 (*Bowers* v. *Hardwick*).

For a strong liberal, restrictions of these sorts are unacceptable, as clear violations of individual rights. But again, the problem for liberal consensus is finding means to support a strong conception of rights. In a diverse society many citizens will not value rights highly, while, once again, philosophical defences of strong rights require appeal to controversial premisses.

This is of course not to say that liberal consensus would allow rights to be cast aside altogether. I have posited support for some reasonable conception of rights as central to any acceptable liberal theory and we have seen that, on a general level, rights are all but unanimously supported. The problem of course is that the content of rights principles must be filled in democratically, which leaves open the possibility of enactments which strong liberals would reject.

Obviously, I cannot address particular troublesome issues in this context or try to draw precise boundary lines. To a large extent, what we mean by procedural liberalism is that such lines must be drawn democratically, with the implication that in certain areas rights will be no stronger than the moral views the populace can support. The fact that a portion of the populace heavily favours moralistic restrictions does not mean that they will necessarily pass. Controversial issues must be debated and voted upon, and strong liberal views may prevail. On the issue of homosexual sex, for instance, it seems that the presumption in favour of liberty makes it difficult justifiably to outlaw consensual (non-harmful) activities among adults. The fact that they are outlawed in many states is an objectionable feature of American democracy. Arguments concerning the inherent wrongfulness of such conduct require premisses drawn from particular comprehensive views and so are unlikely to be sustainable within the constraints of liberal justification. But this is not to say that severe restrictions on practices such as gay marriage and adoption could not pass muster, if defended on neutral grounds (see above, Chapter 3 n. 19). Without being able to invoke a strongly liberal conception of rights, liberal consensus is open to decisions that strong liberals could find difficult to accept.

Although the principles of liberal consensus are not as robust as some liberals might like, they have important egalitarian implications. For instance, as we saw in Chapter 6, in American society there is little support for policies to increase economic equality directly. But, as we also saw, requirements of equal opportunity could justify significant redistribution to provide children relatively equal opportunities to compete in later life. Equalizing school funding is one possible implication. Let us assume that Jones is opposed to redistributive policies in general and against equalizing school funding but supports equality of opportunity (in some sense) and also supports the American political system. Clearly, if the government generates a law in favour of greater equality of funding, this can be justified to him.

We can take this one step further. Support for equality of opportunity creates a general requirement to equalize resources throughout society—though this must be balanced against principles of distribution based on merit. People should support policies required by equal opportunity to some extent and insist that their political leaders implement them—although, again, equality of opportunity could be filled in in myriad ways. Disagreements about what constitutes appropriate equality in school funding should be settled by democratic procedures. But the blatant absence of equal opportunity that characterizes much of American society at the present time would be difficult to defend and so would require ameliorative measures. It is difficult to construct a credible argument that children have reasonably equal opportunities to compete in later life if their school systems have vastly different resources, if school buildings in one neighbourhood have up-to-date technological equipment, but in another are dilapidated and falling apart.

If we grant that Jones's acceptance of principles of equal opportunity implies a range of social policies, a more basic question can be raised about the nature of his commitment.[2] As we have seen, public opinion research shows that most Americans support democracy and equality of opportunity. Let us assume that Jones's views are in accord with those of the majority. But still, one could ask why descriptive statements about his beliefs commit him to *anything*. One could say that the fact that public opinion research shows that Jones supports democratic procedures and equal opportunity is merely a description of his beliefs. And so the question is, what is the normative significance of a description of his beliefs?

To this there is a two-part response. In order to keep matters relatively simple, I will focus on support for democracy. First, moral principles concerning the desirability of and need to support democratic procedures could be justified to Jones as fitting closely with his existing beliefs. Democratic principles are not beliefs that he just happens to hold. They

---

[2] I am indebted to Colin Bird for discussion on this point.

are important components of his overall moral and political belief system. For him to endorse principles opposed to democracy would cause significant problems of coherence in his overall views. Thus if Jones is actively to endorse any principles bearing on the political realm, he should accept these.

To some extent, this line of argument is perhaps based on unrealistic assumptions. It is likely that many liberal citizens hold views that are not clearly articulated, which may suffer from significant incoherence. Accordingly, my justificatory assumption is that, properly sorted out and developed into an integrated structure, the views of the typical liberal citizen would feature principles of democracy and equality of opportunity as prominent components. Once again, this is not to prejudge the exact sense these ideas would receive. But on the basis of the evidence we have seen, support for variants of democracy, equality of opportunity, and basic rights, including democratic rights, is central to the beliefs of virtually all modern liberal citizens.

Secondly, if we wish to dig further, we would likely see that Jones's commitment to democracy is not an accident. The data we have reviewed do not allow us to say exactly why people in general, or any given person, support(s) democracy. What is necessary here would be in-depth interviews. But we can presume that Jones's support of democracy is not only a component of his political views, but bound up with fundamental aspects of his overall philosophy or world-view, especially some conception of human beings as possessing particular rights, dignity, and autonomy. Because people are entitled to be treated with respect, they should be allowed to govern themselves and to compete on reasonably equal terms with others.

Once again, it is not unlikely that Jones's views are not held with sufficient self-consciousness for him to be fully aware of the relevant connections. But if his views were properly sorted out and clarified, he would see how they fit together. Belief that human beings have value along these lines is central to the liberal tradition. In Converse's sense, belief in democracy, equality of opportunity, and basic rights are 'constraining' in this direction (see above, pp. 141–2).

Once again, the requirement of justification itself is bound up with the idea that people have inherent dignity and should be treated with respect. People are entitled to be governed according to principles they could accept, for much the same reasons they are entitled to rule themselves, to have equality of opportunity, and basic rights. These views are of a piece; they are all bound up with beliefs concerning human dignity and the need for respect, and can be presumed to be components of a consistent philosophy.

In a pluralistic society people with different comprehensive views will disagree about why they and others should be treated with respect. Some might advance religious reasons, e.g. that we are all God's children. Others might argue along Kantian lines concerning man's autonomy and rational nature. The American Declaration of Independence of course proclaims that beliefs along these lines are self-evident. Along with disagreements about underlying reasons, liberal citizens are unlikely to agree about what exactly treating people with respect entails. But, as Rawls says, such profound underlying questions can be largely avoided as long as society's disparate comprehensive views converge on similar basic principles. The evidence I have examined of course shows this to be the case. Therefore 'by staying on the surface', we are able to generate a measure of agreement in spite of wider underlying disagreements.

In the absence of detailed examination of Jones's particular beliefs we cannot rule out the possibility that he would reject justifications of liberal principles. It could be the case that his views are inconsistent at a deep level. Though he subscribes to principles of democracy and equality of opportunity, he also supports other principles that conflict with these values, which are more deeply integrated into his overall belief system and to which he is committed more deeply. In a case of this kind, carefully sorting out and systematizing his views would lead him to set aside democratic values. Although I view possibilities along these lines as remote, we cannot rule them out, and people with such views would present severe problems for liberal consensus (but see Appendix, below). However, in the absence of detailed evidence that people's commitments to liberal principles are vulnerable in these ways, we can presume that they are not. The fact that people profess adherence to these principles can be taken at face value and provides a presumption that such principles can be justified to them. At the end of the day it may turn out that, for certain people, this presumption is not true. But again, in the absence of evidence to the contrary, we should assume that it holds. In any event, the true test of liberal consensus is not its ability to encompass all citizens, regardless of their views, but whether other acceptable versions of political liberalism could appeal to more. If liberal consensus is not able to accommodate people like Jones, it remains to be shown that another conception could, and a larger percentage of the overall population as well.

The fact that the principles of liberal consensus would not be accepted by everyone is obviously a shortcoming, as is the fact that principles developed democratically could leave certain classes of people unprotected. These problems touch on difficulties as old as political theory itself. Liberal consensus as developed throughout this book is liberal in two senses:

(*a*) according to the means through which principles are developed, i.e. that they can be justified to a large majority of democratic citizens; and

(*b*) in terms of content, which must be appropriately liberal, i.e. protecting important values of individual liberty, dignity, and autonomy.

These requirements need not conflict. As long as the principles that can be justified are of the desired sort, there is no real problem, and one will not be forced to choose between these priorities. But in other cases severe difficulties ensue.

If there is conflict between principles people can accept and principles with appropriate content (between 'form' and 'content', as these are frequently referred to), then the theorist must attempt to balance these values, or perhaps to choose between them. We can posit a continuum of possible responses, ranging from complete sacrifice of individual autonomy, at one end, to complete sacrifice of content to form, at the other. At the former pole, we might posit Plato's political theory, in the *Republic*. Though this falls well beyond the liberal tradition, it should be useful for purposes of illustration. Having significant doubts about people's ability to attain virtue themselves, Plato has little interest in their existing beliefs and values. People have been so corrupted that, when the philosophers take over a city, they must rusticate everyone over the age of 10 (*Republic* 541a), in order to allow creation of an environment in which children can be raised properly. Plato argues for extremely repressive political and educative institutions, which are intended to bring people as far along the path to virtue as they are able to go. At the opposite pole are views according to which people are free to do what they want, without restrictions. As it says in the book of Judges, in ancient Israel, before the advent of the monarchy, everyone did what was right in his own eyes (Judges 21: 25). The implication is that people did not believe there were standards higher than each person's own judgement.

Of course most reasonable political theories attempt to balance the two values. Different ways of combining them are possible. Liberal consensus could be viewed as one way among others of generating an appropriate balance. Not surprisingly, however, I think it is more than this: that it is probably the best accommodation possible under present circumstances.

The value of liberal consensus can perhaps be represented visually. Imagine a graph. On the x axis would be some simplified view of the liberal content of principles, in terms of a rough combination of range of individual rights protected and amount of economic equality guaranteed. On the y axis would be percentage of the population able to accept the principles—in terms stated above (Chapter 2, Section 3), i.e. based on systematizing and working out subjects' existing views, but with little intensive education required. Clearly, there is a trade-off between the two values. To raise the content of prospective principles would be to lessen the percentage of the population able to accept them. To increase popular acceptability would require reducing liberal content. If we accept that the two values must be balanced, then liberal consensus is arguably the most advantageous balance possible. The graph we have imagined is obviously crude. People would doubtless disagree about appropriate units for liberal values and degrees of popular consensus, while configuring these differently would give the graph widely varying looks. But still, if we employ the graph merely as an illustrative device, it helps to show the advantages of liberal consensus.[3]

If we connect horizontal and vertical lines from the two axes to the point of intersection, the area encompassed beneath the two lines by liberal consensus is probably as large if not larger than what would result from any other way of balancing the values in accordance with political liberalism. Taking the requirement of justification seriously must weaken the liberal content of resulting principles. This of course is not a mathematical demonstration, and one could question the validity of an area-covered standard altogether. But the research reviewed throughout this volume should disabuse us of the idea that trade-offs between the two sets of values can be avoided. Given the present state of liberal societies and the present mindset of liberal citizens, it is a fantasy to believe that markedly more robust liberal principles could be generally accepted. Of course Rawls, in the most important contribution to political liberalism, makes claims along these lines. But, as we saw, in both approach and on substantive grounds Rawls's argument cannot withstand scrutiny.

I will conclude by looking briefly at an approach quite different from Rawls's but with similar implications in regard to consensus. While Rawls's view can be criticized for principles that are indefensibly robust in terms of normative content, 'deliberative democracy' can be faulted for excessive expectations in regard to the potential of democratic procedures. There are many variants of deliberative democracy, although, for obvious reasons, discussion here must be brief.[4] What is common to these views are claims that the political processes in existing liberal democracies are inad-

---

[3] For justifying the principles of liberal consensus to a larger share of the population, see the Appendix, below.

[4] In my discussion here it is not necessary to distinguish 'deliberative democracy', 'discourse democracy', and other forms of 'radical democracy', and I will move between them. My discussion concentrates on elements that different forms of all these views have in common.

equate and should be supplemented with additional mechanisms that would allow widespread public discussion of and participation in the formulation of public policies. A simple definition of a deliberative democracy is 'an association whose affairs are governed by the public deliberation of its members' (Cohen 1989: 17). According to Mark Warren, in such a polity formal procedures such as elections and political rights are not 'definitive of democracy' but are 'mechanisms that empower and protect democratic deliberations' (Warren 1996: 241–2). In general, proponents of deliberative democracy assert that opportunities for appropriate participation are necessary for the moral acceptability of a regime.[5]

Requirements for widespread deliberative possibilities raise a host of problems, especially whether these must be actual processes involving existing citizens, and percentages of the population that must be afforded realistic opportunities. According to Jurgen Habermas, the conduct of actual dialogue is necessary: 'Whether a controversial norm is equally good for everyone concerned is a question that has to be decided in accordance with pragmatic rules in the context of real discourses' (Habermas 1990: 69). The establishment of an 'ideal communication community' is to provide guidance in '*setting up* discourses that have to be carried through *in fact* and cannot be replaced by monological mock dialogue' (Habermas 1987: 95; see Chambers 1996, ch. 11).[6] Obviously, in a society of 260 million there are insuperable bars to real participation by more than a small fraction of the population.[7] But we can set this issue aside and turn to questions concerning what deliberative democracy is to accomplish. For our purposes, the most interesting claim here is that free and unconstrained discourse, in which only the force of the better argument determines outcomes, will generate consensus in society. We should distinguish two versions of what we can call the 'consensus principle'. According to a

[5] For instance, according to Seyla Benhabib: 'legitimacy in complex modern democratic societies must be thought to result from the free and unconstrained public deliberation of all about matters of common concern' (1994: 26; see Benhabib 1996). According to Bernard Manin: 'These decisions are legitimate because they are, in the last analysis, the outcome of the deliberative process taking place before the universal audience of all the citizens' (Manin 1987: 359).

[6] It is to be noted that in Habermas (1996) the requirements of actual participation are significantly diluted, as Habermas argues that the legitimizing functions of discourse are accomplished by more conventional democratic political institutions, especially the rule of law.

[7] Cohen argues that deliberative procedures do not have to afford direct participation to a large percentage of the population (Cohen 1989: 30–2); for a more radical perspective, see Wolff (1970). The nature and feasibility of the institutional structures that would make real deliberation possible raise challenging issues. For an interesting possible proposal, see Fishkin (1991), although the extent to which this would bring about large-scale change in society is subject to doubt.

weak version, increased deliberation will lead to increased agreement throughout society. According to a strong version, implementation of appropriate deliberative mechanisms will lead to a strong measure of general agreement. For our purposes, it is not necessary to specify precise boundaries between the two versions. We can discuss them in turn, beginning with the strong principle.

For our concerns in this study, a strong consensus principle is more important than a weak. Only a strong principle would generate a measure of agreement sufficient to bridge the differences between diverse moral, religious, and philosophical views. But of course a supporter of such a principle must explain how it would work in practice. People with different comprehensive views see things quite differently and would be unlikely to agree. The evidence I have examined concerning the nature of their disagreements creates a powerful prima-facie case that changes in democratic procedures to allow increased deliberation or other forms of participation would not generate deep consensus on the moral issues I have explored. This is a simple point, but I believe it does considerable damage to a strong consensus principle.[8]

To counter this, a proponent must appeal to the transformative power of discourse. For instance, according to Warren, theorists of radical democracy hold that, with increased democratic participation, 'Individuals would become more public spirited, more tolerant, more attentive to the interests of others, and more probing of their own interests' (Warren 1996: 241). Warren argues that, properly formulated, what he calls the 'self-transformation thesis' is 'both defensible and essential to democratic theory' (1992: 8). Confronted with claims of this sort, I do not contend that people's preferences and motivational structures are ineluctably set, and so that democratic participation could not alter them. Nor is this necessary. The burden of proof is on proponents of strong consensus to explain exactly how the transformation would come about.[9] Reasons of space rule out detailed discussion of possible mechanisms in this context. Briefly, according to perhaps the most celebrated account, Habermas argues that democratic deliberation causes subjects to reflect

[8] For discussion, see Moon (1995), Walzer (1989–90), and Chambers (1995); for a pessimistic view of how public debate on controversial issues tends actually to work, see Hunter (1990).

[9] Warren provides a brilliant counter to standard liberal arguments to the effect that self-transformation is impossible (see Warren 1992). But this is far removed from showing that it is likely. Note the difficult preconditions for radical change that Warren allows (p. 21). In spite of his clear account of the self-transformation thesis, Warren should not be identified as a proponent of strong consensus. Because of the pluralism of modern societies, he does not pursue this ideal, but favours more limited goals of self-transformation; see Warren (1996: 243).

upon their existing moral beliefs and preferences. Increased self-consciousness performs an unmasking function, especially in regard to affording insight into the origins of different beliefs, which are shown to be ideological and false by making their holders aware of the forces responsible for them.[10] However, although this may be conceivable in theory, and may well operate as expected for particular individuals, even many individuals, the extent to which democratic processes would so affect a large percentage of the population is an empirical question, which must be settled on the basis of evidence. Clearly, the likelihood of large-scale transformations remains to be established. Especially in regard to the main division discussed in this volume, between religious and deeply secular members of society, strong evidence is necessary to demonstrate the likelihood that deliberation would cause the former to reconfigure their moral epistemologies.

Powerful evidence against the transformative power of discourse is provided by studies of how actual deliberations tend to work, even under conditions that are highly advantageous. Lynn Sanders provides a valuable analysis of empirical studies of American juries (Sanders 1997). As she notes, juries are widely believed to epitomize what is best in American democracy (p. 363). Citizens are given adequate time and resources to deliberate on a problem in which they do not have personal interests. Briefly, however, the literature shows that jurors do not confront each other as rational equals. Rather, citizens defer to one another 'in ways that are entirely unsurprising and predictable given the inequalities familiar in the broader society' (p. 364).

Patterns of social dominance are replicated in jury deliberations. For example, men are more influential than women, better-educated people more influential than the less educated. Jurors who are privileged in terms of race, gender, and economic background have been seen to hold views different from the non-privileged, and it is their views that tend to predominate (p. 369). Under these conditions, rather than building community, deliberation often instils a sense of alienation (pp. 368–9). As Sanders says, improving the quality of democratic discussion appears to require 'interventions in the structure of group deliberations' (p. 366). For our purposes here, it is not necessary to argue that jury deliberations exhaust the possibilities of democratic discourse. But clearly, the observations Sanders recounts add to the burden of proof proponents of strong consensus must meet.

This leaves us with weak consensus principles. These are more defensible. Nothing in this volume should be taken to imply that increased

---

[10] For discussion, see Geuss (1981, ch. 3).

participation in the political process—as it is or in newly configured delib- erative forums—is not desirable. Nor is it unlikely that increased discus- sion would generate agreement in certain areas—particularly in areas of public policy. Evidence shows that participation in deliberative processes can cause people to alter certain beliefs and reorder particular preferences (Miller 1992*a*).[11] In their recent book Amy Gutmann and Dennis Thompson provide several examples of policy disputes that were brought closer to resolution by increased public deliberation (Gutmann and Thompson 1996). But, once again, developments along these lines fall far short of achieving a high level of societal consensus on basic principles. Examination of the evidence concerning the range of moral and political views throughout society should make clear the formidable obstacles attaining this sort of agreement must overcome.

APPENDIX

THE argument of this study is that the principles of liberal consensus are the best possible that could be justified to a large majority of liberal citizens. Principles that could be justified to a larger percentage of the population would fall beyond liberal constraints. Throughout this work I have viewed the standard for liberal consensus as relative rather than absolute. The prin- ciples to be preferred need not be ideal, but should be better than others that could be advanced. Even though the principles I have discussed would not be universally accepted, it is unlikely that other liberal principles could be justi- fied to a higher percentage of the population. But still, even if the principles of liberal consensus could be accepted by the largest possible majority, this falls short of the entire population. And so in this brief Appendix we can see whether liberal consensus can be justified to people who do not subscribe to its tenets and so would not readily accept them.[12]

---

[11] Once again, in this regard, nothing in this work should be taken to rule out the possibility of the democratic procedures to which we appeal having significant delib- erative components. Research on procedural justice supports the idea that, in them- selves, increased opportunities for participation would increase the legitimacy of a given political system, although problems of the kind noted by Sanders (1997) must be addressed.

[12] One could perhaps argue that since the principles of liberal consensus fall within the fundamental commitments of liberal theory, people who do not accept them place themselves beyond the bounds of requiring justification. In accordance with the particular sense of 'reasonable' principles discussed above (Ch. 2, Sect. 1), if the prin- ciples that people adhere to are not consistent with their living peaceably with their fel- lows, then they cannot claim rights to be governed according to principles they could

Although the principles of liberal consensus could not be justified to all people directly, on the basis of their existing beliefs, other resources are available. For ease of reference, let us call supporters of liberal consensus 'proponents', and those who do not accept its principles 'dissenters'. Proponents would be able to show that a given dissenter, Smith, has political obligations to obey the laws passed by and to support the democratic procedures of their territory. As we will see, properly fleshed out, political obligations entail support of liberal consensus. Political obligation is a large subject, which cannot be explored fully in this context. But I will briefly outline an approach that I believe would be able to justify the requisite principles.[13]

The approach to political obligation that I believe would work is the principle of fairness, originally formulated by H. L. A. Hart:[14] 'when a number of persons conduct any joint enterprise according to rules and thus restrict their liberty, those who have submitted to these restrictions when required have a right to a similar submission from those who have benefited by their submission' (Hart 1955: 185). The moral basis of the principle is the mutuality of restrictions. Under specified conditions, the sacrifices made by members of a co-operative scheme in order to produce benefits also benefit non-co-operators, who do not make similar sacrifices. According to the principle, this situation is unfair, and it is intended to justify the obligations of non-co-operators. According to David Lyons, the underlying moral principle at work in the principle of fairness is 'the just distribution of benefits and burdens' (Lyons 1965: 164). According to Rawls: 'We are not to gain from the cooperative labors of others without doing our fair share' (Rawls 1971: 112).

The principle of fairness operates clearly in certain cases. If we assume that three neighbours co-operate in order to dig a well, a fourth who refuses to share their labours but later goes to the well for fresh water is subject to condemnation by the co-operators. There are complexities here which for reasons of space we cannot explore, but it seems clear that when a person takes steps to procure benefits generated by the ongoing co-operative labour of others, he incurs an obligation to share the labour through which the benefits are provided. However, the principle is of greatest interest as it concerns the supply of benefits that, because of their nature, cannot be procured, or even

accept. However, if their principles would allow them to live peaceably, then for both reasons of political stability and the liberal commitment to govern people according to principles they can accept, it is important to be able to justify acceptable principles to them. As cases along these lines show, this commitment holds even for people who do not recognize it.

[13] For detailed elaboration and defence of the view presented here, see Klosko (1992). The main criticisms of the view outlined here concern difficulties in 'accepting' public goods, as discussed below. For additional criticisms, see Klosko (1992: 91), Simmons (1993, ch. 8, 1996), and Green (1996). Language used in the description of the principle of fairness presented here is at points taken from Klosko (1992).

[14] Hart was anticipated by Broad (1915–16) and Ewing (1953).

accepted. These benefits are important public goods produced by the co-operative efforts of large numbers of people, co-ordinated by government. The clearest instances are public goods bearing on physical security, most notably national defence and law and order. Because public goods such as these are non-excludable, and so must be made available to a wider population (or the entire population of some territory) if they are supplied to only certain members, there is an immediate problem in explaining how individuals who have not accepted them incur obligations. Certain scholars argue that, because public goods are not accepted, they cannot generate obligations under the principle of fairness.[15]

I believe the principle of fairness is able to generate powerful obligations to contribute to non-excludable goods if three main conditions are met. Goods supplied must (i) be worth the recipients' effort in providing them; (ii) indispensable for satisfactory lives; and (iii) be have benefits and burdens that are fairly distributed.[16]

Roughly and briefly, if a given benefit is indispensable to Smith's welfare, as, for example (and most notably), physical security, then we can assume that she benefits from it, even if she has not sought to attain it. This is especially important in the case of public goods such as security, the pursuit of which is not required for their receipt. Because of the importance of such goods, unusual circumstances would have to obtain for Smith not to benefit. Though the class of indispensable public goods is perhaps small, it undoubtedly encompasses crucial benefits concerning physical security, notably national defence and law and order, protection from a hostile environment, and provisions for satisfying basic bodily needs.[17] What I mean by calling such goods presumptively beneficial is that, in almost all cases, people can be presumed to benefit from them at a high level. That we all need these public goods, regardless of whatever else we need, is a fundamental assumption of liberal political theory. It is notable that liberal theorists generally view providing them as a central purpose of the state.

The high level of benefit associated with presumptively beneficial public goods (hereafter, presumptive goods) is necessary for the generation of political obligations under the principle of fairness. To illustrate this, we can ask whether an individual, Smith, incurs obligations to co-operative scheme X by virtue of receiving indispensable public goods from it, even if she does not accept them or otherwise seek them out. The example we can concentrate on is national defence.

[15] The need to accept benefits is noted by Rawls (1971: 113–16); similarly Nozick (1974: 95), Dworkin (1986: 192–3), Sartorius (1981: 14 ff.).

[16] For reasons of space, I will discuss only (ii) in this context. In the following discussion, I assume that (i) and (iii) are met. For discussion of these and other important aspects of the principle, see Klosko (1992).

[17] Though I will not discuss other possible members of this class, I do not rule them out.

A strong argument can be made for Smith's obligations in a case of this sort. Because national security is a public good, she receives it whether or not she pursues it. In fact, the benefits of national defence are unavoidable as well as non-excludable; she cannot avoid receiving them, and so it is not clear how she could pursue them even if she wished to. Because the benefits of national defence are indispensable, we can presume that Smith *would* pursue them (and bear the associated costs) if this were necessary for their receipt. If we imagine an artificial choice situation analogous to a state of nature, it seems clear that under almost all circumstances she would choose to receive the benefits at the prescribed cost, if she had the choice. Because of the indispensability of national defence, it would not be rational for her to choose otherwise. But in the case under consideration, Smith's obligation to the members of X does not stem from hypothetical consent—that she would consent to receive the benefits under some circumstances—but from the fact that she receives them.[18]

Thus an argument along these lines should be able to justify to Smith her requirement to obey the laws of X and contribute her share to the supply of presumptive goods. Unless she can present morally relevant distinctions between herself and other inhabitants of X, her unwillingness to do her share would be a clear instance of free-riding and in violation of the principle of fairness.

Smith would incur obligations under the principle only if all three necessary conditions were satisfied, including (iii) the fair distribution requirement, that the benefits and burdens of X must be distributed fairly to all inhabitants. Reasons of space rule out full discussion of this complex matter here. But roughly and simply, because of widespread disagreements among liberal citizens as to what constitutes fair distribution, this requirement can best be satisfied procedurally. Benefits and burdens of X should be assigned by tolerably fair democratic procedures, as long as resulting distributions are reasonably fair.[19] Because of disagreements about distributive principles, this requirement should be operationalized negatively. As long as a given distribution is rationally defensible and not egregiously unfair, it should be accepted. Its imperfections should be recognized as part of the costs of supplying presumptive goods in pluralistic liberal societies.

An argument along these lines should be able to justify political obligations to virtually all citizens, including dissenters. Dissenters too should accede to democratic procedures, which include democratic definition of the principles of liberal consensus. Even if they do not directly support principles (*a–e*) (see p. 230), approximations of these principles can be derived from dissenters' political obligations to obey the law and support democratic procedures. These principles, then, can be justified to virtually all citizens.

---

[18] Discussion here draws on Klosko (1992, ch. 2), where I also consider and counter other possible arguments against obligations in these cases.

[19] For discussion, see Klosko (1992, ch. 3).

Accordingly, arguments for liberal consensus and for political obligations under the principle of fairness converge and are mutually reinforcing. An important reason for this is that central to the principle of fairness is a view of individuals as having worth and dignity and as entitled to respect. As these qualities generate requirements that people not be governed by principles that cannot be justified to them, so it is wrong for others to take advantage of them by receiving the great benefits of their co-operative endeavours while not doing their own fair shares.

REFERENCES

ABRAMSON, PAUL R. (1983). *Political Attitudes in America*. San Francisco: W. H. Freeman.

ADLER, JANE, DEBORAH HENSLER, and CHARLES NELSON (1983). *Simple Justice: How Litigants Fare in the Pittsburgh Court Arbitration Procedure*. Santa Monica, Calif.: Rand.

ADORNO, T. W., ELSE FRENKEL-BRUNSWIK, DANIEL J. LEVINSON, and R. NEVITT SANFORD (1950). *The Authoritarian Personality*. New York: W. W. Norton.

ALLEN, J. W. (1928). *A History of Political Thought in the Sixteenth Century*. London: Methuen.

ALLEN, RUSSELL, and BERNARD SPILKA (1967). 'Committed and Consensual Religion: A Specification of Religion–Prejudice Relationships'. *Journal for the Scientific Study of Religion*, 6: 191–206.

ALLPORT, GORDON (1954). *The Nature of Prejudice*. Reading, Mass.: Addison-Wesley.

—— (1966). 'The Religious Context of Prejudice'. *Journal for the Scientific Study of Religion*, 5: 447–57.

—— and MICHAEL ROSS (1967). 'Personal Religious Orientation and Prejudice'. *Journal of Personality and Social Psychology*, 5: 432–43.

ALMOND, GABRIEL A., and SIDNEY VERBA (1965). *The Civic Culture*. Boston: Little, Brown.

ALTEMEYER, BOB (1981). *Right-Wing Authoritarianism*. Winnipeg: University of Manitoba Press.

—— (1988). *Enemies of Freedom*. San Francisco: Jossey-Bass Publishers.

—— (1996). *The Authoritarian Spector*. Cambridge, Mass.: Harvard University Press.

—— and BRUCE HUNSBERGER (1992). 'Authoritarianism, Religious Fundamentalism, Quest, and Prejudice'. *International Journal for the Psychology of Religion*, 2: 113–33.

—— —— (1993). 'Commentary: Reply to Gorsuch'. *International Journal for the Psychology of Religion*, 3: 33–7.

ALVES, WAYNE, and PETER ROSSI (1978). 'Who should Get What? Fairness Judgment of the Distribution of Earnings'. *American Journal of Sociology*, 84: 541–64.

AMMERMAN, NANCY (1991). 'North American Protestant Fundamentalism'. In Martin Marty and R. Scott Appleby (eds.), *Fundamentalisms Observed*. Chicago: University of Chicago Press.

ARISTOTLE (1981). *The Politics*. Ed., and trans. T. A. Sinclair and T. Saunders. Rev. edn. Harmondsworth: Penguin.

AUDI, ROBERT (1989). 'The Separation of Church and State and the Obligations of Citizenship'. *Philosophy and Public Affairs*, 18: 209–37.

—— (1991). 'Religious Commitment and Secular Reason: A Reply to Professor Weithman'. *Philosophy and Public Affairs*, 20: 66–76.

BACHRACH, PETER (1967). *The Theory of Democratic Elitism*. Boston: Little, Brown.

BAIER, KURT (1989). 'Justice and the Aims of Political Philosophy'. *Ethics*, 99: 771–90.

BARNUM, DAVID G., and JOHN L. SULLIVAN (1989). 'Attitudinal Tolerance and Political Freedom in Britain'. *British Journal of Political Science*, 19: 136–46.

—— —— (1990). 'The Elusive Foundations of Political Freedom in Britain and the United States'. *Journal of Politics*, 52: 719–39.

BARRETT-HOWARD, EDITH, and TOM TYLER (1986). 'Procedural Justice as a Criterion in Allocation Decisions'. *Journal of Personality and Social Psychology*, 50: 296–304.

BARRY, BRIAN (1989). *Theories of Justice. A Treatise of Social Justice*, i. Berkeley: University of California Press.

—— (1995a). Review of John Rawls, *Political Liberalism. Ethics*, 105: 874–915.

—— (1995b). *Justice as Impartiality. A Treatise of Social Justice*, ii. Oxford: Oxford University Press.

BATSON, C. DANIEL (1976). 'Religion as Prosocial: Agent or Double Agent?' *Journal for the Scientific Study of Religion*, 15: 29–45.

—— and LYNN RAYNOR-PRINCE (1983). 'Religious Orientation and Complexity of Thought about Existential Concerns'. *Journal for the Scientific Study of Religion*, 22: 38–50.

—— and W. LARRY VENTNIS (1982). *The Religious Experience*. New York: Oxford University Press.

—— STEPHEN NAIFEH, and SUZANNE PATE (1978). 'Social Desirability, Religious Orientation, and Racial Prejudice'. *Journal for the Scientific Study of Religion*, 17: 31–41.

—— CHERYL FLINK, PATRICIA SCHOENRADE, JIM FULTZ, and VIRGINIA PSYCH (1986). 'Religious Orientation and Overt versus Covert Racial Prejudice'. *Journal of Personality and Social Psychology*, 50: 175–81.

BAYLES, MICHAEL (1990). *Procedural Justice: Allocating to Individuals*. Dordrecht: Kluwer Academic.

BEAN, CLIVE (1991). 'Are Australian Attitudes to Government Different?' In Francis Castle (ed.), *Australia Compared: People, Policies and Politics*. Sydney: Allen & Unwin.

BEATTY, KATHLEEN MURPHY, and B. OLIVER WALTER (1984). 'Religious Preference and Practice: Reevaluating their Impact on Political Tolerance'. *Public Opinion Quarterly*, 48: 318–29.

—— and B. OLIVER WALTER (1988). 'Fundamentalists, Evangelicals, and Politics'. *American Politics Quarterly*, 16: 43–59.

BENHABIB, SEYLA (1994). 'Deliberative Rationality and Models of Democratic Legitimacy'. *Constellations*, 1: 26–52.

—— (1996). 'Toward a Deliberative Model of Democratic Legitimacy'. In Seyla Benhabib (ed.), *Democracy and Difference: Contesting the Boundaries of the Political*. Princeton: Princeton University Press.

BENN, S. I., and PETERS, R. S (1959). *Social Principles and the Democratic State*. London: Allen & Unwin.

BERAN, HARRY (1987). *The Consent Theory of Political Obligation*. London: Croom Helm.

BERLIN, ISAIAH (1969). 'Two Concepts of Liberty'. In *Four Essays on Liberty*. Oxford: Oxford University Press.

BIES, ROBERT, and JOSEPH MOAG (1986). 'Interactional Justice: Communication Criteria of Fairness'. In R. J. Lewicki, B. H. Sheppard, and B. H. Bazerman (eds.), *Research on Negotiation in Organizations*, i. Greenwich, Conn.: JAI Press.

—— and DEBRA L. SHAPIRO (1987). 'Interactional Fairness Judgments: The Influence of Causal Accounts'. *Social Justice Research*, 1: 199–218.

BOCK, DAVID C., and NEIL CLARK WARREN (1972). 'Religious Belief as a Factor in Obedience to Destructive Commands'. *Review of Religious Research*, 13: 185–91.

BOHMAN, JAMES (1995). 'Public Reason and Cultural Pluralism'. *Political Theory*, 23: 253–79.

BORK, ROBERT H., RUSSELL HITTINGER, HADLEY ARKES, CHARLES COLSON, and ROBERT GEORGE (1996). 'The End of Democracy: The Judicial Usurpation of Politics'. *First Things*, 67.

BRADY, HENRY E., and GARY R. ORREN (1992). 'Polling Pitfalls: Sources of Error in Public Opinion Surveys'. In Thomas E. Mann and Gary R. Orren (eds.), *Media Polls in American Politics*. Washington: Brookings Institution.

BROAD, C. D (1915–16). 'On the Function of False Hypotheses in Ethics'. *International Journal of Ethics*, 26: 377–97.

BROCKNER, JOEL, and BATIA M. WIESENFELD (1996). 'An Integrative Framework for Explaining Reactions to Decisions: Interactive Effects of Outcomes and Procedures'. *Psychological Bulletin*, 120: 189–208.

—— TOM TYLER, and ROCHELLE COOPER-SCHNEIDER (1992). 'The Influence of Prior Commitment to an Institution on Reactions to Perceived Unfairness'. *Administrative Science Quarterly*, 37: 241–61.

—— BATIA M. WIESENFELD, and CHRISTOPHER MARTIN (1995). 'Decision Frame, Procedural Justice, and Survivors' Reactions to Job Layoffs'. *Organizational Behavior and Human Decision Processes*, 63: 59–68.

CALDEIRA, GREGORY A., and JAMES L. GIBSON (1992. 'The Etiology of Public Support for the Supreme Court'. *American Journal of Political Science*, 36: 635–64.

CASTBERG, FREDE (1960). *Freedom of Speech in the West*. New York: Oceana.

CHAMBERS, SIMONE (1995). 'Discourse and Democratic Practices'. In Stephen White (ed.), *The Cambridge Companion to Habermas*. Cambridge: Cambridge University Press.

CHAMBERS, SIMONE (1996). *Reasonable Democracy: Jurgen Habermas and the Politics of Discourse*. Ithaca, NY: Cornell University Press.

CHONG, DENNIS (1993). 'How People Think, Reason, and Feel about Rights and Liberties'. *American Journal of Political Science*, 37: 867–99.

CITRIN, JACK (1974). 'Comment: The Political Relevance of Trust in Government'. *American Political Science Review*, 68: 973–88.

COHEN, JOSHUA (1989). 'Deliberation and Democratic Legitimacy'. In A. Hamlin and P. Pettit (eds.), *The Good Polity: Normative Analyses of the State*. Oxford: Blackwell.

—— (1993). 'Moral Pluralism and Political Consensus'. In David Copp, Jean Hampton, and John Roemer (eds.), *The Idea of Democracy*. Cambridge: Cambridge University Press.

—— (1994). 'Pluralism and Proceduralism'. *Chicago-Kent Law Review*, 69: 589–618.

—— (1996). 'Procedure and Substance in Deliberative Democracy'. In Seyla Benhabib (ed.), *Democracy and Difference: Contesting the Boundaries of the Political*. Princeton: Princeton University Press.

CONNOLLY, WILLIAM (1983). *The Terms of Political Discourse*. 2nd edn. Princeton: Princeton University Press.

CONVERSE, PHILIP E. (1964). 'The Nature of Belief Systems in Mass Publics'. In David E. Apter (ed.), *Ideology and Discontent*. Glencoe, Ill.: Free Press.

CRAIG, STEPHEN C. (1993). *The Malevolent Leaders*. Boulder, Colo.: Westview.

—— RICHARD NIEMI, and GLENN SILVER (1990). 'Political Efficacy and Trust: A Report on the NEW Pilot Study Items'. *Political Behavior*, 12: 289–314.

CROPANZANO, RUSSELL, and ROBERT FOLGER (1991). 'Procedural Justice and Worker Motivation'. In R. Steers and L. Porter (eds.), *Motivation and Work Behavior*. New York: McGraw Hill.

DAHL, ROBERT (1961). *Who Governs?* New Haven: Yale University Press.

—— (1971). *Polyarchy*. New Haven: Yale University Press.

—— (1989). *Democracy and its Critics*. New Haven: Yale University Press.

DELLI CARPINI, MICHAEL X., and SCOTT KEETER (1996). *What Americans Know about Politics and Why it Matters*. New Haven: Yale University Press.

DEVLIN, PATRICK (1965). *The Enforcement of Morals*. Oxford: Oxford University Press.

DONAHUE, MICHAEL (1985*a*). 'Intrinsic and Extrinsic Religiousness: The Empirical Research'. *Journal for the Scientific Study of Religion*, 24: 418–23.

—— (1985*b*). 'Intrinsic and Extrinsic Religiousness: Review and Meta-Analysis'. *Journal of Personality and Social Psychology*, 48: 400–19.

DUCH, RAYMOND M., and JAMES L. GIBSON (1992). 'Putting up with Fascists in Western Europe: A Comparative, Cross-Level Analysis of Political Tolerance'. *Western Political Quarterly*, 45: 237–73.

DWORKIN, RONALD (1978). *Taking Rights Seriously*. Cambridge, Mass.: Harvard University Press.

—— (1985). *A Matter of Principle*. Cambridge, Mass.: Harvard University Press.

—— (1986). *Law's Empire*. Cambridge, Mass.: Harvard University Press.

EASTON, DAVID (1965a). *A Framework for Political Analysis*. Chicago: University of Chicago Press.

—— (1965b). *A Systems Analysis of Political Life*. Chicago: University of Chicago Press.

—— (1975). 'A Re-assessment of the Concept of Political Support'. *British Journal of Political Science*, 5: 435–57.

EISINGA, ROB, ALBERT FELLING, and JAN PETERS (1990). 'Religious Belief, Church Involvement, and Ethnocentrism in the Netherlands'. *Journal for the Scientific Study of Religion*, 29: 54–75.

—— REUBEN KONIG, and REER SCHEEPERS (1995). 'Orthodox Religious Beliefs and Anti-semitism: A Replication of Glock and Stark in the Netherlands'. *Journal for the Scientific Study of Religion*, 34: 214–23.

ELLIS, RICHARD J. (1993). *American Political Cultures*. New York: Oxford University Press.

EMIG, ARTHUR G., MICHAEL B. HESSE, and SAMUEL H. FISHER III (1996). 'Black–White Differences in Political Efficacy, Trust, and Sociopolitical Participation'. *Urban Affairs Review*, 32: 264–76.

ERIKSON, ROBERT S., NORMAN R. LUTTBEG, and KENT L. TEDIN (1991). *American Public Opinion*. New York: Macmillan.

EWING, A. C. (1953). 'What would Happen if everyone Acted like Me?' *Philosophy*, 28: 16–29.

EXDELL, JOHN (1994). 'Feminism, Fundamentalism, and Liberal Legitimacy'. *Canadian Journal of Philosophy*, 24: 441–63.

FEAGIN, JOE R. (1964). 'Prejudice and Religious Types: A Focused Study of Southern Fundamentalists'. *Journal for the Scientific Study of Religion* 4: 3–13.

FEINBERG, JOEL (1984). *The Moral Limits of the Criminal Law: Harm to Others*. New York: Oxford University Press.

—— (1985). *The Moral Limits of the Criminal Law: Offense to Others*. New York: Oxford University Press.

—— (1986). *The Moral Limits of the Criminal Law: Harm to Self*. New York: Oxford University Press.

—— (1988). *The Moral Limits of the Criminal Law: Harmless Wrongdoing*. New York: Oxford University Press.

FINKEL, STEVEN E., LEE SIGELMAN, and STAN HUMPHRIES (forthcoming). 'Democratic Values and Political Tolerance'. In John Robinson and Lawrence Wrightsman (eds.), *Measures of Political Attitudes*. New York: Academic Press.

FISHKIN, JAMES (1991). *Democracy and Deliberation*. New Haven: Yale University Press.

FOLGER, ROBERT (1986). 'Rethinking Equity Theory'. In H. W. Bierhoff, R. L. Cohen, and J. Greenberg (eds.), *Justice in Social Relations*. New York: Plenum.

—— (1987). 'Distributive and Procedural Justice in the Workplace'. *Social Justice Research* 1: 143–59.

—— and JERALD GREENBERG (1985). 'Procedural Justice: An Interpretive Analysis of Personnel Systems'. In K. Rowland and G. Ferris (eds.), *Research in Personnel and Human Resources Management*, iii. Greenwich, Conn.: JAI Press.

FOLGER, ROBERT and MARY KONOVSKY (1989). 'Effects of Procedural and Distributive Justice on Reactions to Pay Raise Decisions'. *Academy of Management Journal*, 32: 115–30.

—— DAVID ROSENFIELD, JANET GROVE, and LOUISE CORKRAN (1979). 'Effects of "Voice" and Peer Opinions on Responses to Inequity'. *Journal of Personality and Social Psychology*, 37: 2253–61.

FOSSATI, THOMAS E., and JAMES W. MEEKER (1997). 'Evaluations of Institutional Legitimacy and Court System Fairness: A Study of Gender Differences'. *Journal of Criminal Justice*, 25: 141– 54.

FRANKLIN, JULIAN (1969). *Constitutionalism and Resistance in the Sixteenth Century*. New York: Pegasus.

FRENKEL-BRUNSWICK, ELSE, and R. NEVITT SANFORD (1945). 'Some Personality Factors in Anti-semitism'. *Journal of Psychology*, 20: 271–91.

FROHLICH, NORMAN, and JOE A. OPPENHEIMER (1992). *Choosing Justice: An Experimental Approach to Ethical Theory*. Berkeley: University of California Press.

FUCHS, DIETER, GIOVANNA GUIDOROSSI, and PALLE SVENSSON (1995). 'Support for the Democratic System'. In Hans-Dieter Klingemann and Dieter Fuchs (eds.), *Citizens and the State*. Oxford: Oxford University Press.

FULLERTON, J. TIMOTHY, and BRUCE HUNSBERGER (1982). 'A Unidimensional Measure of Christian Orthodoxy'. *Journal for the Scientific Study of Religion*, 21: 317–26.

GALLIE, W. B (1955–6). 'Essentially Contested Concepts'. *Proceedings of the Aristotelian Society*, 56: 167–98.

GALLUP, GEORGE, and JIM CASTELLI (1989). *The People's Religion*. New York: Macmillan.

GALSTON, WILLIAM (1989). 'Pluralism and Social Unity'. *Ethics*, 99: 711–26.

—— (1991). *Liberal Purposes*. Cambridge: Cambridge University Press.

—— (1995). 'Two Concepts of Liberalism'. *Ethics*, 105: 516–34.

GAUS, GERALD (1996). *Justificatory Liberalism*. New York: Oxford University Press.

GEORGE, ROBERT P (1997). 'Public Reason and Political Conflict: Abortion and Homosexuality'. *Yale Law Journal*, 106: 2475–504.

GEUSS, RAYMOND (1981). *The Idea of a Critical Theory: Habermas and the Frankfurt School*. Cambridge: Cambridge Univesity Press.

GIBSON, JAMES L (1987). 'Homosexuals and the Ku Klux Klan: A Contextual Analysis of Political Tolerance'. *Western Political Quarterly*, 40: 427–48.

—— (1988). 'Political Intolerance and Political Repression during the McCarthy Red Scare'. *American Political Science Review*, 82: 511–29.

—— (1989*a*). 'The Policy Consequences of Political Intolerance: Political Repression during the Vietnam War Era'. *Journal of Politics*, 51: 13–35.

—— (1989*b*). 'The Structure of Attitudinal Tolerance in the United States'. *British Journal of Political Science*, 19: 562–70.

—— (1989c). 'Understandings of Justice: Institutional Legitimacy, Procedural Justice, and Political Tolerance'. *Law and Society Review*, 23: 469–96.

—— (1992a). 'Alternative Measures of Political Tolerance: Must Tolerance be "Least-Liked"?' *American Journal of Political Science*, 36: 560–77.

—— (1992b). 'The Political Consequences of Intolerance: Cultural Conformity and Political Freedom'. *American Political Science Review*, 86: 338–56.

—— and GREGORY A. CALDEIRA (1992). 'Blacks and the United States Supreme Court: Models of Diffuse Support'. *Journal of Politics*, 54: 1120–45.

—— and KENT L. TEDIN (1988). 'The Etiology of Intolerance of Homosexual Politics'. *Social Science Quarterly*, 69: 587–604.

GLOCK, CHARLES Y., and RODNEY STARK (1966). *Christian Beliefs and Anti-semitism*. New York: Harper & Row.

GOODIN, ROBERT, and ANDREW REEVE (eds.) (1989). *Liberal Neutrality*. London: Routledge.

GORSUCH, RICHARD (1993). 'Religion and Prejudice: Lessons not Learned from the Past'. *International Journal for the Psychology of Religion*, 3: 29–31.

—— and DANIEL ALESHIRE (1974). 'Christian Faith and Ethnic Prejudice: A Review and Interpretation of Research'. *Journal for the Scientific Study of Religion*, 13 3: 281–307.

GREEN, JOHN, JAMES GUTH, LYMAN KELLSTEDT, and CORWIN SMIDT (1994). 'Uncivil Challenges? Support for Civil Liberties among Religious Activists'. *Journal of Political Science*, 22: 25–49.

GREEN, LESLIE (1996). 'Who Believes in Political Obligation?' In John T. Sanders and Jan Narveson (eds.), *For and Against the State*. Savage, Md.: Rowman & Littlefield.

GREENBERG, JERALD (1986). 'Determinants of Perceived Fairness of Performance Evaluations'. *Journal of Applied Psychology*, 71: 340–2.

—— (1987). 'Reactions to Procedural Injustice in Payment Distributions: Do the Means Justify the Ends?' *Journal of Applied Psychology*, 72: 55–61.

—— (1988). 'Cultivating an Image of Justice: Looking Fair on the Job'. *Academy of Management Executive*, 2: 155–7.

—— (1990). 'Looking Fair vs. Being Fair: Managing Impressions of Organizational Justice'. In B. M. Staw and L. L. Cummings (eds.), *Research in Organizational Behavior*. Greenwich, Conn.: JAI Press.

—— (1994). 'Using Socially Fair Treatment to Promote Acceptance of a Work Site Smoking Ban'. *Journal of Applied Psychology*, 79: 288–97.

GREENBERG, JERALD, and CLAIRE MCCARTY (1990). 'The Interpersonal Aspects of Procedural Justice: A New Perspective on Pay Fairness'. *Labor Law Journal*, 41: 580–6.

GRIFFIN, GLENN, RICHARD GORSUCH, and ANDREA-LEE DAVIS (1987). 'A Cross-cultural Investigation of Religious Orientation, Social Norms and Prejudice'. *Journal for the Scientific Study of Religion*, 26: 358–65.

GUTMANN, AMY (1995). 'Civic Education and Social Diversity'. *Ethics*, 105: 557–79.

—— and DENNIS THOMPSON (1996). *Democracy and Disagreement*. Cambridge, Mass.: Harvard University Press.

HABERMAS, JURGEN (1987). *The Theory of Communicative Action*, ii. Trans. Thomas McCarthy. Boston: Beacon Press.

—— (1990). *Moral Consciousness and Communicative Action*. Trans. Christian Lenhardt and Shierry Nicholson. Cambridge, Mass.: MIT Press.

—— (1995). 'Reconciliation through the Public Use of Reason: Remarks on John Rawls's *Political Liberalism*'. *Journal of Philosophy*, 92: 109–31.

—— (1996). *Between Facts and Norms: Contributions to a Discourse Theory of Law and Democracy*. Trans. William Rehg. Cambridge, Mass.: MIT Press.

HAMILTON, ALEXANDER, JOHN JAY, and JAMES MADISON (n.d.). *The Federalist*. New York: Modern Library.

HAMPSHIRE, STUART (1989). *Innocence and Experience*. Cambridge, Mass.: Harvard University Press.

HART, H.L.A (1955). 'Are there any Natural Rights?' *Philosophical Review*, 64: 175–91.

—— (1963). *Law, Liberty, and Morality*. Stanford, Calif.: Stanford University Press.

HARTZ, LOUIS (1955). *The Liberal Tradition in America*. New York: Harcourt Brace.

HEREK, GREGORY (1987). 'Religious Orientation and Prejudice: A Comparison of Racial and Sexual Attitudes'. *Personality and Social Psychology Bulletin*, 13: 34–44.

HIBBING, JOHN R., and ELIZABETH THEISS-MORSE (1995). *Congress as Public Enemy*. Cambridge: Cambridge University Press.

HOBHOUSE, L. T. (1994). *Liberalism and Other Writings*. Ed. James Meadowcraft. Cambridge: Cambridge University Press.

HOCHSCHILD, JENNIFER (1981). *What's Fair: American Beliefs about Distributive Justice*. Cambridge, Mass.: Harvard University Press.

HOGE, DEAN, and JACKSON CARROLL (1973). 'Religiosity and Prejudice in Northern and Southern Churches'. *Journal for the Scientific Study of Religion*, 12: 181–97.

HOGGE, JAMES, and S. THOMAS FRIEDMAN (1967). 'The Scriptural Literalism Scale: A Preliminary Report'. *Journal of Psychology*, 66: 275–9.

HOOD, RALPH W. (1971. 'A Comparison of the Allport and Feagin Scoring Procedures for Intrinsic/Extrinsic Religious Orientation'. *Journal for the Scientific Study of Religion*, 10: 370–4.

HOULDEN, PAULINE, STEPHEN, LATOUR, LAURENS WALKER, and JOHN THIBAUT (1978). 'Preference for Modes of Dispute Resolution as a Function of Process and Decision Control'. *Journal of Experimental Social Psychology*, 14: 13–30.

HUBER, J., and WILLIAM FORM (1973). *Income and Ideology*. New York: Free Press.

HUNSBERGER, BRUCE (1989). 'A Short Version of the Christian Orthodoxy Scale'. *Journal for the Scientific Study of Religion*, 28: 360–5.

—— (1995). 'Religion and Prejudice: The Role of Religious Fundamentalism, Quest, and Right–Wing Authoritarianism'. *Journal of Social Issues*, 51: 113–29.

—— MICHAEL PRATT, and S. MARK PRANCER (1994). 'Religious Fundamentalism and Integrative Complexity of Thought: A Relationship for Existential Content Only?' *Journal for the Scientific Study of Religion*, 33: 335–46.

HUNTER, JAMES (1990). *Culture Wars*. New York: Basic Books.

—— (1994). *Before the Shooting Begins*. New York: Free Press.

—— and CARL BOWMAN (1996). *The State of Disunion: 1996 Survey of American Political Culture*. 2 vols. Ivy, Va.: In Media Res Educational Foundation.

JACKMAN, MARY R. (1973). 'Education and Prejudice, or Education and Response-Set?' *American Sociological Review* 38: 327–39.

—— (1978). 'Does Education Increase Commitment to Racial Integration?' *American Journal of Political Science*, 22: 302–24.

JACKMAN, ROBERT (1972). 'Political Elites, Mass Publics, and Support for Democratic Principles'. *Journal of Politics*, 34: 753–73.

JELEN, TED G. (1989). 'Biblical Literalism and Inerrancy: Does the Difference Make a Difference?' *Sociological Analysis*, 49: 421–9.

JONES, PETER (1995). 'Review Article: Two Conceptions of Liberalism and Two Conceptions of Justice'. *British Journal of Political Science*, 25: 515–50.

KANT, IMMANUEL (1964). *Groundwork of the Metaphysic of Morals*. Trans. H. J. Paton. New York: Harper & Row.

—— (1970). *Kant's Political Writings*. Ed. Hans Reiss. Cambridge: Cambridge University Press.

KELLSTEDT, LYMAN (1989). 'The Meaning and Measurement of Evangelicalism: Problems and Prospects'. In Ted Jelen (ed.), *Religion and Political Behavior in the United States*. New York: Praeger.

—— and CORWIN SMIDT (1991). 'Measuring Fundamentalism: An Analysis of Different Operational Strategies'. *Journal for the Scientific Study of Religion*, 30: 259–78.

KEY, V. O. (1964). *Public Opinion and American Democracy*. New York: Alfred A. Knopf.

KINDER, DONALD, and LYNN SANDERS (1996). *Divided by Color*. Chicago: University of Chicago Press.

—— and DAVID O. SEARS (1981). 'Prejudice and Politics: Symbolic Racism versus Threats to the Good Life'. *Journal of Personality and Social Psychology*, 40: 414–31.

KIRKPATRICK, LEE, RALPH HOOD, and GARY HARTZ (1991). 'Fundamentalist Religion Conceptualized in Terms of Rokeach's Theory of the Open and Closed Mind: New Perspectives on Some Old Ideas'. *Researching the Scientific Study of Religion*, 3: 157–79.

KLOSKO, GEORGE (1986). *The Development of Plato's Political Theory*. New York: Methuen.

—— (1991). 'Reformist Consent and Political Obligation'. *Political Studies*, 39: 676–90.

—— (1992). *The Principle of Fairness and Political Obligation*. Savage, Md.: Rowman & Littlefield.

KLOSKO, GEORGE (1993*a*). *History of Political Theory: An Introduction*. 2 vols. Vol. i: *Ancient and Medieval Political Theory*. Fort Worth: Harcourt Brace.

—— (1993*b*). 'Rawls's "Political" Philosophy and American Democracy'. *American Political Science Review*, 87: 348–59.

—— (1994). 'Rawls's Argument from Political Stability'. *Columbia Law Review*, 94: 1882–97.

—— (1995). *History of Political Theory: An Introduction*. 2 vols. Vol. ii: *Modern Political Theory*. Fort Worth: Harcourt Brace.

—— (1997). 'Political Constructivism in Rawls's *Political Liberalism*'. *American Political Science Review*, 91: 635–46.

KLUEGEL, JAMES R., and ELIOT R. SMITH (1986). *Beliefs about Inequality*. New York: Aldine de Gruyter.

KONOVSKY, MARY, and ROBERT FOLGER (1991). 'The Effects of Procedures, Social Accounts, and Benefits Level on Victims' Layoff Reactions'. *Journal of Applied Social Psychology*, 21: 630–50.

KOPER, GERDA, AAAN VAN KNIPPENBERG, FRANCIEN BOUHUIJS, RIEL MERMUNT, and HENK WILKE (1993). 'Procedural Fairness and Self-Esteem'. *European Journal of Social Psychology*, 23: 313–25.

KRASNOFF, LARRY (1998). 'Consensus, Stability, and Normativity in Rawls's *Political Liberalism*'. *Journal of Philosophy*, 105: 269–92.

KUKLINSKI, JAMES, ELLEN RIGGLE, VICTOR OTTATI, NORBERT SCHWARTZ, and ROBERT S. WYER (1991). 'The Cognitive and Affective Bases of Political Tolerance Judgments'. *American Journal of Political Science*, 35: 1–27.

—— MICHAEL D. COBB, and MARTIN GILENS (1997). 'Racial Attitudes and the "New South" '. *Journal of Politics*, 59: 323–49.

KYMLICKA, WILL (1988). 'Liberalism and Communitarianism'. *Canadian Journal of Philosophy,* 18: 181–203.

LARMORE, CHARLES (1987). *Patterns of Moral Complexity*. Cambridge: Cambridge University Press.

—— (1996). *The Morals of Modernity*. Cambridge: Cambridge University Press.

LATOUR, STEPHEN, PAULINE HOULDEN, LAURENS WALKER, and JOHN THIBAUT (1976). 'Some Determinants of Preference for Modes of Conflict Resolution'. *Journal of Conflict Resolution*, 20: 319–56.

LAWRENCE, DAVID (1976). 'Procedural Norms and Tolerance: A Reassessment'. *American Political Science Review*, 70: 80–100.

LEAK, GARY K., and STANLEY FISH (1989). 'Religious Orientation, Impression Management, and Self-Deception: Toward a Clarification of the Link between Religiosity and Social Desirability'. *Journal for the Scientific Study of Religion*, 28: 355–9.

LEUNG, KWOK (1987). 'Some Determinants of Reactions to Procedural Models for Conflict Resolution: A Cross-National Study'. *Journal of Personality and Social Psychology*, 53: 898–908.

—— and E. ALLAN LIND (1986). 'Procedural Justice and Culture: Effects of Culture, Gender, and Investigator Status on Procedural Preferences'. *Journal of Personality and Social Psychology*, 50: 1134–40.

LEVENTHAL, GERALD (1980). 'What should be Done with Equity Theory?' In K. J. Gergen, M. S. Greenberg, and R. H. Willis (eds.), *Social Exchange: Advances in Theory and Research*. New York: Plenum Press.

LIND, E. ALLAN (1994). 'Procedural Justice and Culture: Evidence for Ubiquitous Process Concerns'. *Zeitschrift für Rechtssozologie*, 15: 24–36.

—— and ROBIN LISSAK (1985). 'Apparent Impropriety and Procedural Fairness Judgments'. *Journal of Experimental Social Psychology* 21: 19–29.

—— and TOM TYLER (1988). *The Social Psychology of Procedural Justice*. New York: Plenum.

—— BONNIE ERICKSON, NEHEMIA FRIEDLAND, and MICHAEL DICKENBERGER (1978). 'Reactions to Procedural Models for Adjudicative Conflict'. *Journal of Conflict Resolution*, 22: 318–41.

—— RUTH KANFER, P. CHRISTOPHER EARLEY (1990). 'Voice, Control, and Procedural Justice: Instrumental and Noninstrumental Concerns in Fairness Judgments'. *Journal of Personality and Social Psychology*, 59: 952–9.

—— YUEN J. HUO, and TOM R. TYLER (1994). '. . . And Justice for All: Ethnicity, Gender, and Preferences for Dispute Resolution Procedures'. *Law and Human Behavior*, 18: 269–89.

—— TOM TYLER, and YUEN HUO (1997). 'Procedural Context and Culture: Variations in the Antecedents of Procedural Justice Judgments'. *Journal of Personality and Social Psychology*, 73: 767–80.

LIPSET, SEYMOUR (1960). *Political Man: The Social Bases of Politics*. Garden City, NY: Anchor Books.

LISSAK, ROBIN, and BLAIR SHEPPARD (1983). 'Beyond Fairness: The Criterion Problem in Research on Dispute Intervention'. *Journal of Applied Social Psychology*, 13: 45–65.

LOCKE, JOHN (1955). *A Letter Concerning Toleration*. Indianapolis: Bobbs-Merrill.

—— (1988). *Two Treatises of Government*. Ed. Peter Laslett. Student edn. Cambridge: Cambridge University Press.

LYONS, DAVID (1965). *Forms and Limits of Utilitarianism*. Oxford: Oxford University Press.

MACCALLUM. GERALD (1967). 'Negative and Positive Freedom'. *Philosophical Review*, 76: 312–34.

MCCLOSKY, HERBERT (1964). 'Consensus and Ideology in American Politics'. *American Political Science Review*, 58: 361–82.

—— and ALIDA BRILL (1983). *Dimensions of Tolerance*. New York: Russell Sage Foundation.

—— and JOHN ZALLER (1984). *The American Ethos*. Cambridge, Mass.: Harvard University Press.

MCCONAHAY, JOHN B. (1982). 'Self-Interest versus Racial Attitudes as Correlates of Anti-busing Attitudes in Louisville'. *Journal of Politics*, 44: 692–720.

—— and JOSEPH C. HOUGH (1976). 'Symbolic Racism'. *Journal of Social Issues*, 32: 23–45.

MACEDO, STEPHEN (1990). 'The Politics of Justification'. *Political Theory*, 18: 280–304.

258 References

MACEDO, STEPHEN (1995). 'Liberal Civic Education and Religious Fundamentalism: The Case of God v. John Rawls?' *Ethics*, 105: 468–96.
—— (1998). 'Transformative Constitutionalism and the Case of Religion'. *Political Theory*, 26: 56–80.

McEWEN, CRAIG, and RICHARD MAIMAN (1981). 'Small Claims Mediation in Maine: An Empirical Assessment'. *Maine Law Review*, 33: 237–68.
—— —— (1984). 'Mediation in Small Claims Court: Achieving Compliance through Consent'. *Law and Society Review*, 8: 11–49.

McFARLAND, SAM G. (1989). 'Religious Orientations and the Targets of Discrimination'. *Journal for the Scientific Study of Religion*, 28: 324–36.

MANIN, BERNARD (1987). 'On Legitimacy and Political Deliberation'. Trans. Elly Stein and Jane Mansbridge. *Political Theory*, 15: 338–68.

MANN, MICHAEL (1970). 'The Social Cohesion of Liberal Democracy'. *American Sociological Review*, 35: 423–39.

MARCUS, GEORGE E., JOHN L. SULLIVAN, ELIZABETH THEISS-MORSE, and SANDRA L. WOOD (1995). *With Malice toward Some*. Cambridge: Cambridge University Press.

MARSDEN, GEORGE (1971). 'Defining Fundamentalism'. *Christian Scholar's Review*, 1: 141–51.
—— (1980). *Fundamentalism and American Culture*. Oxford: Oxford University Press.

MEIKELJOHN, ALEXANDER (1948). *Free Speech and its Relation to Self Government*. New York: Harper & Brothers.

MENENDEZ, ALBERT (1993). *Visions of Reality: What Fundamentalist Schools Teach*. Buffalo: Prometheus Books.

MILL, JOHN STUART (1978). *On Liberty*. Ed. Elizabeth Rapaport. Indianapolis: Hackett.

MILLER, ARTHUR (1974a). 'Political Issues and Trust in Government: 1964–1970'. *American Political Science Review*, 68: 951–72.
—— (1974b). 'Rejoinder to "Comment" by Jack Citrin: Political Discontent or Ritualism?' *American Political Science Review*, 68: 989–1001.

MILLER, DAVID (1992a). 'Deliberative Democracy and Social Choice'. *Political Studies*, 40: 54–67.
—— (1992b). 'Distributive Justice: What the People Think'. *Ethics*, 102: 555–92.

MINOW, MARTHA, JOHN RAWLS, MICHAEL SANDEL, RONALD THIEMANN, and CORNELL WEST (1995). 'Political Liberalism, Religion, and Public Reason'. *Religion and Values in Public Life*, 3: 1–11.

MOON, J. DONALD (1993). *Constructing Community*. Princeton: Princeton University Press.
—— (1995). 'Practical Discourse and Communicative Ethics'. In Stephen White (ed.), *The Cambridge Companion to Habermas*. Cambridge: Cambridge University Press.

MOORE, LEROY (1968). 'Another Look at Fundamentalism: A Response to Ernest R. Sandeen'. *Church History*, 37: 195–203.

MULLER, EDWARD N. (1979). *Aggressive Political Participation*. Princeton: Princeton University Press.

—— and THOMAS O. JUKAM (1977). 'On the Meaning of Political Support'. *American Political Science Review*, 71: 1561–95.

—— —— and MITCHELL SELIGSON (1982). 'Diffuse Political Support and Antisystem Political Behavior: A Comparative Analysis'. *American Journal of Political Science*, 26: 240–64.

MURPHY, WALTER, and JOSEPH TANENHAUS (1969). 'Public Opinion and the United States Supreme Court'. In J. Grossman and J. Tanenhaus (eds.), *Frontiers of Judicial Research*. New York: Wiley.

NAGEL, THOMAS (1987). 'Moral Conflict and Political Legitimacy'. *Philosophy and Public Affairs*, 16: 215–40.

—— (1991). *Equality and Partiality*. Oxford: Oxford University Press.

NOELLE-NEUMANN, ELISABETH, and RENATE KÖCHER (1993). *Allensbacher Jahrbuch der Demoskopie, 1984–1992*. Munich: K. G. Saur.

NOZICK, ROBERT (1974). *Anarchy, State, and Utopia*. New York: Basic Books.

NUNN, CLYDE Z., and HARRY J. CROCKETT, and J. ALLEN WILLIAMS (1978). *Tolerance for Nonconformity*. San Francisco: Jossey- Bass Publishers.

PERKINS, H. WESLEY (1983). 'Organized Religion as Opiate or Prophetic Stimulant: A Study of American and English Assessments of Social Justice in Two Urban Settings'. *Review of Religious Research*, 24: 206–24.

—— (1985). 'A Research Note on Religiosity as Opiate or Prophetic Stimulant among Students in England and the United States'. *Review of Religious Research*, 26: 269–80.

PITKIN, HANNAH (1965). 'Obligation and Consent'. *American Political Science Review*, 59: 990–9.

PONTON, MARCEL, and RICHARD GORSUCH (1988). 'Prejudice and Religion Revisited: A Cross-cultural Investigation with a Venezuelan Sample'. *Journal for the Scientific Study of Religion*, 27: 260–71.

PROTHRO, JAMES, and CHARLES GRIGG (1960). 'Fundamental Principles of Democracy: Bases of Agreement and Disagreement'. *Journal of Politics*, 22: 276–94.

PROVENZO, EUGENE (1990). *Religious Fundamentalism and American Education*. Albany, NY: State University of New York Press.

PRUITT, DEAN, ROBERT PIERCE, NEIL MCGILLICUDDY, GARY WELTON, and LYNN CASTRIANNO (1993). 'Long-Term Success in Mediation'. *Law and Human Behavior*, 17; 313–30.

QUINN, PHILIP (1995). 'Political Liberalisms and their Exclusion of the Religious'. *Proceedings and Addresses of the American Philosophical Association*, 69: 35–56.

RAWLS, JOHN (1958). 'Justice as Fairness'. *Philosophical Review*, 67: 164–94.

—— (1971). *A Theory of Justice*. Cambridge, Mass.: Harvard University Press.

—— (1980). 'Kantian Constructivism in Moral Theory'. *Journal of Philosophy*, 77: 515–72.

260 *References*

RAWLS, JOHN (1982). 'The Basic Liberties and their Priority'. In Sterling MacMurrin (ed.), *The Tanner Lectures on Human Values*. Cambridge: Cambridge University Press. Repr. as Rawls (1993, lecture 8).

—— (1985). 'Justice as Fairness: Political not Metaphysical'. *Philosophy and Public Affairs*, 14: 223–51.

—— (1987). 'The Idea of an Overlapping Consensus'. *Oxford Journal of Legal Studies*, 7: 1–25.

—— (1988). 'The Priority of Right and Ideas of the Good'. *Philosophy and Public Affairs*, 17: 251–76.

—— (1989). 'The Domain of the Political and Overlapping Consensus'. *New York University Law Review*, 64: 233–55.

—— (1993). *Political Liberalism*. New York: Columbia University Press.

—— (1995). 'Reply to Habermas'. *Journal of Philosophy*, 92: 132–80.

—— (1996). *Political Liberalism*. Paperback edn. New York: Columbia.

—— (1997). 'The Idea of Public Reason Revisited'. *University of Chicago Law Review*, 64: 765–807.

REEHER, GRANT (1996). *Narratives of Justice*. Ann Arbor: University of Michigan Press.

ROKEACH, MILTON (1960). *The Open and Closed Mind*. New York: Basic Books.

ROLLER, EDELTRAUD (1995). 'Political Agendas and Beliefs about the Scope of Government'. In Ole Borre and Elinor Scarbrough (eds.), *The Scope of Government*. Oxford: Oxford University Press.

RORTY, RICHARD (1988). 'The Priority of Philosophy to Democracy'. In Merrill D. Peterson (ed.), *The Virginia Statute for Religious Freedom*. Cambridge: Cambridge University Press.

ROSETT, ARTHUR (1988). *Contract Law and its Application*. 4th edn. Westbury, NY: Foundation Press.

RUGGIERO, GUIDO DE (1959). *The History of European Liberalism* (1928). Boston: Beacon Press.

RYTINA, JOAN, WILLIAM FORM, and JOHN PEASE (1970). 'Income and Stratification Ideology: Beliefs about the American Opportunity Structure'. *American Journal of Sociology*, 75: 703–16.

SANDEEN, ERNEST (1970). *The Roots of Fundamentalism*. Chicago: University of Chicago Press.

—— (1971). 'Defining Fundamentalism: A Reply to Professor Marsden'. *Christian Scholar's Review*, 1: 227–33.

SANDEL, MICHAEL (1982). *Liberalism and the Limits of Justice*. Cambridge: Cambridge University Press.

—— (1996). *Democracy's Discontent*. Cambridge, Mass.: Harvard University Press.

SANDERS, LYNN (1997). 'Against Deliberation'. *Political Theory*, 25: 347–76.

SAPP, GARY L., and LOGAN JONES (1986). 'Religious Orientation and Moral Judgement'. *Journal for the Scientific Study of Religion*, 25: 208–14.

SARAT, AUSTIN (1975). 'Support for the Legal System: An Analysis of Knowledge, Attitudes, and Behavior'. *American Politics Quarterly*, 3: 3–24.

—— (1977). 'Studying American Legal Culture: An Assessment of Survey Evidence'. *Law and Society Review*, 11: 427–88.

SARTORIUS, ROLF (1981). 'Political Authority and Political Obligation'. *Virginia Law Review*, 67: 3–17.

SCANLON, THOMAS (1982). 'Contractualism and Utilitarianism'. In A. Sen and B. Williams (eds.), *Utilitariianism and Beyond*. Cambridge: Cambridge University Press.

SCHUMAN, HOWARD, and STANLEY PRESSER (1981). *Questions and Answers in Attitude Surveys*. New York: Academic Press.

SHEPPARD, BLAIR, and ROY LEWICKI (1987). 'Toward General Principles of Managerial Fairness'. *Social Justice Research*, 1: 161–76.

SHER, GEORGE (1997). *Beyond Neutrality*. Cambridge: Cambridge University Press.

SIMMONS, A. JOHN (1979). *Moral Principles and Political Obligations*. Princeton: Princeton University Press.

—— (1992). *The Lockean Theory of Rights*. Princeton: Princeton University Press.

—— (1993). *On the Edge of Anarchy*. Princeton: Princeton University Press.

—— (1996). 'Philosophical Anarchism'. In John T. Sanders and Jan Narveson (eds.), *For and Against the State*. Savage, Md.: Rowman & Littlefield.

SMIDT, CORWIN (1988). 'Evangelicals within Contemporary American Politics: Differentiating between Fundamentalist and Non-fundamentalist Evangelicals'. *Western Political Quarterly*, 41: 601–20.

—— and JAMES PENNING (1982). 'Religious Commitment, Political Conservatism, and Political and Social Tolerance in the United States: A Longitudinal Analysis'. *Sociological Analysis*, 43: 231–46.

SMITH, TOM (1989). 'Inequality and Welfare'. In Roger, Jowell, Sharon Witherspoon, and Lindsay Brook (eds.), *British Social Attitudes: Special International Report*. Aldershot: Gower.

SNIDERMAN, PAUL M., JOSEPH F. FLETCHER, PETER H. RUSSELL, and PHILIP E. TETLOCK (1991). 'The Fallacy of Democratic Elitism: Elite Competition and Commitment to Civil Liberties'. *British Journal of Political Science*, 21: 349–70.

—— —— —— —— (1996). *The Clash of Rights*. New Haven: Yale University Press.

SOLUM, LAWRENCE, (1993). 'Constructing an Ideal of Public Reason'. *San Diego Law Review*, 30: 729–62.

—— (1994). 'Inclusive Public Reason'. *Pacific Philosophical Quarterly*, 75: 217–31.

STARK, RODNEY, and CHARLES Y. GLOCK (1968). *American Piety: The Nature of Religious Commitment*. Berkeley: University of California Press.

STERBA, JAMES (1992). Review of Will Kymlicka, *Liberalism, Community, and Culture*. *Ethics*, 103: 152–4.

STOUFFER, SAMUEL A (1955). *Communism, Conformity, and Civil Liberties*. Garden City, NY: Doubleday.

STROZIER, CHARLES B. (1994). *Apocalypse: On the Psychology of Fundamentalism in America*. Boston: Beacon Press.

SULLIVAN, JOHN L., JAMES PIERESON, and GEORGE E. MARCUS (1982). *Political Tolerance and American Democracy*. Chicago: University of Chicago Press.

—— MICHAL SHAMIR, PATRICK WALSH, and NIGEL ROBERTS (1985). *Political Tolerance in Context*. Boulder, Colo. Westview Press.

TATA, JASMINE, and LYNN BOWES-SPERRY (1996). 'Emphasis on Distributive, Procedural, and Interactional Justice: Differential Perceptions of Men and Women'. *Psychological Reports*, 79: 1327–30.

TAYLOR, M. SUSAN, KAY B. TRACY, MONIKA K. RENARD, J. KLINE HARRISON, and STEPHEN J. CARROLL (1995). 'Due Process in Performance Appraisal: A Quasi-experiment in Procedural Justice'. *Administrative Science Quarterly*, 40: 495–523.

TELES, STEVEN (1996). *Whose Welfare? AFDC and Elite Politics*. Lawrence, Kan.: University of Kansas Press.

THIBAUT, J., and L. WALKER (1975). *Procedural Justice: A Psychological Analysis*. Hillsdale, NJ: Lawrence Erlbaum.

—— —— (1978). 'A Theory of Procedure'. *California Law Review*, 66: 541–66.

THOMASSEN, JACQUES (1995). 'Support for Democratic Values'. In Hans-Dieter Klingemann and Dieter Fuchs (eds.), *Citizens and the State*. Oxford: Oxford University Press.

THOMPSON, ANDREW (1974). 'Open-mindedness and Indiscriminate Antireligious Orientation'. *Journal for the Scientific Study of Religion*, 13: 471–7.

TIERNEY, BRIAN (1955). *Foundations of the Conciliar Theory*. Cambridge: Cambridge University Press.

—— (1982). *Religion, Law, and the Growth of Constitutional Thought: 1050–1650*. Cambridge: Cambridge University Press.

TOCQUEVILLE, ALEXIS DE (1969). *Democracy in America*. 2 vols. Trans. George Lawrence. New York: Harper & Row.

TROELTSCH, ERNST (1960). *The Social Teaching of the Christian Churches*. 2 vols. Trans. Olive Wyon. New York: Harper & Row.

TYLER, TOM (1984). 'The Role of Perceived Injustice in Defendants' Evaluations of their Courtroom Experience'. *Law and Society Review*, 18: 1–74.

—— (1988). 'What is Procedural Justice?: Criteria Used by Citizens to Assess the Fairness of Legal Procedures'. *Law and Society Review*, 22: 103–35.

—— (1989). 'The Psychology of Procedural Justice: A Test of the Group-Value Model'. *Journal of Personality and Social Psychology*, 57: 830–8.

—— (1990). *Why People Obey the Law*. New Haven: Yale University Press.

—— (1993). 'Legitimizing Unpopular Public Policies: Does Procedure Matter?' *Zeitschrift für Rechtssoziologie*, 14: 47–54.

—— (1994a). 'Governing Amid Diversity: The Effect of Fair Decisionmaking Procedures on the Legitimacy of Government'. *Law and Society Review*, 28: 809–31.

—— (1994b). 'Psychological Models of the Justice Motive: Antecedents of Distributive and Procedural Justice'. *Journal of Personality and Social Psychology*, 67: 850–63.

—— and ROBERT BIES (1990). 'Beyond Formal Procedures: The Interpersonal Context of Procedural Justice'. In J. Carroll (ed.), *Applied Social Psychology and Organizational Settings*. Hillsdale, NJ: Lawrence Erlbaum.

—— and ANDREW CAINE (1981). 'The Influence of Outcomes and Procedures on Satisfaction with Formal Leaders'. *Journal of Personality and Social Psychology*, 41: 642–55.

—— and PETER DEGOEY (1995). 'Collective Restraint in Social Dilemmas: Procedural Justice and Social Identification Effects on Support for Authorities'. *Journal of Personality and Social Psychology*, 69: 482–97.

—— and ROBERT FOLGER (1980). 'Distributional and Procedural Aspects of Satisfaction with Citizen–Police Encounters'. *Basic and Applied Social Psychology*, 1: 281–92.

—— and E. ALLAN LIND (1992). 'A Relational Model of Authority in Groups'. In M. P. Zanna (ed.), *Advances in Experimental Social Psychology*, xxv. San Diego: Academic Press.

—— and KATHLEEN MCGRAW (1986). 'Ideology and Interpretation of Personal Experience: Procedural Justice and Political Quiescence'. *Journal of Social Issues*, 42: 115–28.

—— and GREGORY MITCHELL (1994). 'Legitimacy and the Empowerment of Discretionary Legal Authority: The United States Supreme Court and Abortion Rights'. *Duke Law Journal*, 43: 703–815.

—— and KENNETH RASINSKI (1991). 'Procedural Justice, Institutional Legitimacy, and the Acceptance of Unpopular US Supreme Court Decisions: A Reply to Gibson'. *Law and Society Review*, 25: 621–30.

—— —— and KATHLEEN MCGRAW (1985). 'The Influence of Perceived Injustice on the Endorsement of Political Leaders'. *Journal of Applied Social Psychology*, 15: 700–25.

—— JONATHAN CASPER, and BONNIE FISHER (1989). 'Maintaining Allegiance toward Political Authorities: The Role of Prior Attitudes and the Use of Fair Procedures'. *American Journal of Political Science*, 33: 629–52.

—— ROBERT BOECKMANN, HEATHER SMITH, and YUEN HUO (1997). *Social Justice in a Diverse Society*. Boulder, Colo.: Westview Press.

US DEPARTMENT OF COMMERCE (1996). *Statistical Abstract of the United States*. 116th edn. Washington.

VERBA, SIDNEY, and GARY ORREN (1985). *Equality in America*. Cambridge, Mass.: Harvard University Press.

VIDMAR, NEIL (1990). 'The Origins and Consequences of Procedural Justice'. *Law and Social Inquiry*, 15: 877–92.

VLASTOS, GREGORY (1984). 'Justice and Equality'. In Jeremy Waldron (ed.), *Theories of Rights*. Oxford: Oxford University Press.

WALD, KENNETH, DENNIS OWEN, and SAMUEL HILL Jr (1989). 'Habits of the Mind? The Problem of Authority in the New Christian Right'. In Ted Jelen (ed.), *Religion and Political Behavior in the United States*. New York: Praeger.

WALDRON, JEREMY (1987). 'Theoretical Foundations of Liberalism'. *Philosophical Quarterly*, 37: 127–50.

WALDRON, JEREMY (1989). 'Legislation and Moral Neutrality'. In Robert Goodin and Andrew Reeve (eds.), *Liberal Neutrality*. London: Routledge.

WALL, STEVEN (1998). *Liberalism, Perfectionism, and Restraint*. Cambridge: Cambridge University Press.

WALZER, MICHAEL (1989–90). 'A Critique of Philosophical Conversation'. *Philosophical Forum*, 21: 182–96.

WARREN, MARK (1992). 'Democratic Theory and Self-transformation'. *American Political Science Review*, 86: 8–23.

—— (1996). 'What should we Expect from More Democracy?' *Political Theory*, 24: 241–70.

WATSON, P. J., RONALD MORRIS, JAMES FOSTER, and RALPH HOOD (1986). 'Religiosity and Social Desirability'. *Journal for the Scientific Study of Religion*, 25: 215–32.

WEITHMAN, PAUL J. (1991). 'The Separation of Church and State: Some Questions for Professor Audi'. *Philosophy and Public Affairs*, 20: 52–65.

WENAR, LEIF (1995). '*Political Liberalism*: An Internal Critique'. *Ethics*, 106: 32–67.

WESTIE, FRANK R. (1965). 'The American Dilemma: An Empirical Test'. *American Sociological Review*, 30: 524–38.

WESTLE, BETTINA (1989). *Politische Legitimität: Theorien, Konzepte, empirische Befunde*. Baden-Baden: Nomos Verlagsgesellschaft.

WILCOX, CLYDE (1992). *God's Warriors*. Baltimore: Johns Hopkins University Press.

—— and TED JELEN (1990). 'Evangelicals and Political Tolerance'. *American Politics Quarterly*, 18: 25–46.

WOLFF, ROBERT P. (1970). *In Defense of Anarchism*. New York: Harper & Row.

—— (1977). *Understanding Rawls*. Princeton: Princeton University Press.

WRIGHT, JAMES D. (1981). 'Political Disaffection'. In Samuel L. Long (ed.), *The Handbook of Political Behavior*, iv. New York: Plenum.

WULFF, DAVID M. (1991). *Psychology of Religion: Classic and Contemporary Views*. New York: Wiley.

WUTHNOW, ROBERT (1973). 'Religious Commitment and Conservatism: In Search of an Elusive Relationship'. In Charles Glock (ed.), *Religion in Sociological Perspective*. Belmont, Calif.: Wadsworth.

YOUNG, JAMES P. (1996). *Reconsidering American Liberalism*. Boulder, Colo.: Westview Press.

ZALLER, JOHN R. (1992). *The Nature and Origin of Mass Opinion*. Cambridge: Cambridge University Press.

INDEX